NEW CONCEPTS IN LATINO AMERICAN CULTURES
A Series Edited by Licia Fiol-Matta & José Quiroga

Ciphers of History: Latin American Readings for a Cultural Age
by Enrico Mario Santí

Cosmopolitanisms and Latin America: Against the Destiny of Place
by Jacqueline Loss

Remembering Maternal Bodies: Melancholy in Latina and Latin American Women's Writing
by Benigno Trigo

The Ethics of Latin American Literary Criticism: Reading Otherwise,
edited by Erin Graff Zivin

Modernity and the Nation in Mexican Representations of Masculinity: From Sensuality to Bloodshed
by Héctor Domínguez-Ruvalcaba

White Negritude: Race, Writing, and Brazilian Cultural Identity
by Alexandra Isfahani-Hammond

Essays in Cuban Intellectual History
by Rafael Rojas

Mestiz@ Scripts, Digital Migrations, and the Territories of Writing
by Damián Baca

Confronting History and Modernity in Mexican Narrative
by Elisabeth Guerrero

Forthcoming Titles

Cuba in the Special Period: Culture and Ideology in the 1990s,
edited by Ariana Hernandez-Reguant

Cuban Women Writers: Imagining A Matria
by Madeline Cámara Betancourt

The Mestizo State
by Joshua Lund

Telling Ruins in Latin America,
edited by Michael J. Lazzara and Vicky Unruh

Other Worlds: New Argentinean Film
by Gonzalo Aguilar

NEW DIRECTIONS IN LATINO AMERICAN CULTURES
Also Edited by Licia Fiol-Matta & José Quiroga

New York Ricans from the Hip Hop Zone
by Raquel Rivera

The Famous 41: Sexuality and Social Control in Mexico, 1901,
edited by Robert McKee Irwin, Edward J. McCaughan, and
Michele Rocío Nasser

Velvet Barrios: Popular Culture & Chicana/o Sexualities,
edited by Alicia Gaspar de Alba, with a foreword by Tomás Ybarra Frausto

Tongue Ties: Logo-Eroticism in Anglo-Hispanic Literature
by Gustavo Perez-Firmat

Bilingual Games: Some Literary Investigations,
edited by Doris Sommer

Jose Martí: An Introduction
by Oscar Montero

New Tendencies in Mexican Art
by Rubén Gallo

*The Masters and the Slaves: Plantation Relations and Mestizaje in American
Imaginaries,*
edited by Alexandra Isfahani-Hammond

The Letter of Violence: Essays on Narrative and Theory
by Idelber Avelar

Intellectual History of the Caribbean
by Silvio Torres-Saillant

None of the Above: Contemporary Puerto Rican Cultures and Politics,
edited by Frances Negrón-Muntaner

Queer Latino Testimonio, Keith Haring, and Juanito Xtravaganza: Hard Tails
by Arnaldo Cruz-Malavé

Forthcoming Titles

The Portable Island: Cubans at Home in the World,
edited by Ruth Behar and Lucía M. Suárez

Puerto Ricans in America: 30 Years of Activism and Change,
edited by Xavier F. Totti and Felix V. Matos Rodriguez

Confronting History and Modernity in Mexican Narrative

Elisabeth Guerrero

palgrave
macmillan

First published in 2008 by
PALGRAVE MACMILLAN®
in the US—a division of St. Martin's Press LLC,
175 Fifth Avenue, New York, NY 10010.

Where this book is distributed in the UK, Europe and the rest of the world,
this is by Palgrave Macmillan, a division of Macmillan Publishers Limited,
registered in England, company number 785998, of Houndmills,
Basingstoke, Hampshire RG21 6XS.

Palgrave Macmillan is the global academic imprint of the above companies
and has companies and representatives throughout the world.

Palgrave® and Macmillan® are registered trademarks in the United States,
the United Kingdom, Europe and other countries.

ISBN-13: 978–0–230–60637–1
ISBN-10: 0–230–60637–7

Library of Congress Cataloging-in-Publication Data

Guerrero, Elisabeth, 1964–
    Confronting history and modernity in Mexican narrative / Elisabeth
Guerrero.
        p. cm.—(New concepts in Latino American cultures series)
        Includes bibliographical references and index.
        ISBN 0–230–60637–7
        1. Historical fiction, Mexican—History and criticism. 2. Mexican
fiction—History and criticism. 3. Literature and history—Mexico.
    I. Title.

PQ7207.H5G84 2008
863'.08109972—dc22   2007052844

A catalogue record for this book is available from the British Library.

Design by Newgen Imaging Systems (P) Ltd., Chennai, India.

First edition: July 2008

10 9 8 7 6 5 4 3 2 1

Printed in the United States of America.

Contents

Acknowledgments

The cover photograph, "Ángel del Temblor" by Manuel Álvarez Bravo, appears courtesy of the Samek Art Gallery of Bucknell University.

An earlier version of the second half of chapter 1 appeared in Volume 133, Issue 1 (2001) of *Hispanófila*. A version of the last part of chapter 3 is reprinted by permission from the publisher, *Latin American Literary Review*, Volume 34, Issue 67, 2006. Earlier versions of portions of chapter 2 were originally published as an article in *The Rocky Mountain Review of Language and Literature*, Volume 56, Issue 2 (2002) and in *Chasqui: revista de literatura iberoamericana*, Volume 31, Issue 2 (2002). Index is by Denise E. Carlson and copyediting by the team at Newgen.

I am grateful to many for reading drafts or responding to ideas, especially my loyal interlocutor Anne Lambright. Thanks also go to Sandra Cypess, Naomi Lindstrom, Roger Rothman, Marcy Schwartz, and Nick Shumway. I also want to thank those who may not have been directly involved in the book but who shared joy, support, and companionship while I was writing it: family Kit, Carolyn, Elaine, Pete, Oscar, Sebastian, and Sophia, and friends Anne, Coralynn, Douglas, Elizabeth, Ghislaine, Jasmine, Jaxi, dance buddies Joe and Kelly, flute teacher Leslie, and also Mara, María across the ocean, Robin, Rolando, Susan across the country, and Virginia across the hall. Finally, I am grateful to the excellent staff at Palgrave Macmillan, to Bucknell University and my colleagues in the Department of Spanish, Alice, Ana Mercedes, Collin, Isabel, and Manuel, to Cindy on the custodial staff, and to administrative assistant Ruth Robenolt (Ruth, you deserve to have your name in a book!).

Introduction: Confronting History and Modernity in Mexican Narrative

Two motifs of an angel of history, one European and one Mexican, provide a theoretical framework for this book about contemporary Mexican narrative. The first is Walter Benjamin's interpretation of the Klee painting *angelus novus*, an angel of history that gazes upon the ruins of the past, powerless to repair the broken pieces as it keels into the future. Although Benjamin envisions history as catastrophe piled upon catastrophe, he also sees in this angel the possibility for redemption in divine destruction. Mexico's Angel of Independence also embodies redemption and destruction through history; standing tall in the nation's capital, the "Ángel" holds powerful symbolic resonance in Mexico, marking moments of staggering transformation beyond the conquest. The monument commemorates national independence (1821), was erected on the cusp of the revolution (1910), and today stands amidst a swirl of traffic and smog in the federal district, a vital yet troubled link in today's network of global cities. Together these two theoretical angels guide *Confronting History and Modernity in Mexican Narrative's* examination of a selection of historical novels from Mexico that reflect upon history as an allegory of the present.

During the last twenty-five years, Mexican intellectuals have responded to the rapid shifts of today's global age with a reassessment of national historical traditions. Today's historical novels mark moments of political and economic transition, responding to major changes such as explosive urban growth, the neoliberal economy, globalization, and escalating criminal violence. In the midst of the tumultuous 1970s and 1980s, a period of military dictatorships in the Southern Cone, civil wars in Central America, and single-party rule in Mexico, Nobel Prize–winning poet and essayist Octavio Paz wrote in 1986, "The history of our countries, since independence, is the history of different attempts at modernization" (*Tiempo nublado* 119).[1]

The goal of modernization that Paz describes would open Latin America to full access to the world's cultural resources through advancements both political (democracy) and technological (rapid transit, information technology).[2] Particularly from the 1980s to the present, novelists have responded to these changes in their works by engaging in a lively dialogue between past and present, which recasts notions of history and modernity.[3] Their works thereby provide valuable insights into how questions of heterogeneity such as class, ethnicity, and gender are as crucial today as they were, in different guises, when the nation first came into being. *Confronting History and Modernity in Mexican Narrative* examines this balancing act of Mexican writers today as they juggle past and present in an attempt to delineate a national identity in the face of globalization, and to respond to modernization on their own terms. The analysis focuses on a selection of historical novels from Mexico that were published between 1980 and 2008; the novels chosen for this study are particularly revealing of literary trends and of the shifting representations of regional character.

The historical novel was the favored prose genre during the period of nation formation in nineteenth-century Latin America. This period roughly corresponds with the European scheme that Georg Lukács traced in his classic study, *The Historical Novel* (1937); the Hungarian Marxist critic marks the rise of the historical novel at the beginning of the nineteenth century, near the time of the fall of Napoleon, with the publication of Sir Walter Scott's *Waverley* (1815); thus, the historical novel was born as the result of massive socioeconomic change, documenting the transition from feudalism to democracy.

For Lukács, the historical novels of Scott and Balzac are exemplary, democratic works in which grand historical figures hold merely a secondary role; the popular hero stars in the narrative, representing ordinary folk in a great historical moment. Nevertheless, comparable works throughout the nineteenth century in Latin America tended not to diminish prominent figures but rather to monumentalize them in the romantic tradition as either grand heroes or appalling villains. For example, in his novel *Sacerdote y caudillo* (1868), Juan Mateos exalts Father Miguel de Hidalgo, transforming foibles into virtues for the leader of Mexico's 1810 independence uprising, while on the other side of the spectrum, historian Lucas Alamán's nonfiction work *Historia de México* (1849) converts Hidalgo into a depraved evildoer.

At the time that these works were published, the elite of what Uruguayan critic Ángel Rama calls the "lettered city" was in the process of creating a national identity through the design and promotion of symbols such as independence days and founding fathers.[4] As Noé Jitrik points out in his sketch of the historical novel, *Historia e imaginación literaria*, the genre emerges during this period from the desire to comprehend, through the past, a present moment that is unclear, chaotic, or enigmatic: "As romanticism turns to answers from the past to palliate its anguish for the present, the historical novel similarly attempts to clarify current enigmas" (19). The Romantic literary movement was a key moment in the development of a modern epistemology. While a sense of modernity began to take root in the renaissance as the legitimacy of knowledge came under question, the trend developed more fully during the industrial revolution of the late eighteenth and early nineteenth centuries, in which faith in technology seemed to replace faith in divinity. This produced a sense of estrangement for many writers, and romanticism emerged from these circumstances. Thus, as Cathy Jrade describes it, "The first major movement to focus on issues of fragmentation and alienation was European romanticism. Its principal exponents sought to recreate the lost ethical totality of society by reappropriating premodern visions of life and language" (3). Jitrik explains, in accordance with this theory, that the romantic historical novel explores earlier periods in order to answer questions of national identity such as, "What does it mean to be Mexican?" For Jitrik, then, the focus of these narratives is not the formation of an individual subject but rather that of a community, a sociopolitical entity. As Jitrik also makes clear, while today's historical novels vary—"archaeological" ones excavate the distant past, "cathartic" versions address recent traumas, and "functional or systematic" variants analyze politically and morally ambiguous historical situations—each of these subcategories is subordinated to the basic endeavor of understanding a collective identity (60).

Doris Sommer's study *Foundational Fictions* provides further insights into the nation-building role of romanticism in her analysis of nineteenth-century Brazilian and Spanish American historical novels; her study traces the use of romance as a metaphor for founding the nation, equating *eros* with *polis* in the collective consciousness. In Sommer's analysis, narratives such as the Cuban writer Gertrudis Gómez de Avellaneda's *Sab* (1841) and Mexican Ignacio Altamirano's *El Zarco* (1888) projected ideals of national conciliation through the lovers' yearnings across racial, class, or regional barriers. Sommer's study makes an invaluable contribution to understanding the nineteenth-century genre; however, the novel of the Mexican Revolution in the first decades of the twentieth century indicates that the unity sketched out in the nineteenth-century novels did not come to be. They indicate instead that violence, division, and exclusion can supersede romance and unity in the process—and rhetoric—of nation formation.

Now, nearly two centuries after Mexico's independence from Spain in 1821 and the publication of the first Latin American historical novel, *Xicoténcatl* (a narrative of the conquest of Mexico, with conquistador Hernán Cortés as a villain), in 1826, writers are using the historical novel, with a postmodern twist, to create a new national imaginary that often signals the rhetorical powers of both romance and violence.[5] The genre's resurgence is not surprising; as Karl Kohut observes, "Postmodernity and a manifest interest in history are parallel expressions of our time" (20).[6] Novels such as *Xicoténcatl* documented a moment of transition from colonialism to independence, and they created a new national imaginary. Today's historical novels similarly mark moments of political and economic transition. However, the genre has changed enough that some writers, in order to disassociate themselves from romanticism, insist that their works should not be called historical novels.

While I still consider such narratives of recent decades to be "historical novels" (my definition appears later), their differences are manifest; while nineteenth-century heroes and villains were larger than life, fiction in recent decades demonumentalizes these figures. Furthermore, while nineteenth-century novels were stylistically straightforward, generally including a linear chronology and a third-person omniscient narrator, today's historical novels tend to incorporate innovative stylistic devices such as the use of anachronisms and contradictory narrative voices. Influenced by the deliberations of Hayden White and Michel de Certeau, writers today generally accept the idea that historiography, while based on real events, is a literary creation subject to question.[7] In the postmodern historical novel, this perspective has led to the frequent use of techniques such as pastiche, parody, and the incorporation of multiple registers, metaliterary techniques that invite the reader to reflect upon the creation of the text itself. Linda Hutcheon has termed this phenomenon "historiographic metafiction," a genre that incorporates both a nostalgia for and a parody of the texts and motifs of the past.

While implicitly responding to the theorists mentioned earlier, this book is informed throughout by Walter Benjamin and by Wilhelm Friedrich Hegel's philosophy of history, and also further develops the work of Noe Jitrik, Seymour Menton, and Fernando Aínsa, the three major theorists of Latin America's "new historical novel." Menton notes accurately that the 500th anniversary of the 1492 conquest is the most important factor to have stirred up writers' interest in exploring history once again, and Aínsa credibly argues that the increasing interdisciplinarity of thinking today inspires works of historical fiction in which social sciences and humanities cross boundaries. However, Jitrik's theory has proven the most instructive for this study; for Jitrik, the historical novel appears during times of political crisis. Frenzied periods such as independence, revolution, or today's neoliberal transition motivate writers to reflect upon the past in order to better understand the chaotic present. Therefore, a well-conceived historical novel is not an escapist genre but rather an attempt to grapple with the present.[8]

In order to explain what I mean by "historical fiction," for the purposes of this study, I define the historical novel simply as a work of fiction in which a substantial portion of the narrative takes place in the past in a historically identifiable moment or period. This category includes works such as Nicaraguan writer Gioconda Belli's *La mujer habitada* (1988) and Mexican writer Brianda Domecq's *La vida insólita de Santa Teresa de Cabora* (1990), in which the narratives shift through a character from the present who reflects extensively on past events and figures.

Furthermore, in my definition, "the past" depicted does not necessarily have to be remote in order for the work to be a historical novel; narratives of earlier events within the author's lifetime can be included within this category if they address significant milestones (such as the 1968 student massacre in Tlatelolco, for instance) and if they make use of oral testimony or historical documentation concerning the event.[9] Examples of the latter category would include, for instance, Tomás Eloy Martínez's depictions of mid-twentieth-century Argentina in *La novela de Perón* (1985) and *Santa Evita* (1995).

Finally, the writer's use of historiography can vary significantly; while some, such as Mexican novelist Fernando del Paso in *Noticias del Imperio* (1987), take pains with the accuracy of documentation, others, such as Uruguayan Alejandro Paternain's *Crónica del descubrimiento* (1980) make use of history to create an entirely apocryphal text (in this case, a reversal of the conquest in which natives of the Americas discover Europe). This element of liberty is key; after all, both novelists who are careful with historiographic accuracy and those who disregard historical precision generally assert that their principal aim is to write a work of fiction, not of social science.

Confronting History and Modernity in Mexican Narrative delineates three major narrative tendencies in Latin American works of historical fiction from 1980 to the present; first, as Aínsa has asserted, humanizing canonized heroes and making them accessible is the foremost characteristic of today's historical novels in Latin America. Second, in addition to refraining from villainizing or monumentalizing historical figures, these narratives also demonumentalize the European legacy, renegotiating Europe's 500-year bequest of conquest and colonialism in the Americas. Third, the novels addressed here have begun to recover secondary figures previously lost to history, particularly women and people of color, moving them from the margins to the center of the story. While these three fundamental tendencies apply throughout Latin America, they are particularly pronounced in Mexican literary production.

I have chosen seven texts from Mexico that are particularly representative of these intellectual trends. Chapter 1, "Humanizing the Hero," addresses the most predominant change in the historical novel since the nineteenth century: the demonumentalization of both heroes and villains, who are now traced more subtly and made more accessible to the reader. The dead body—or rather, the remaining consciousness—of Francisco I. Madero, the first president of the Mexican revolution of 1910, is the unusual protagonist of Ignacio Solares's *Madero, el otro* (1989). In death, Madero is at his most human and vulnerable, belying any possibility of heroic immortality as the narrator guides him through the process of death with the help of the *Tibetan Book of the Dead* and the *Bhagavad Gita*. The link between Madero's time and the time of the publication of the novel is key; in the 1980s the Miguel de la Madrid administration sponsored the publication of a series of books about the revolution in order to spread the "revolutionary culture" ostensibly bequeathed to the triumphant "Revolutionary" party, the PRI. However, an unanticipated result of this reawakening of interest in the history of the revolution was the reassessment of such heroes as Madero and, implicitly, a questioning of the heroes' revolutionary bequest to the ruling party and to the nation as a whole. In the novel, the narrator's familiarity with Madero's most intimate gestures and memories permits him to question each of the former president's steps and to concede the losses Mexico may have suffered up to the present day from his political mistakes. Jorge Ibargüengoitia's novel *Los pasos de López* (1982) also humanizes a national hero, but it does so through parody rather than sobriety, using earthy humor to poke fun at the independence leader Miguel Hidalgo's human frailties.

Chapter 2, "Highlighting Women in History," examines the resurgence of feminine figures and domestic spaces in historical fiction. Although María Cristina Pons noted in a 1996 study that lamentably few women were producing the genre at that time and that "one of the most important social agents in the construction of history, woman, is nearly invisible, even at present" (13), the tide has been turning, particularly in the last ten years, and both women and men are penning historical narratives that often depict female subjectivities; to give a few examples, María Esther de Miguel's (Argentina) *La amante del restaurador* (2001), Tomás Eloy Martínez's *Santa Evita* (1995), Mercedes Valdivies's (Chile) *Maldita yo entre las mujeres* (1993), and Elena Poniatowska's (Mexico) *Tinísima* (1992) turn their gaze to the influences and experiences of female historical figures.

Chapter 2 is divided into two sections that examine the work of two different Mexican writers that address women in history. The first is Rosa Beltrán, a peer of the relatively young "Crack Generation" of Mexican writers and "McOndo" generation of South American writers. This group has responded to the anxiety of influence[10] with a new paradigm of writing that diverges from the novels of the highly successful "boom" of the 1960s, particularly the earlier works of Colombian writer and Nobel Prize winner Gabriel García Márquez: monumental, magical-realist, metaliterary novels set in rural Latin America.[11] In contrast with this paradigm, the new generations' work reflects the present-day globalization of the region; the narrative often takes place in urban settings, is replete with international pop-culture references, and focuses more on the individual subject rather than the epic of a community.

However, the historical novel is also still going strong among this generation, as evidenced, for example, in Beltran's award-winning *La corte de los ilusos* [*Court of the Deluded*, 1995]. Her work narrates female subjectivities and women's experiences of history on the outskirts of influence. *La corte de los ilusos* traces the brief reign (1822–1823) of Agustín de Iturbide, controversial liberator and emperor of newly independent Mexico. In accordance with Josefina Ludmer's classic article on Sor Juana, "Las tretas del débil," minor genres such as letters and recipes can speak eloquently to power from the margins. This "technique of the weak" appears on several levels in the novel, as the character of the royal seamstress begins and finishes the "seams" of the novel, and the camp aesthetic of Iturbide's sister, Princess Nicolasa, parodies the use of luxury objects to mark noble status.

The second section of chapter 2 examines a second novel that recenters women, Brianda Domecq's *La insólita historia de la Santa de Cabora* (1990). The protagonist is Teresa Urrea (1873–1906), a Sonoran mystic, healer, and anti-Porfirian activist whose life ended in exile in the United States. Domecq revives Urrea in light of feminist theory, producing what activist historian Aurora Levins Morales calls history as *curandera*, a healing history. *The Astonishing Story* puts into practice a number of Levins Morales's observations, such as telling untold or undertold stories, centering women to change the landscape, identifying and contradicting strategic pieces of misinformation, showing agency rather than victimization, and embracing complexity and ambiguity.

Resolving and recuperating the conflict-ridden European legacy is the third of the key tendencies addressed in this book, discussed in chapter 3, "Mourning the European Legacy." As is examined further in the Conclusion, the European legacy is central to Mexican modernity and to questions of center and periphery; it is thus appropriate to place the European chapter at the center of this study. The 500th anniversary of the Spanish conquest (1492–1521) has provided fertile ground for dozens of revisitations throughout Latin America such as Libertad Demitrópulos's *El río de las congojas* (Argentina, 1981), Juan José Saer's *El entenado* (Argentina, 1983), Abel Posse's *El largo atardecer del caminante* (Argentina, 1992), Herminio Martínez's *Diario maldito de Nuño de Guzmán* (Mexico, 1990), and Alicia Freilich's *Colombina descubierta* (Venezuela, 1991), to name just a few.

Poet and ecological activist Homero Aridjis, in turn, focuses on the Spanish Inquisition's legacy of state-sponsored violence in his novels *1492: Vida y tiempos de Juan Cabezón de Castilla* [*1492: The Life and Times of Juan Cabezón of Castile*, 1985] and *Memorias del Nuevo Mundo* [*Memories of the New World*, 1991]. As I discuss more fully in chapter 3, Aridjis's narrative tells a tale of peril and loss, imparting a fitting response to Walter Benjamin's warning; for Benjamin, the storyteller has a responsibility to tell history as an act of resistance against totalitarianism, to "seize hold of a memory as it flashes up at a moment of danger" ("Theses" 255). In this case, the moment of danger is the apocalyptic memory of 1492. My analysis of Aridjis's narrative in this chapter indicates how the violence of the Inquisition was not an ancient form of barbarism incomprehensible to the modern observer; on the contrary, in its very brutality administered through bureaucracy, the Holy Office was a sign of the future, the biopolitical tool of a modern state. We shall see how in Aridjis's novels, this synthesis of violence and power is manifested in the Inquisition's punishment of the body and censorship of thought.

The second part of chapter 3 explores a later phase of mourning for the painful European legacy during the empire of Maximilian and Carlota (1864–1867) in del Paso's novel *Noticias del Imperio* [*News of the Empire*, 1987]. I examine mourning in the novel as a means of mediating between tradition and modernity as well as between Europe and the Americas. The mad Charlotte ("Carlota") negotiates these relations as she mourns for the losses caused by the French intervention in Mexico, serves as a diplomat of transculturation, and moderates modernity from both shores. Storytelling and transculturation, both on the part of the characters Maximilian and Charlotte and as seen in the novel as a whole, represent a process of collective mourning for Mexico.

While *Confronting History and Modernity* emphasizes the importance of recognizing and commemorating the brutalities of history, the book ends with an analysis of the possibility of redemption, which is also a recurring theme in the works studied here. In chapter 4, "Redemption of the Present," I examine novelist and essayist Carlos Fuentes's *Los años con Laura Diaz* [*The Years with Laura Díaz*, 1999], a novel that merits attention for its ambitious overview of Mexico's twentieth century and the history that it shares with Europe and the United States. In counterpoint with his familiar cyclical, mythical view of history, in this novel Fuentes traces a progressive outlook that offers the possibility of transformation and redemption. In the wake of destruction, we can imagine Benjamin's Angel of History gazing upon the remains of the Angel de la Independencia, toppled and broken in the 1957 earthquake but raised again to become what is now a gathering place both for jubilant soccer fans and for vexed political protestors. Looking back from the twenty-first century upon the horrors of the twentieth, is Hegel's early nineteenth-century optimistic representation of historical progress still credible? Benjamin's early twentieth-century Angel of History may offer the possibility of redemption and yet despairs for what lies ahead; in contrast, at the turn of the twenty-first century, Fuentes links the promise of redemption to creation rather than destruction, as the "everywoman" protagonist of Fuentes's novel, Laura Díaz, is restored and redeemed like the Angel of Independence—in her case, through artistic production and participation in civil society. Narratives such as that of Fuentes and the other writers studied here thus turn to the past as an allegory of a present rife with troubles but also replete with possibilities.

Fuentes's many works of historical fiction such as *Los años con Laura Díaz* are just a sampling of how new fictional approaches to history have mushroomed throughout the globe in recent decades; the genre has particularly flourished in Latin America and even more so in the specific case of Mexico. Writer Eugenio Aguirre pointed out in 1997, "It's indisputable that, during the last fifteen years, the historical novel has reached a zenith without precedence in Mexico" (93). Why does the historical novel occupy such a prominent position in Mexican literary production? Jitrik would turn to sociopolitical volatility for the answer: while the middle class is growing, times are still tough for many in Mexico; violent crime has soared in recent decades, as current and former police officers are often involved or in collusion with crime networks, a corrupt justice system usually turns a blind eye, and the rate of brutal kidnappings of both the wealthy and the poor exploded following the 1995 fall of the peso, and has not abated (Preston and Dillon 387–388). Furthermore, despite the high hopes of both Right and Left when the "one-party dictatorship" of the PRI was overturned in the 2000 election of Vicente Fox, the legacy of his presidency and the promise of the disputed Felipe Calderón presidency (2006–2012) is far from utopian, and protests at the base of the Angel of Independence are frequent, as if shoring up Benjamin's Angel of History as it is thrust from the ruins into an uncertain future.

Throughout this selective sampling of historical novels from the region, several distinctive elements have emerged in these creative responses to uncertain times. The novels studied here center women and other marginal figures and genres in works such as Rosa Beltrán's *La corte de los ilusos* and Brianda Domecq's *La insólita historia de la Santa de Cabora*. They demonumentalize national heroes in novels such as Ignacio Solares's *Madero, el otro* and Jorge Ibargüengoitia's *Los pasos de López*. They explore violence as well as romance as nation-building enterprises, and mourn for the detritus left by the European legacy, in works such as Homero Aridjis's *1492: Vida y tiempos de Juan Cabezón* and *Memorias del Nuevo Mundo* and Fernando del Paso's *Noticias del Imperio*. Yet they also offer possibilities of redemption despite these failures, as we see in Carlos Fuentes's *Los años con Laura Díaz*. In this manner, these writers stir some freshness of thought into the smog of Mexico City, where the air was once legendarily clear.

1

Humanizing the Hero: Ignacio Solares's *Madero, el otro* and Jorge Ibargüengoitia's *Los pasos de López*

Mythical violence is bloody power over mere life for its own sake, divine violence pure power over all life for the sake of the living. The first demands sacrifice, the second accepts it.

—Walter Benjamin, "Critique of Violence," 295

Madero, el otro

The dead body—or rather, the remaining consciousness—of Francisco I. Madero, the first president of the Mexican Revolution of 1910, is the unusual protagonist of Ignacio Solares's *Madero, el otro* (1989) [*Madero's Judgment*].[1] In death, Madero is at his most human and vulnerable, belying any possibility of heroic immortality. Such humanization of the hero is a common characteristic of the new historical novel in Latin America; witness, for example, the Nobel Prize–winning Colombian writer Gabriel García Márquez's *El general en su laberinto* (1989), a narrative that brings South American independence liberator Simón Bolívar down to earth through the depiction of his most abject bodily functions, or Mexican writer Jorge Ibargüengoitia's novel *Los pasos de López* (1982) (López's Steps), a parodic representation of independence leader Miguel Hidalgo that uses humor to poke fun at Hidalgo's human frailties.

Critic Fernando Aínsa calls the humanization of the hero the most important characteristic of the new historical novel in Latin America: "buscar entre las ruinas de una historia desmantelada al individuo perdido detrás de los acontecimientos, descubrir y ensalzar al ser humano en su dimensión más auténtica, aunque parezca inventado, aunque en definitivo lo sea" (9) [to look for the individual among the ruins of a dismantled history, to discover and exalt the human being in his/her most authentic dimension, although it may seem, and may indeed be, invented].[2] Solares's narrative exemplifies this trend of demonumentalizing the hero, but in contrast with Ibargüengoitia's *Los pasos de López*, Solares's sober, contemplative novel lowers the hero from his pedestal through a close spiritual and psychological examination rather than through earthy humor.

As part of this intimacy, the narrator addresses Madero as "hermano," or brother. While literary critics have identified the narrator as the spirit of Raúl, Madero's brother who died in childhood, he is more likely a part of Madero himself or perhaps even a Mexican "everyman," uniting with Madero as he says, for example, "look down at the body of you/me." This voice seems to know the protagonist's every movement, his every weakness. Here, for instance, he notices Madero's nervousness when he is transported to the penitentiary, where he suspects he may be shot: "No lograbas dejar las piernas quietas—a pesar de tanta disciplina física y el yoga nunca lograste dominar del todo tus nervios—y estrujabas el portafolios con unas manos sudorosas, que hormigueaban" (13). [You could not keep your legs from trembling—you never did manage to control your nerves entirely in spite of so much physical discipline and yoga—and you gripped your briefcase with nervous, sweaty hands (9).] This familiarity with Madero's most intimate gestures permits the narrator to question each of his motives and his decisions, and to concede the losses Mexico may have suffered up to the present day as a result of his political mistakes.

The link between Madero's time and the time of the publication of the novel (1989) is key; in the 1980s the Miguel de la Madrid administration sponsored the publication of a series of books about the revolution in order to spread "revolutionary culture." Such a culture was ostensibly the legacy that revolutionary heroes bequeathed to the triumphant "Revolutionary" party with a capital R, the PRI.[3] However, an unanticipated result of this reawakening of interest in the history of the revolution was the reassessment of such heroes as

Madero and, implicitly, a questioning of the heroes' revolutionary bequest to the ruling party and to the nation as a whole.

A particular subtlety of Solares's novelistic reassessment of Madero lies in its imbrication of Madero's defective humanity with his belief in divine guidance. The pacifist Madero struggles with the carnage and suffering of the revolution, and yet the "other," political Madero of the novel's title is responsible for unleashing violence for the sake of the poor and for the sake of democracy. This sacrifice is in keeping with Benjamin's description in the epigraph to this chapter: divine violence "for the sake of the living." The insurrectionist Madero justifies taking up arms in order to create a more just Mexican state; however, the mystic Madero struggles with the risks of activism.

The narrator guides Madero the spiritual seeker through the process of death, reviewing even his most guilty, painful, and brutal memories. Yet the novel avoids lingering on any of these reminiscences, as the narrator also cautions him to steer clear of fixating on any one image: "Acuérdate: no te detengas en una sola imagen: podrías después no salir de ella" (193). [But do not focus on a single image: you may get trapped there forever (24).] This practice of releasing memories is in accordance with a key Buddhist text cited at the beginning of the novel, the *Bardo Thodol*, or *Tibetan Book of the Dead*: "Antes de subir a más altas regiones...observa tu pobre cuerpo un instante más. Recuerda la 'sabiduría del espejo,' que leíste en *El Bardo Thodol*, uno de tus libros predilectos. Estás solo (tú y yo), el espejo no refleja sino un rostro—contraído por una mueca de dolor—con el que hablas (hablamos)" (8). [Before ascending to higher regions...look at your poor body a moment longer. Remember the "wisdom of the mirror" that you read about in one of your favorite books, the *Bardo Thodol*. You are alone (you and I); the mirror reflects only one face—contorted in a grimace of pain—through which you (we) speak (7).] In the novel, Madero's consciousness looks down at his own dead body as if watching a film of his life screened on the face of a mirror.

According to the *Bardo Thodol* [*Book of the Dead*], the mind passes through several stages following physical death. At this point the devotee is instructed to engage in Buddhist practices that include the fostering of lucidity, the liberation from desires, attachments, and anger, and the cultivation of compassion. Through these means the practioner aims to free him/herself from the cycle of birth and death. In the novel, it is particularly important that Madero undergo this process of reflection in order to release his sense of responsibility for bloodshed and

suffering in Mexico: "Por eso, espera: entiende, entiéndete, entién-
deme. No intentes marchar con esta gran culpa a cuestas. Aférrate al
último latido, al recuerdo del último latido: permanece en él, no lo
olvides, eternízalo" (9). [Then, at least wait. Understand, understand
yourself, understand me. Don't try to go forward with this great guilt
hanging over you. Hang onto the last heartbeat, to the memory of the
last heartbeat. Stay with it, don't forget it, eternalize it (8).] Madero's
spiritual process of navigating the *bardo* (liminal, in-between states)
involves weighing his good and bad deeds in the mirror of karma and
relinquishing his attachments to the material world.

The northern landholder Francisco I. Madero (1873–1913) was an
unlikely hero. A vegetarian and spiritist who not only would seek to
comply with the *Bardo Thodol* as seen earlier but who also studied
and wrote commentaries on the Hindu sacred text the *Bhagavad Gita*,
Madero entered the annals of history when he published *La sucesión
presidencial* [*The Presidential Succession*] in 1910. His book called
for democratic elections to end Porfirio Díaz's thirty-five-year dictatorship. Madero proclaimed a revolution to begin in November of
that same year, a call that was answered and led by the Aquiles Serdán
brothers, who lost their lives in the uprising. When Díaz resigned in
1911, Madero was elected president. However, his leadership disappointed not only Díaz supporters but also chief revolutionary com-
manders such as Emiliano Zapata, who lamented Madero's lack of
initiative in land reform and his misguided trust in such figures as the
treacherous Victoriano Huerta. Within a year and a half of Madero's
presidency, Huerta unleashed the *decena trágica*, or "ten tragic days."
During the "ten tragic days" in 1913, Huerta's soldiers fired on civilians in the capital, brutalized and killed Madero's brother Gustavo,
and assassinated Madero and vice president Pino Suárez. This assassination inspired tremendous popular support for Madero's memory
and was the catalyst for further armed uprisings, unleashing several
more years of violence before the revolution ended in 1920.

Given the violent human losses of the armed uprising that Francisco I.
Madero tipped off, is the reader to see him as a quixotic figure, mis-
guided by his fervent belief in communicating with spirits?
Alternatively, does Madero fulfill a necessary role in Mexican his-
tory? The novel cites the early twentieth-century intellectual José
Vasconcelos regarding Madero's loss of lucidity:

Vasconcelos, quien será de los pocos que *casi* entendieron lo que te
sucedió, escribió: "El destino, al consumar fines tortuosos, ciega a los

más lúcidos en el instante en que va a destruirlos. Sobreviene una especie de parálisis la víspera de las derrotas injustas, pero inevitables. La maldición que pesa sobre nuestra patria oscureció la mente del más despejado de sus hijos. Entorpeció la acción del más ágil de sus héroes. A Madero le envolvió la sombra." (224)

[Vasconcelos, who will be one of the few who almost understood what happened to you, wrote, "Destiny, to realize its tortuous ends, blinds the most brilliant men at the very instant in which it will destroy them. It overcomes them with a form of paralysis on the eve of their unjust but inevitable defeat. The curse that hangs over our country darkened the minds of the most innocent of its children. It hindered the actions of its most able hero. Its shadow engulfed Madero." (108)]

For Vasconcelos, Madero was confused, misled by his belief in spirits, and led blindly into a ruinous fate for himself and his country. On the other hand, we can recall Wilhelm Friedrich Hegel's philosophy of history from the introduction to this book; for Hegel, a hero such as Madero would be unconsciously guided not by the spirits of the dead but by a rational world spirit: "Reason rules the world" (408). Thus, in the Hegelian view, Madero's impulses and ideals would form part of the evolution of world history as guided by reason: "All these expressions of individual and national life, in seeking and fulfilling their own ends, are at the same time the means and instruments of a higher purpose and wider enterprise of which they are themselves ignorant and which they nevertheless unconsciously carry out" (408). Hegel offers the example of Caesar as such a historical agent whose actions transcend his conscious intentions: "...his work was the product of an impulse which accomplished the end for which his age was ready. Such are the great men of history: the substance of their own particular ends is the will of the world spirit" (410). In attempting to conserve his own power and status, Caesar won an initial victory over his rivals that had a much greater impact, consolidating the Roman Empire and changing world history.

However, the narrator in the novel does not make clear whether the greater changes that Madero's sacrifices brought about have affected Mexican history for better or for worse. On the one hand, both his initiation of the revolution and his assassination unleashed waves of violence, suffering, and death throughout the region. On the other hand, the novel concedes implicitly that inaction may also have been inacceptable, as the conditions under Díaz's long presidency were dire for most, with extreme poverty, little access to education, the suppression of strikes and killing or virtual enslavement of strikers, the absence of democratic elections, and censorship of the press.

Given these conditions, was the revolution indeed worth its human costs? We can examine closely the narrator's review of Madero's errors and see what this appraisal indicates about Mexico in his time and at the time of the novel's publication in the late twentieth century. Do Madero's weaknesses make him seem more noble because of what he attempts to accomplish despite them? Madero makes two principal mistakes that appear repeatedly throughout the novel and that resonate in the years to follow his death:

1. Forgiving and trusting the wrong people and failing those that he should have most trusted.
2. Launching a political, public life, a step that would cause him and countless others to lose their lives.

Let us begin with the first error. The narrator makes it clear that Madero fails Emiliano Zapata, the revolutionary "general of the south," by not supporting him. Madero succumbs to his own class prejudices; in his view, Zapata's peasant soldiers are merely uncontrolled agents of violence. Madero also disappoints Zapata by failing to back his plans of agrarian reform, permitting officials not worthy of trust to disarm Zapata, and even going so far as to encourage them to "put him in his place." For the narrator, this merits a stronger word than error—betrayal: "Pero tú traicionaste a Zapata. Aunque lo reconocieras como "mi mayor error," según le confesaste a Ángeles en la prisión de la tendencia, ¿por qué no nombrarlo con la palabra adecuada? Traición" (110). [But you betrayed Zapata. And it made no difference that you recognized it as "my biggest mistake," as you confessed to Angeles when you were both prisoners in the supply depot at the National Palace. But why don't you call it what it is? Betrayal (54–55).] Madero betrays Zapata and the zapatistas because, despite his avowed compassion for the poor, for him the zapatistas represent brutal, uneducated peasant multitudes.

Ironically, after Madero relinquishes his support for Zapata, the federal soldiers then respond to Zapata's *Plan de Ayala* demanding land reform (and denouncing Madero) with cruelty rather than the civilized mercy that the president had counted on. The federals proceed to burn down entire villages and hang suspected rebels from the trees, "destruir y quemar todo sitio en donde los rebeldes pudieran encontrar refugio y armas" (143) [burning and destroying every structure where the rebels could find weapons or shelter (69)]. The narrator again obliges Madero to gaze into the mirror of his memories and to witness the people of Morelos defending their homes with shovels and hoes; he sees the federals burning peasant rebels alive or decapitating them, and the insurgents doing the same to the federals in revenge—in sum, a brutal scene for a man working through the phases of the *Bardo Thodol* to have to face: "Y mientras más saña muestran unos, peor es la venganza de otros. Finalmente nadie se salva, hermano, en la tierra abrasada de ese estado. En la tierra abrasada de todo tu país" (144). [And the more ruthless one side is with the other, the greater the vengeance of the other. In the end, Brother, no one escapes, no one is saved in the burning earth of that state—in the scorched earth of your entire country (69).] The consequences of the president's abandonment of Zapata are devastating in the novel.

Madero not only fails those who merit his trust; he also trusts those who will betray him. His decisions as a historical figure resonate throughout the remainder of the twentieth century, during which PRI leaders continued to appoint individuals whose strengths often lay in the reach of their power rather than in their ethics, in accordance with the Machiavellian philosophy of keeping one's friends close and one's enemies closer. Witness, for example, the case of Carlos Hank González (1927–2001), former governor of the state of Mexico, former mayor of Mexico City, and former secretary of tourism, and secretary of agriculture under Carlos Salinas de Gortari. Beginning in the 1970s under President López Portillo and continuing through the 1990s under Salinas de Gortari, Carlos Hank González wielded his PRI connections to consolidate a massive financial empire, "Grupo Hank," with multimillion-dollar reaches in transportation, banking, and construction. The Drug Enforcement Administration (DEA) and the Central Intelligence Agency (CIA) have linked the family business (now run by sons Jorge Hank Rhon and Carlos Hank Rhon) to drug trafficking and money laundering; perhaps even more alarming is the suspicion that Carlos Hank González may be linked to masterminding the assassination of the PRI's own presidential candidate Luis Donaldo Colosio in 1994, an assassination that recalls the political betrayals and murders among revolutionary leaders.

In the novel, although warned not to have faith in Huerta, a ruthless political figure, Madero nevertheless grants him more autonomy and even names him to lead the armed forces instead of the more trustworthy Felipe Ángeles. Pancho Villa, Emiliano Zapata, his brother Gustavo, and his mother warn Madero "porque hasta tu propia madre te había prevenido contra él" (15) [because even your own mother had warned you against him (10)]. The narrator insinuates that the president has forgiven Huerta his previous treachery and granted him greater military authority because he has chosen Huerta as the agent to hasten his own death: "Tenía que ser él, ¿verdad hermano?" (15). [It had to be Huerta. Right, Brother? (10)] The narrative voice further suggests that Madero has set himself up for betrayal in a quest for martyrdom:

> ¿Querías precipitarlo todo de una buena vez? Porque ya sólo tu sangre salvaría quizás esta revolución truncada en la que tú mismo habías perdido la fe, y no podías más con ella, y los errores cometidos a esas alturas no tenían remedio, y ansiabas beber el cáliz hasta las heces porque siempre tuviste vocación para ello y sabías que era tu destino. (16)

> [Did you just want it all to end and be done with it? Because by now only your blood could save this aborted revolution, the revolution in which you yourself had lost faith; you couldn't handle it anymore; and at this stage there was no way to right the errors that had already been committed. You yearned to drain the last bitter drops from the chalice because this was always your calling and you knew it was your destiny. (10)]

Perhaps, the narrator finally challenges Madero, in trusting Huerta he was simply seeking a selfish end to his own disillusionment and his guilty conscience.

On the one hand, Madero does not command respect because he is not willing to imprison or execute figures who later returned to slaughter his allies. The narrator continuously chastises Madero for his naiveté in believing in the basic goodness of all humanity and for his insistence on loving and forgiving his enemies: "¿De veras creías que terminarías por redimirlos? Salvo contadas excepciones, ¿iba a poder con ellos tu suave bondad?" (21). [Did you really believe that you would wind up saving your enemies? Except for a few, were you going to win them over with your goodness? (13)] On another occasion Madero's disingenuous faith in humanity gets him into trouble when he attempts to convince an official to respect the democratic vote, but instead the official orders his colleague's arrest: "¿Por qué no te convenciste nunca de que apelar a la buena voluntad de la gente era sólo una ilusión?" (16). [Why weren't you ever convinced that appealing to people's good will was just an illusion? (11)] The narrator again laments Madero's lack of skepticism.

On the other hand, the leader's compassion and calm are admirable qualities with a certain strength of their own that draw others to him: "hasta que tu imperturbabilidad, a falta de otra fuerza, les demostró quién era el jefe del movimiento revolucionario. Fuerza que, diría Felipe Ángeles, tenías en lo más profundo de tu mirada dulce" (19). [Your immutability, more than any other force, showed them who was the leader of the revolution. This strength, as Felipe Ángeles would later say, shone from the depths of your tender gaze (12).] Despite Madero's indecisiveness, his tranquility and benevolence earn him the troops' loyalty. Indeed, not only does Madero's kindness win him the respect of a well-educated revolutionary general such as Felipe Ángeles; his "big soul" also earns the admiration of a tough rebel such as the northern leader Pancho Villa: "Este hombre es un rico que pelea por el bien de los pobres. Yo lo veo chico de cuerpo, pero creo que es muy grande su alma" (19). [This is a rich man who fights for the good of the poor. I see he is a small man physically, but I believe he has a very big heart (12).] As the narrator concedes, Madero does win over a few in life—and perhaps many more after his death—with his example of compassion.

However, those who endeavor to earn the forgiveness he has granted them are few, and Huerta is not among them. For the narrator, Madero's mistake of believing in the loyalty of Huerta leads to the worst possible outcome; he leaves the country in Huerta's hands:

> Y ahora tu dolor—un dolor mucho más agudo que el que nunca imaginaste—es porque ésa tu pretensión de redentor ha dejado a tu país en manos de gente como él. Y es que, no tenía remedio, la culminación de tu bondad debía ser el martirio, el tuyo y el del pueblo; pueblo que no se perdonaría tampoco el haber permitido que te mataran, a ti su Presidente bueno que lo liberó de la tiranía y creyó en él en su libertad y en su responsabilidad. (21)

> [And now your pain—a more intense pain than you ever imagined—comes from the fact that your aspirations to become a savior put your country in the hands of such men. And the thing is, there could be no other outcome. The culmination of your goodness had to be martyrdom, yours and your countrymen, they who would not forgive themselves for having allowed your enemies to kill you, their good President who freed them from tyranny and who believed in them, in their freedom and responsible behavior. (13)]

Particularly painful for the president's conscience to face is the panorama of endless corpses hung from the trees as the fighting intensifies after his assassination: "y las piernas balanceándose como péndulos, con los huaraches enlodados. ¿Quiénes son, hermano? ¿Y qué punzantes sus miradas extraviadas, plenas de una resignación dulce, aún más insoportable que el odio y el reclamo" (22). [Legs swinging like pendulums shod in mud-caked *huaraches*. Who are they, Brother? And how penetrating are their lost stares full of a tender resignation even more unbearable than their previous cries of protest and hatred (13).] The image is excruciatingly vivid, an image still conserved and commemorated in the jarring photographs found in the Casasola Archives, photos that form part of what Mexican intellectual Carlos Monsiváis terms the collective conscience of Mexico today.

In addition to seeing the lynchings, Madero must witness his own brother Gustavo's suffering, when he is tormented and killed in revenge for having arrested Huerta—and then having released him, on Madero's orders: "Pero, finalmente, ninguna culpa es comparable a la que te provoca recordar la muerte de tu hermano Gustavo. Los cuerpos inánimes colgados en la ristra de árboles, los cientos de miles de muertes que desatará tu muerte misma, se desvanecen—anónimas—en la memoria, ante esa sola imagen calcinante" (33). [In the final analysis there is no guilt that can compare to what you feel when you remember how your brother Gustavo died. The string of motionless bodies hanging from the rows of trees, the hundreds of thousands of deaths that your own death will unleash, they all vanish—anonymous— in your memory before the single burning image of Gustavo's death (18).] The narrator's conclusion is brutally frank: Madero's faith in humanity is answered with criminal ingratitude in the brutalization of his dearly loved brother. "Gustavo era un hombre corpulento, muy sano, que tardaba en morir.... Finalmente, su cadáver fue enterrado bajo un montón de estiercol. ¿No fue esta ceremonia una respuesta...a la fe incondicional que tenías en la bondad humana?" (43). [Gustavo was a strong, very healthy man and it took a long time for him to die.... Finally, they buried his body under a pile of manure. Wasn't this ceremony a response...to the unconditional faith that you had in the goodness of human nature? (23)] In prison before his assassination, Madero appears to recognize his mistake in attempting to please those who did not merit his faith: "Como político he cometido dos graves errores que han causado mi caída: haber querido contentar a todos y no haber sabido confiar en mis verdaderos amigos" (111). [As a politician, I have made two major errors that have brought about my downfall: trying to please everyone and not trusting in my true friends (54).] His lack of fortitude and his poor judgment have come at a high price.

We have seen this misplaced trust as Madero's first error in the novel; the second error that the narrator brings up again and again is his immersion in political, revolutionary life. There are two core narratives with contradictory messages within *Madero, el otro* regarding the protagonist's public dealings. In one narrative, a Tolstoy story cited in the novel as a favorite of Madero's, two hermit brothers find a pile of gold behind their cottage. While one flees, the other uses the gold to feed the poor, heal the sick, and house the homeless, who thank him and praise him for his deeds. However, when he attempts to return to the mountain cottage an angel bars the generous hermit, admonishing him that the gold was a devilish temptation and that his brother's simple life of renunciation, work, and prayer has been of greater service to God.

The narrator's interpretation of the tale in *Madero, el otro* indicates that, like the hermit who shunned the gold, Madero should have stayed on the farm, working simply and administering to local residents. Upon recalling the leader's first public act in 1904, in which he exhorts citizens to vote, the narrator pauses: "Pero si regresara el tiempo, ¿no te detendrías ahí, en pleno llano, e irías a reducirte a atender los negocios de tu hacienda, a ayudar a tu grupito de pobres— muy pocos, ¿pero no decías que con salvar a uno solo justificabas tu vida?—y a continuar con tus retiros místicos?" (70) [But again, if you could turn back the hands of time, wouldn't you choose to stop there in the middle of the plain and limit yourself to attending to the affairs of your small *hacienda*, to helping your small group of poor folks? They were few, but didn't you say that if you saved even one life, this action justified your own life? Wouldn't you go back to your mystic retreats? (35)] In this sense, the narrator indicates that Madero will later regret his decision to engage in public life, a choice that would lead to many more betrayals and assassinations of major leaders during the revolutionary period: Zapata, Villa, and Obregón were all handed over and shot. Even in the late twentieth century such a public life in Mexico put a major leader at risk for assassination from within his own party; witness, as mentioned earlier, the mysterious shooting of PRI presidential candidate Luis Donaldo Colosio in 1994, a shooting that was rumored to have been masterminded by the same party leaders that had designated him as their candidate in the famous "dedazo," or "big finger," when the departing president points to his choice of successor.

On the other hand, in contrast with Tolstoy's message to refrain from public life, the novel also cites a second core narrative with a spiritual theme that contradicts Tolstoy, as it finds a proper place in life for public battle. In a key section of the *Bhagavad Gita*, the divinity

Krishna, disguised as a charioteer, explains to the prince-warrior Arjun that it is useless for him to lament battling his kinsmen. After all, it is Arjun's ordained role to fight; furthermore, his relatives' and neighbors' deaths are no cause for worry. Earthly mortality is meaningless, Krishna explains; death is simply a phase in the cycle of rebirth: "Those who are wise lament neither for the living nor the dead" (21). Therefore, as also advised in the *Bardo Thodol*, Madero must relinquish his anguished recollections of suffering and death that the revolution has unleashed. The narrator's interpretation of this story in *Madero, el otro* is in accordance with both the *Gita* and with the Hegelian approach to history, indicating that Madero's revolutionary acts are the fulfillment of his destined role, and that like Arjun, rather than lamenting the deaths and violent losses that result from his actions, he must learn to accept them.

Indeed, in the novel, Madero's attempts to reject violence simply bring about more violence, as when, as we have seen, he refuses to have the traitor Huerta shot and Huerta subsequently unleashes waves of human destruction: "el loco Madero...aceptó y generó una violencia que temía y rechazaba, que lo desconcertó y culpó tanto que terminó por hacer exactamente lo contrario a aquello que debería haber hecho para evitarla" (246). [The crazy Madero...accepted and generated a violence that he both feared and rejected, a violence that confused him and made him feel so guilty that he ended up doing the exact opposite of what he should have done to avoid it (118).] In effect, the narrator indicates that there were times when a stronger hand may have prevented more brutality and suffering in the long run. An example could be that of the astute president Lázaro Cárdenas, who led a radicalization period from 1934 to 1940 by wielding complete power through the revolutionary party (then called the PRM rather than the PRI), but who also is fondly remembered in Mexico for distributing land more effectively than subsequent presidents and for nationalizing an economic jewel, the petroleum industry.

Would an interior life of study, prayer, and contemplation have been preferable to a life of public service for the mystical Madero, a less pragmatic individual than Cárdenas? The narrator again interrogates the protagonist: "¿A partir de qué momento—determinante en tu vida y en la de tu país—te creíste destinado a una más alta misión? Eso es, búscalo: ¿en qué momento te conquistó el resplandor del oro, lo tomaste y bajaste con él a la ciudad?" (50). [What was the moment—the fatal moment of your life and of your country—when you began to believe you were destined for a higher mission? That's it, look for it: what was the moment when the glitter of gold overcame you, when you took the gold and came down from the mountain to the city? (27)] When Madero's spirit sessions reveal to him that he should take action and lift the yoke from his people, the narrator again questions his decision: "Ya estaba ahí: el resplandor del oro en la hierba, brillando como el sol. Por eso 'aspira a hacer el bien a tus conciudadanos realizando tal o cual obra útil, trabajando por algún ideal que venga a elevar el nivel moral de la sociedad, a sacarla de la opresión, de la esclavitud, del fanatismo' "(59). [And there it was, the glitter of gold, shining like the sun over the fields. Raúl's urgings made the temptation greater: "Strive to do good work for your fellow citizens by carrying out this or that useful deed, by working for some ideal that will raise the moral standard of society, that will free it from oppression, from slavery, from fanaticism" (31).] For the narrator, Madero's decision to become involved in public service entails his succumbing to the temptation of the gold behind the hut. Again, the narrator asks, is Madero the pacifist corrupted by power? Or is he doomed to lose power and unleash bedlam because of his hesitancy to act?

> ¿Será que el poder es, finalmente, incompatible con hacer el bien? ¿Y por eso, porque lo supiste desde siempre, no te restaba sino el sacrificio para demostrarlo, para demostrar que un presidente bueno, que no fusila, que no reprime, que cree en la libertad individual e intenta la pacificación a toda costa, es irreconciliable con el poder absoluto que corrompe absolutamente? (211)

> [Could it be that, in the final analysis, power is incompatible with doing good? And because you believed this from the start, you had no choice but to sacrifice yourself to prove it, to prove that a good president—one who does not have people shot, one who does not repress them, one who believes in the rights of the individual, one who tries to impose peace at all costs—is irreconcilable with absolute power that corrupts absolutely? (101)]

A fundamental question of the novel is, then, whether power is incompatible with doing good, a question of continued relevance throughout the PRI-powered, ostensibly well-intentioned series of governments of twentieth-century Mexico. However, we can recall that in the narrator's interpretation of the Arjun episode, the warrior must fulfill his destined role, and that for Hegel as well, monumental figures are simply carrying out their destiny to transform history. Even if it means great personal sacrifice, they are compelled to do so.

The figure in the novel most compatible with Hegel's paradigm is perhaps the "other" Madero, the one who takes political action, prompting citizens to take up arms on November 20, 1910. This is the Madero seduced by the splendor of his destiny:

> Ya no había regreso, hermano, caíste (te hicimos caer) en tentación y la verdad es que esto de asumir un destino con un sabor tan agridulce... producía en ti una euforia que nunca, ni remotamente, produjeron las escapadas furtivas a los burdeles en París, o el vino, o el tabaco, o el baile. Nada. Si tuvieras que elegir un vicio, uno solo—bien te lo dictó Raúl: "los espíritus superiores gozan sobre todo con el triunfo de sus ideas"—sería éste: transformar la realidad. (72)

> [There was no turning back now, Brother. You fell (we made you fall) into temptation. The truth is, this business of assuming such a bitter-sweet destiny... produced in you a euphoria not experienced before, not even remotely: not from your furtive escapades in the brothels of Paris, nor from consuming wine or tobacco, nor from dancing. Nothing else. If you had to choose a vice, only one—Raúl said it well when he dictated it to you: "What gives the spirits their greatest pleasure is the realization of their ideas"—it would be this: changing reality. (36)]

Was he tempted by the glory of his deeds? Or the possibility of transforming reality? Was this the dream of the insurrectionist, of "el *otro* Madero, el que implicaba sin remedio desatar las amarras de la furia y la sangre contenida?" (163) [the *other* Madero, the dream that implied the inevitable unleashing of a suppressed rage and the spilling of blood (79).] The violence required to bring about revolutionary change is the responsibility of the "other" Madero, the one who initiates the military attack in 1911 in northern Mexico: "el *otro* Madero, que desde tu retiro ascético, desde el estrecho tapanco de la hacienda, concebía la gran acción redentora, la acción fascinante que te (nos) sacaba al mundo lanza en ristre: 'Eres el último de los soldados, pero soldado de la libertad y el progreso'" (172). [The *other* Madero. The one who from your ascetic retreat in the small attic of the hacienda had conceived the great redeeming action, the fascinating action that thrust you (us) into the world, lance at the ready. "You are the last of the soldiers, but you are a soldier of freedom and progress" (83).] This Madero sees as his role as a soldier of God, saving his people from oppression.

This sense of divine violence stands in opposition to the Tolstoy story, again appearing instead in the *Bhagavad Gita* tale mentioned earlier. Significantly, Madero, a rare intellectual president followed by a long line of strongmen, businessmen, and U.S.-trained economists, carries to his assassination a briefcase holding the valued commentaries that he has been writing on the sacred Hindu text. The narrator rebukes him, stating that his commentaries misinterpret the passage cited earlier in which the divinity Krishna admonishes Arjun to stop fretting because it is his duty to go to battle: "Interpretaste el pasaje como un símbolo de la batalla que debemos emprender contra nosotros mismos, contra nuestras pasiones más bajas…¿Cómo pudiste engañarte así, hermano? ¿Cuánto dolor te hubieras ahorrado, les hubieras ahorrado a todos, si interpretaras el pasaje, no como un símbolo, sino como una realidad?" (90) [You interpreted the passage as a symbol of the battle we must wage against our own selves, against our basest passions.…How could you fool yourself like that, Brother? How much pain would you have spared yourself, and everyone else, if you had interpreted the passage not as a symbol, but as reality? (45)]

The reality for the narrator is that, as the *Gita* denotes, a revolutionary must not only struggle with his inner passions but must also at times fight hand to hand against his own neighbors. Caught up in his own spiritual quest, Madero has overlooked the practical realities of the external world, and his action, or his inaction, affects multitudes of people beyond himself.

During the final tragic ten days, the narrator quotes Madero, like Arjun, lamenting the wasted blood between brothers:

"Toda la sangre derramada por un conflicto entre hermanos es inútil, se lo aseguro."—¿Cómo podía hablar así el jefe de una revolución triunfante, que además él mismo inició? Pero aquel había sido *otro* Madero, ¿no es verdad?, y para entonces—como ahora—sólo te provocaba culpa y no querías ya saber de él. 'No más víctimas, no más víctimas, por favor,' resumía tu súplica a Sánchez Azcona. (220)

["I assure you, any blood spilled because of conflict among brothers is useless." How could the leader of a triumphant revolution, especially the one who started it, talk like that? But that had been the *other* Madero talking, right? Because since then—like now—that *other* only made you feel guilty, and you did not want to even think about him anymore. Your plea to Sánchez Azcona summed it up in these words: "No more victims, no more victims, please." (105–106)]

The president regrets the steps taken by the "other" Madero the leader of a revolution, one willing to shed blood; he attempts to reject that part of his own history, but the *Gita* passage reminds him that the "other," fighting Madero is a necessary part of his destined role.

Despite the overwhelming sense of guilt, at the end of the novel the narrator provides Madero with a more comforting memory with which to depart the world. When facing Huerta, the memories of his own words pass through his mind like the soundtrack of a film. Then the catharsis comes:

> Mira, las escenas que desentrañas dejan de culparte y de fijarse en ti como un mal sueño. Sin embargo, no creo que debas quedarte con esa últimas imagen de Félix Díaz, tan grotesca...Busca otra, quizá años más adelante. Ésa, por ejemplo, de noviembre de 1914....Quédate con esa última imagen, hermano: Villa, Ángeles y Zapata llorando, los tres, ante tu tumba. (245)

> [Look! The scenes that you can make out now seem to have lost their power to make you feel guilty and are no longer clinging to you like a bad dream. Be that as it may, I don't think it's a good idea for your last image to be of Félix Díaz; it's so grotesque....Look for a different image, perhaps something from years later. For example, in November 1914....Let this be your last image, Brother: Villa, Angeles and Zapata, the three of them together, crying at your grave. (117–118)]

In his final memory he is granted a picture of the affection and admiration of those left behind. Although it must also be said that, amidst the violent reprisals, betrayals, and assassinations that followed Madero's death, neither of the three generals survived for more than a few years beyond Madero himself to carry on his legacy as a "compassionate revolutionary."

With this funerary image in mind, we can now retrace the connection from the revolution to the novel's time of publication in 1989. From a late twentieth- and early twenty-first-century perspective, were the sacrifices of Madero's time fruitful and worthwhile? General Felipe Ángeles is quoted in the novel as concluding that Francisco I. Madero's death was a positive force for change in Mexico: " 'la muerte de Madero hizo más bien al país que todas las gestiones que hizo en su vida' " (87). [" 'Madero's death did more for the good of the country than all his actions during his lifetime' " (43).] Was the revolution indeed a success? Was the bloodshed worth overcoming the thirty-five-year Díaz presidency? Had Mexico achieved Madero's dream of democracy, Zapata's dream of agrarian reform, or Villa's dream of social justice? While Solares sets the novel in 1911, the story contains implicit political links with Solares's own time. We know that the Partido Revolucionario Institucional (PRI) was in power continuously from the revolution until the year 2000, and the faction appropriated the revolution as a party icon. Because the idealization of revolutionary heroes such as Madero has been part and parcel of PRI rhetoric, the demythification of such a hero in the novel was daring. As critic William Martínez explains,

> La frustración que México vivió (y todavía vive) por conservar los ideales de libertad, justicia y paz, ha creado una exaltación de la valoración de figuras icónicas....Específicamente, en el caso de México, los héroes revolucionarios han sido elevados a tal grado, tanto por la cultura oficial, como por la popular, que es imposible concebir ni siquiera la mera implicación de alguna falla en ellos. (79)

> [The frustration that Mexico lived (and still does) for conserving the ideals of liberty, justice, and peace, has created an exaltation of the valuation of iconic figures....Specifically, in the case of Mexico, revolutionary heroes have been elevated to such a degree, as much by official culture as by popular culture, that it is impossible to even conceive the mere implication of a fault in them.]

Every year on September 15, upon the celebration of Mexico's independence, the president cries from the balcony of the National Palace "¡Viva México! ¡Viva la revolución!" and shouts the names of historical figures such as "¡Viva Madero!" However, despite this yearly ritual, the public exaltation of revolutionary heroes has not been sufficient to cover up the failings of the revolution's promises.

Under the PRI, extreme poverty and economic disparity did not abate. Indeed, today, alongside the poverty-level majority and the smaller middle class, Mexico boasts of some of the richest families in the world, families that are not generally known for generous philanthropy. To give one example of this disparity, Carlos Slim Helú, the telecom magnate and the business associate of Carlos Salinas de Gortari (president 1988–1994) ranks third place in the world in *Fortune* magazine's 2007 list of billionaires, yet only recently has he begun to be involved in philanthropic causes such as donating eyeglasses for schoolchildren. Meanwhile, on the outskirts of Mexico City, citizens erect colonies next to open sewage canals, and *pepenadores* scrounge a living picking through the steaming garbage in the nearby dumps. These individuals continue to arrive from the countryside to the city, where they hope to eke out a better living. The PRI government's fulfillment of the revolution's promise of land reform more often than not entailed the

disappointing distribution of arid, unworkable terrain; furthermore, competing with U.S. agribusiness under the free-trade agree-
ment passed in 1994 has made it increasingly challenging for small
Mexican growers to succeed economically.

There were also numerous cases of ineffectiveness, fraud, and
repression in the decades leading up to the publication of *Madero, el
otro*. The party's wrongs included government-sponsored shootings
at the student protest in 1968 in the Plaza de Tlatelolco and police
repression of a student protest again in 1971. Porfirio Díaz's suppression of strikes in the early twentieth century also resonates with the
PRI's repression of the 1968 student protest: "la política de Díaz:
estimular la inversión del capital extranjero en detrimento de los
intereses nacionales, sofocar brutal y sistemáticamente los brotes de
rebeldía que pudieran alterar la paz y que se traducía en la represión
de obreros en Cananea y Río Blanco, o en la esclavitud del pueblo
Yaqui" (147). [Don Porfirio's policies: fostering foreign investment at
the expense of the national interests, and brutally and systematically
suffocating any sign of rebellion that could disturb the peace, as was
the case with the repression of the workers in Cananea and Río
Blanco, or with the slavery of the Yaqui Indians (71).]

Indeed, the 1968 shootings led to poet and essayist Octavio Paz's
resignation from his diplomatic position in India, where he had been
composing poetry inspired by the same Eastern philosophies that
Madero had studied while seeking a pacifist response to Díaz's strong-
handed policies. Finally, corruption and mismanagement of funds
were also evidenced during the 1985 earthquake, when government
aid was notably missing from what were largely civilian rescue
efforts.

In an additional link between Díaz's regime and the PRI's disap-
pointments, censorship came into play when, in 1976, journalists
critical of the government were fired from *Excelsior*, a major national
newspaper. The censorship case in 1976 particularly resonates with
the novel's mention of Díaz's censorship: "Sólo faltó agregar: de la
censura, añorándola como al resto del régimen porfirista" (178).
[They conveniently failed to mention the other side of the Díaz regime,
its censorship (86).] Ironically, although the newspapers had been
unable to critique Díaz while he was in power, under Madero's newly
instated freedom of the press they mocked Madero and reminisced
about the prosperity and stability they had enjoyed under Díaz.

While Díaz's presidency was a dictatorship that lasted for 35 years,
during the decades that followed the revolution's triumph Mexico

was ruled by what Peruvian writer Mario Vargas Llosa famously called the "dictatorship of the party." At the time of the novel's publication, Carlos Salinas de Gortari was president, one of an uninterrupted series of PRI leaders since the end of the revolution; his election in 1988 was disputed when a majority of citizens claimed they had voted for his rival Cuauhtemoc Cárdenas (son of Lázaro Cárdenas). Then, as in 1910 under Díaz, democratic, fraud-free elections appeared to be a farce. Salinas's neoliberal economic policies likewise were not dissimilar from Díaz's promotion of European investment, industry, and development, beneficial to the privileged but at a cost to the poor. Salinas's presidency was, however, the beginning of the end for the PRI; he had artificially inflated the peso, which subsequently fell in crisis proportions after his presidency ended in 1994. Scandals and arrests followed the 1995 economic crash: Salinas's brother Raúl was detained and is serving a fifty-year prison term, and PRI presidential candidate Colosio was assassinated under suspicious circumstances. Ernesto Cedillo's presidency (1994–2000) finally cleared the path for the democratic election of a president from another party, conservative PAN candidate Vicente Fox, in 2000. However, the public's jubilation in response to the historic electoral change and Fox's attempts at a coalition across party lines was soon followed by disappointment in the ineffectiveness of the Fox administration as well.

To further emphasize this link between Madero's time and our own, historian Enrique Krauze wrote in 1987 of the continued relevancy of Madero's political manifesto, *La sucesión presidencial*: "Muchas de las llagas políticas y morales que Madero señaló en aquel fogoso libro se han perpetuado. Vale la pena vernos ahora mismo en ellas y recordar que la medicina democrática de aquel sonriente apóstol no tiene—ni tendrá—fecha de caducidad" (108). [Many of the political and moral wounds that Madero pointed out in that spirited book have perpetuated. It is worth seeing ourselves in them now and remembering that the democratic medicine of that smiling apostle does not have—nor will it have—an expiration date.] Krauze indicates that despite Madero's insight, his efforts did not accomplish enough to change Mexico's political panorama in the twentieth century.

Hegel wrote his philosophy of history in the early nineteenth century, long before twentieth-century totalitarians such as Hitler would forever change our perception of world leaders who can only be seen as a destructive force. In the Hegelian view, the course of history is

always linked to its context of time and place, and figures such as
Madero are destined to be the sages of their time:

> They are the far-sighted ones; they have discerned what is true in
> their world and in their age, and have recognized the concept, the
> next universal to emerge....They have made themselves the instru-
> ments of the substantial spirit...they are irresistibly driven on to ful-
> fill their task....There is a power within them that is stronger than
> they are. (411)

In this interpretation, a hero would be driven by world spirit to bring
about the changes of his age, even though his actions would lead to
his own demise: "Caesar had to do what was necessary to overthrow
the decaying freedom of Rome; he himself met his end in the struggle, but necessity triumphed: in relation to the Idea, freedom was
subordinate to the external event" (413). Perhaps the fictional
Madero, struggling with guilt for the violence his life and death
unleashed, would be consoled by this Hegelian analysis of heroes.
Like Krishna simultaneously reassuring and admonishing Arjun in
Madero's dog-eared copy of the *Bhagavad Gita*, in the Hegelian
interpretation Madero had no choice but to fulfill his role as a historical catalyst for a new era in Mexican history, even when that
meant many failures and deaths alongside the limited successes of
the decades to come.

Los pasos de López

Jorge Ibargüengoitia's *Los pasos de López* (1982) focuses on a hero's
gaffes in another key moment one hundred years before Madero's
demise: the independence battles of 1810. Like Solares, Ibargüengoitia
also takes a figure from the Mexican pantheon and humanizes him
for the reader, but he does so from an ironic perspective. The main
character, Periñón, closely resembles Father Miguel Hidalgo y Costilla,
the insurgent celebrated today as independence hero and father of the
nation. However, unlike the works it reelaborates, *Los pasos* does not
iconize Hidalgo; nor does it demonize him. Instead, the novel brings
the hero down to scale; Periñón fumbles as a military leader and falters as a man of the cloth. Like Solares's *Madero, el otro, Los pasos*
reduces the epic distance that has separated today's reader from the
revolutionary icon, but Ibargüengoitia achieves this with a lighter
touch, through parody.

Fernando Aínsa recognizes the vital function of parody in new historical narrative: "La escritura paródica nos da, tal vez, la clase en que puede sintetizarse la nueva narrativa histórica. La historiografía, al ceder a la mirada demoledora de la parodia ficcional…permite recuperar la olvidada condición humana" (9). [Parodic writing gives us, perhaps, the class in which the new historical narrative can be synthesized. Historiography, upon ceding the destructive gaze of fictional parody, permits the recuperation of the forgotten human condition.] Ibargüengoitia employs humor to humanize Hidalgo through the use of stylistic elements of language, narrative perspective, naming, and collapsing. Parody also brings to light the inherent political commentary within *Los pasos de López*: the novel shows the priest and his coconspirators as privileged *criollos* who manipulate the indigenous masses as their military pawns in a poorly planned game of politics. As Jaime Castañeda Iturbide observes, beneath Ibargüengoitia's seemingly lighthearted style lies a powerful critique: "Decía Kierkegaard que el verdadero humorista debe hacer de la risa un despertar de la conciencia. Creo que es el caso de Jorge Ibargüengoitia" (44). [Kierkegaard used to say that a true humorist should make laughter an act of consciousness raising. I believe that's the case of Jorge Ibargüengoitia.] Ibarguengoitia's novel uses humor to raise trenchant questions about political and social mores of past and present.

Between the deceptively simple lines of *Los pasos de López* appears a critical commentary that diminishes the motives of the conspirators who initiated the revolution and reduces the previously amplified virtues and flaws of Hidalgo. Works such as Juan Mateos's popular serial novel *Sacerdote y caudillo* (1869) and Luis Castillo Ledón's biography *Hidalgo: La vida del héroe* (1945), as well as today's civic ceremonies and official festivities, have molded Hidalgo into a heroic statue. At the time when Mateos published his novel in 1869, the liberal elite was in the process of creating a cohesive sense of national identity. Mateos and his peers worked toward building a nation by establishing state symbols such as the Virgin of Guadalupe, civic holidays such as the sixteenth of September, and historical patron saints such as Hidalgo.

In contrast with Mateos's epoch, *Los pasos de López* appears at an opportune time for reassessing national myths. On the fifteenth and sixteenth of September, Mexico commemorates Hidalgo's call for independence with parades; the president emerges to reenact the ringing of the bell and the shout for independence. Institutional power affirms itself through such gestures. Barrientos comments that for the youth of Mexico today Hidalgo has become an empty symbol of the ruling party: "la demagogia oficial ha erizado de estatuas y monu-mentos los parques y las plazas del país; los símbolos patrios se han desgastado—los colores de la bandera son también los del partido oficial—y por eso la reacción general de niños y adolescentes frente a estos símbolos es de indiferencia, cuando no de franco rechazo" ("El grito" 23). [Official demogoguery has pockmarked the parks and pla-zas of the country with statues and monuments; the national symbols have worn out—the colors of the flag are also those of the ruling party—and because of that, the general reaction of children and ado-lescents before these symbols is one of indifference, if not outright rejection.] The oversaturated youth mistrust the national symbols.

Los pasos de López endeavors to rescue Hidalgo from the pedestals of "la demagogia oficial," using humor to bring him down to today's public. In this sense, Ibargüengoitia is a jester who breaks down national archetypes. Castañeda Iturbide notes that his novels are "Las únicas en la literatura mexicana contemporánea que logran mostrarnos la otra cara—quizás la auténtica—de nuestra realidad actual y pretérita. Las únicas que se atreven a desacralizar a los héroes nacionales, despoján-dolos del oropel y describiéndolos de carne y hueso, con sus virtudes y defectos" (11). [The only ones in contemporary Mexican literature that manage to show us the other face—perhaps the authentic one—of our current and previous reality. The only ones that dare to desacralize national heroes, stripping them of tinsel and describing them as flesh and bone, with their virtues and defects.] He maintains that critics have minimized Ibargüengoitia's work precisely because it is funny and because they find him "irrespetuoso de nuestros héroes, irreverente de la historia patria, mal mexicano" (99) [disrespectful of our heroes, irreverent toward national history, a bad Mexican]. Contrary to official glorification of the revolutionary leader, the "bad Mexican" Periñón of *Los pasos* is refashioned as a more everyday figure. Hidalgo as Periñón is more accessible. He is jollier, less intellectual, more youthful.

In the novel, Matías Chandón, an artillery soldier who joins the conspiracy and revolution, retells the plotting of the revolution among a group of associates who meet under the guise of a literary club. He narrates the discovery of the conspiracy, the ensuing battles, and the execution of Periñón and other leaders of the insurgency. Chandón speaks from the perspective of thirty years after the fateful days he recounts. His name resembles "chambón," indicating an awkward, clumsy bumbler as well as someone who has won by a fluke. Chandón's voice is educated but informal and colloquial. Although directly involved in the events he retells, the narrator looks back with an ironic gaze upon the arbitrariness of the heroes' actions that provoked the unfolding of the revolution. His stance blends irreverence and respect to reveal Periñón as utterly human. Whereas his defenders Mateos, Castillo Ledón, and conservative historian Lucas Alamán's works position themselves to judge Hidalgo from above or below, Ibargüengoitia's novel appears not to judge but simply to reveal the events from the perspective of a peer.

The consciousness of this eyewitness narrator calls attention to historical inconsistencies that had been previously unnoticed. For example, Chandón questions Periñón's choice to confide in the drum major of the Guanajuato (here Cuévano) batallion, who promises to turn over the troops of his town. He points out the rare likelihood that someone of drum major rank would have any such power; the decision "me pareció extraña, porque en el orden natural de las cosas un tambor mayor rara vez llega a estar en condiciones de entregar una plaza" (77) [seemed odd to me, because in the natural order of things a drum major is rarely in the position to hand over a plaza]. As the narrator suspects, the drum major later betrays the conspiracy.

Northrop Frye's interpretation of irony offers a useful approximation to the narrator's voice in *Los pasos de López* and helps to illuminate how Ibargüengoitia situates himself at an ironic distance before national history. The colloquial language and quiet distance of Chandón's voice make his opinions difficult to pinpoint. Frye says of the ironic perspective:

> The conception of irony meets us in Aristotle's *Ethics*, where the *eiron* is the man who deprecates himself, as opposed to the *alazon* [who aspires to be more than he is]. Such a man makes himself invulnerable, and, though Aristotle disapproves of him, there is no question that he is a predestined artist, just as the alazon is one of his predestined victims. The term irony, then, indicates a technique of saying as little and meaning as much as possible, or, in a more general way, a pattern of words that turns away from direct statement. . . . The ironic fiction writer, then, deprecates himself and, like Socrates, pretends to know nothing, even that he is ironic. Complete objectivity and suppression of all explicit moral judgements are essential to his method . . . sophisticated irony merely states, and lets the reader add the ironic tone himself. (40)

Such an ironic writer as Ibargüengoitia leaves it to the reader to make her own inferences from the narrator's self-deprecating style.

The irony inherent in *Los pasos* undermines the heroic power that Hidalgo yields in the romance of Mateos's *Sacerdote y caudillo*. Frye suggests that the romantic mode proffers an analogy of innocence; Periñón deviates from this model. *Sacerdote y caudillo* shares many characteristics with romance, a mode that avoids subtlety and complexity in favor of polarized good and evil. Simple binary relations appear as universal values. As Frye explains, "The mode of romance presents an idealized world: in romance heroes are brave, heroines beautiful, villains villainous, and the frustrations, ambiguities, and embarrassments of ordinary life are made little of" (151). Furthermore, romance tends to sanctify the hero and demonize the villain; in *Sacerdote y caudillo*, Hidalgo is a Moses or Christ figure. *Los pasos* parodies the romantic elements of such depictions. The hero combines both transcendent qualities, such as Hidalgo's passionate egalitarianism, and lowly qualities, such as his pride and his prodigal sexuality. He must contend with the everyday details of the conspiracy and revolution: his faltering attempts to make a functional cannon, for instance. Such moments travesty the romance of *Sacerdote y caudillo*. As Frye writes, "No one in a romance, Don Quixote protests, ever asks who pays for the hero's accommodation" (223). Such mundane struggles as paying for lodging or dragging an unwieldy cannon make for a more realistic hero.

Ibargüengoitia commented in an interview on his novel *Los relámpagos de agosto* that he was weary of "esa gran Vaca Sagrada de México que es su revolución y toda la prosa bastarda que de ella ha nacido" (qtd. in González de León 106) [that great sacred cow of Mexico that is the revolution and all the bastard prose born of it]. Although the writer was referring to the civil war that began in 1910, his declaration serves equally well for the independence war. In its parody of previous accounts of the independence movement, *Los pasos* embodies what Linda Hutcheon has termed "historiographic metafiction," a postmodern version of the historical novel that incorporates both a nostalgia for and a parody of the texts and motifs of the past. Such novels question and challenge the totalizing vision of what Lyotard calls "master fables," yet they refrain from definitively denying these tales. Such self-reflexive texts recognize that as both history and literature are human creations, it is most effective not to praise nor to destruct previous versions of history and ideology, but instead to explore them through techniques of parody and pastiche that juxtapose contradictory systems. Hutcheon emphasizes, "Postmodernism is a contradictory phenomenon, one that uses and abuses, installs and then subverts, the very concepts it challenges" (3). Such parody is a "repetition from a critical distance that permits an ironic signaling of the difference within the same heart of the similarity" (26). The resulting texts are "fundamentally contradictory, decidedly historical and inevitably political" (4).

To facilitate this historical and political parody, *Los pasos* thinly disguises the names of the now famous people and historic places where the events of independence unfolded. The name changes in *Los pasos* reduce the magnitude of historically marked figures and sites. Hidalgo is now "Periñón" and in a play the conspirators present, the "López" of the title. Nationally revered heroes address each other informally as "Pepe" and "Diego." Guanajuato is "Cuévano" and the famous shout or "Grito de Dolores," which initiated the revolution, is now the "Grito de Ajetreo". Rather than bearing the name of the town Dolores, signifying pain and suffering, the historic site is now Ajetreo, meaning bustle, rush, and fatigue. Ibargüengoitia uses this word play to transform a somber event into a poorly planned accident of history. The change in nomenclature in *Los pasos* provides for an escape from the requirement of historical accuracy. It also frees places and individuals from the weight of historical associations. Ibargüengoitia, a native of Guanajuato, mocks local pride by changing the names of sites that boast "Hidalgo was here."

In addition to the changes in place names, the personal names "López" and "Periñón" are significant. "López" is the name of a character that Periñón (Hidalgo) plays in the conspirators' literary group rehearsals of a Golden Age comedy called "La precaución inútil." López is the *gracioso* who maintains the dynamic flow of the action in the play, just as Hidalgo fuels the play of history. The novel reveals a conception of history as a stage in which a series of actors play their assigned roles. This idea of history as a theatrical show eliminates the epic dimension from the tale of the "fathers of independence." "Periñón era López, criado de Lindoro y el personaje más interesante de la comedia, él enredaba y desenredaba la acción, resolvía todos los problemas y al final recibía todos los castigos" (37). [Periñón was López, Lindoro's servant and the most interesting character in the comedy; he entangled and disentangled the action, resolved all of the problems and in the end received all of the penalties.] The name López appears again twice: first, the priest visits a prostibule before dawn and gives the code name "López" to gain entry. Such tongue-in-cheek scenes as this irreverently subvert Hidalgo's somber image. The name "López" returns once more at the end of the novel, when Periñón's prosecutors demand that he sign a confession of contrition before he is put to death. After waiting for six months, the insurgent leader finally concedes and signs the paper. The executioners fail to notice until years later that Periñón has the last laugh. He has signed the confession "López."

In addition to López as a character in a Golden Age play, the name indicates another theatrical reference from that period. Upon first glance, the title of the novel, *Los pasos de López*, appears to indicate that the narrative will follow the character's historical footsteps, or *pasos*. However, there is another hidden reference: the title also alludes to a series of short comedic plays known as "Los pasos de Lope." Lope de Rueda was a Spanish actor, writer, director, and producer with his own theatrical company in the mid-1500s. His *pasos* were simple scenes performed between the acts of longer comedies and designed to induce laughter; a typical skit might involve tricking a simpleton out of his evening meal. Lope de Rueda is known for initiating the transition from Italian-inspired verse works to the use of Spanish speech patterns and popular dialects. *Los pasos de López* shares two principal qualities with "Los pasos de Lope": brevity and agile language. Ibargüengoitia trims down the verbiage of the mythic tale as he trims down the hero.

Along with Hidalgo's subversive pseudonym López, the hero's given name in the novel is "Domingo Periñón." The narrator explains at the conclusion that a cactus with red flowers called *periñona* grows at the spot of the priest's execution. This motif of red flowers in the desert recalls the roses that the Virgin of Guadalupe produced for the indigenous man Juan Diego in the dry cold of winter. Hidalgo astutely used her image in the revolutionary banner to inspire the masses to join his movement. However, Barrientos has a more worldly suggestion; the critic postulates that the name honors Hidalgo's wine cultivation, as in *Dom Perignon*. The connotations of a bubbly French libation correspond to the hero's extroverted personality as well as to his ideas influenced by the French Revolution and by forbidden French thinkers such as Voltaire. Furthermore, Barrientos adds, Hidalgo was a fine winemaker himself, although the critic fails to note that in *Los pasos*, Periñón's wine is quite sour. These playful alterations of Hidalgo's name allow the wordly connotations of both theatre (López) and wine (Periñón) to slip between the letters of the hero's name etched on official plaques.

In addition to changing names, Ibargüengoitia collapses many elements of the independence movement into composites. Rather than adding additional layers of events and characters upon the historical frame, Ibargüengoitia opts for reducing the tale, thereby relaying the essential messages of the story and keeping the narrative simple. As Barrientos observes, "El autor procede así como un dramaturgo o un guionista que reduce a uno tres episodios para ahorrarse gastos; al mismo tiempo desacraliza al padre de la patria, pues su versión se opone a la solemnidad de [otros textos]" (16). [The author proceeds like a playwright or screenwriter who reduces three episodes to one to save expenses; at the same time he desacralizes the father of the nation, as his version opposes the solemnity of other texts.] For instance, the famous events of San Miguel, Dolores, and Atotonilco all come about in one site, the chaotic Ajetreo. *Los pasos* also reduces the mishaps that lead to the conspiracy's discovery. Hidalgo's biographer Castillo Ledón documents several precipitous betrayals of the conspiracy involving the mayor and the magistrate and his wife. In contrast, the unfolding of the conspiracy becomes less significant, more commonplace in *Los pasos*. For example, in the novel, the secretary divulges the secret because of a personal slight: the magistrate's wife had not invited him to a luncheon in her home. The narrator also reassesses the much-recorded ride to warn Hidalgo and the "Grito de Dolores" in which the priest initiates the uprising, slowing down the melodramatic pace and reducing the epic dimensions of the messenger's adventure. The narrator himself, Chandón, carries the message. He rectifies national legend from his own experience:

El episodio que sigue es tan conocido que no vale la pena contarlo. Voy a referirme a él brevemente nomás para no perder el hilo del relato y precisar algunos puntos que la leyenda ha borroneado. Es el que empieza con mi cabalgada nocturna y termina con Periñón en la iglesia dando lo que ahora se llama el "Grito de Ajetreo."

Dicen que yo tenía tanta prisa por avisar a mis compañeros que la Junta de Cañada había sido descubierta, que reventé cinco caballos aquella noche. Que me detuve en Muérdago nomás el tiempo que necesité para dar el mensaje y dejar que Ontananza y Aldaco montaran, desenvainaran espadas y gritaran "¡a las armas!" Luego viene "el abrazo." Un pintor que quiso evocar mi llegada a Ajetreo, me representó sacando el pie de debajo de un caballo muerto, al fondo se ve la iglesia, Periñón está en el atrio y va corriendo hacia mí con los brazos abiertos. Dicen que apenas di la noticia Periñón hizo tocar a rebato, llegaron los fieles corriendo y que cuando se llenó la iglesia, Periñón subió al púlpito y gritó:

—¡Viva México! ¡Viva la independencia! ¡Vamos a matar españoles!

Que la gente le hizo coro, que él sacó una espada, que salió de la iglesia
y que todos lo seguimos. Es una visión inexacta. (107)

[The episode that follows is so well known that it's not worth telling.
I'm going to refer to it briefly just so as not to lose the thread of the tale
and to point out some details that the legend has outlined. It's the one
that begins with my night ride and ends with Periñón in the church
giving what they now call the "Ajetreo Shout." They say that I was in
such a hurry to warn my associates that we'd been discovered that I
rode five horses to death that night. That I stopped in Muérdago just
long enough to give the message and let Ontananza and Aldaco mount,
pull out their swords and shout "To arms!" Then comes "the embrace."
A painter that tried to evoke my arrival at Ajetreo represented me pull-
ing my foot out from under a dead horse. The church appears in the
background, Periñón is in the atrium and is running toward me with
open arms. They say as soon as I gave the news Periñón had the alarm
called, the faithful came running and when the church filled, Periñón
got up in the pulpit and shouted, "Long live Mexico! Long live independence! Let's go kill some Spaniards!" That people called back to
him, that he pulled out a sword, and that we all followed him. It's an
inexact vision.]

Chandón's version of the episode diverges from those designed to
exhalt patriotic passions. Rather than riding seven stallions until they
burst, Chandón proceeds at the leisurely pace of his mare. The ride
ends anticlimactically, as Periñón is not home when the narrator
arrives. And as for the famous *Grito*, "Ni el gritó ¡vamos a matar
españoles! ni matamos a ninguno aquella noche" (108) [he didn't
shout, "Let's go kill Spaniards!" Nor did we kill any that night].
Finally, the insurgent leaders end the evening on a disappointing note
by drinking some of the priest's wine. It is sour.

In this manner, the irreverent first-person narrator avoids the patriotic
hyperbole of Castillo Ledón, who marvels at Hidalgo's deeds, and the
omniscient narrator of *Sacerdote y caudillo*, who upholds Hidalgo as a
demigod, as well as Lucas Alamán's *Historia de México: desde los primeros movimientos que prepararon su independencia en el año de 1808
hasta la época presente* (1849), which decries him as evil. Ibargüengoitia's
characters speak to each other of everyday activities using natural,
informal language rather than the "tono declamatorio y teatral"
[theatrical, declamatory tone] of *Sacerdote y caudillo* (Barrientos 19).
And to further reduce the solemnity of the tale, Ibargüengoitia also plays
with Hidalgo's popularity; not only do the masses adore him but the
prostitutes give him special privileges in the brothel. Ibargüengoitia strips

the priest of his ripened dignity and instead affords him an informal manner and youthful vitality.

In contrast with this informal approach to the hero, Mateos's novel *Sacerdote y caudillo* paints him as a well-read, saintly, and devout elderly celibate, and although Castillo Ledón's novelized biography *Hidalgo: La vida del héroe* does acknowledge that Hidalgo was an imperfect human being, it also maintains a defensive posture. Although Hidalgo initiates an independence movement that will only come to fruition ten years after his death, he appears not only as a brilliant visionary but also as a capable military leader, soaring above George Washington, Simón Bolívar, and José de San Martín. Castillo Ledón does pause in his approbations to acknowledge that the priest broke his vow of chastity and had four children by two different women, but the biographer explains that such activity was common for clerics at the time. Castillo Ledón also recognizes that Hidalgo permitted his masses of soldiers to pillage towns and allowed them to sacrifice Spanish civilians and prisoners. Nevertheless, he maintains that all is fair in war; Hidalgo knew his followers would desert if he did not grant them blood and booty. The biographer admonishes the reader to remember Hidalgo not for his mistakes but for his contribution to the independence of Mexico and his plan for an egalitarian democracy. *Sacerdote y caudillo* magnifies Hidalgo's heroism further. Indeed, the novel grants him biblical proportions, referring to the insurgent as a Moses who leads his people toward the redemption of progress and as a Christlike figure who brings injustice to light: "Llamó como el Salvador al ciego y le hizo ver la luz" (314). [He called out as the savior called to the blind man and made him see the light.] In this romantic version, Hidalgo is a divine hero.

Los pasos de López mocks this hyperbolic image with Periñón's everyday errors. Instead of showing extraordinary military skills he makes mistakes in battle and admits them. He keeps company with three young "nieces" even as the brothel eagerly greets him as a familiar client. Furthermore, in *Los pasos de López* the priest loses his post as school rector for less noble reasons than in *Sacerdote y caudillo*, in which Hidalgo is demoted primarily for reading forbidden works. In *Los pasos*, Periñón is stuck in the remote town of Ajetreo (Dolores) for youthful selfishness and irresponsibility: he has wasted a scholarship to Europe that friends and church benefactors had partially funded. Instead of attending the University of Salamanca as planned, he had spent his stay betting at cards and traveling.[4] The priest later explains to Chandón that the bishop detests him because he never repaid the money the bishop had lent him for his studies. The priest thereby appears more human and contemporary, targeted for smaller reasons than censorship by the inquisition. An ordinary man, his slips are petty, not the great tragic downfall of a hero.[5]

In regard to Periñón's sexual indiscretions, the narrator appears to withhold judgment of his three mysterious "nieces," but the implications are clear. He observes that the young women appear to be the same age and do not look at all like sisters, thereby insinuating that they must be the priest's lovers: "Al rato aparecieron tres mujeres. Las tres eran bellas y las tres parecían tener la misma edad—unos veinte años—pero no parecían hermanas. Estaban muy limpias y vestidas con sencillez.—Son sobrinas mías—explicó" (75). [A while later three women appeared. All three were beautiful and they seemed to be the same age—around twenty—but they didn't look like sisters. They were very clean and dressed plainly. "They're my nieces," he explained.] Ibargüengoitia also makes the Magistrate's wife more exciting and youthful in *Los pasos*, as sexual tension arises between the charming "Carmelita" and the narrator. In this way, the novel subsumes her intellect and her passion for a cause to her flirtatious wiles. In contrast with this technique of trivialization, *Sacerdote y caudillo* aggrandizes the Magistrate's wife just as it sanctifies Hidalgo: "esa mujer sublime, esa heroína" (260) [that sublime woman, that heroine]. She appears as a figure who fomented the revolution in a moment of urgency, sounding the alarm by stomping on the floor to signal her neighbor below when the conspiracy was discovered and thereby entering the glorious pages of history.

The Magistrate also receives little credit in history for his nonviolent principles. Ibargüengoitia humorously presents his careful plan as reminiscent of the royalist officer Agustín de Iturbide's Treaty of Cordoba, the document that sealed Mexico's independence in 1821. The Magistrate claims that they will simply draft and sign a declaration to obtain independence and equality: "Va a ser de lo más sencillo. Basta con firmar un documento" (45). [It will be so simple. It's just a question of signing a document.] He adds that as leaders they will achieve their goals without resorting to violence, and insists that they would not require bullets and machetes:

> La independencia de la Nueva España va a lograrse por medio de un acto pacífico y perfectamente legal. Bastará con redactar un documento y firmarlo. Después daremos a conocer el suceso en todo el país por medio de bandos y estoy convencido de que será recibido con beneplácito

por la mayoría de la población. El verdadero problema que tendremos entonces será el de formar un gobierno. (51)

[The independence of New Spain will be achieved through a peaceful and perfectly legal act. It will suffice to draft a document and sign it. Afterwards we'll let the whole country know via proclamations and I'm convinced that the event will be well received by the majority of the population. The real problem that we'll have after that is forming a government.]

The ironic distancing of a narrator looking back thirty years after the events demonstrates that although the Magistrate's attitude appears idealistic and naive, his method is the one that finally succeeds. By presenting these ideas, *Los pasos* revives the importance of the Magistrate and his wife in the independence movement. After winning their first battle, the insurgents return to release the two, thereby "corrigiendo así los hechos y a los historiadores que, por lo general, no se vuelven a acordar de ellos" (Barrientos 16) [correcting the facts and correcting the historians, who generally do not recall them again]. These characters' return in the narrative underlines their absence in history.

While the novel revives the Magistrate and his wife, it refrains from glorifying the pair. Likewise it refuses to perpetuate Hidalgo as a symbol loaded with mythic meaning. Instead the priest is an imperfect leader who, despite his remarkable vision, does not question his role as a white *criollo* inducing indigenous and mestizo masses to be slaughtered in battle under the banner of a brown-skinned Virgin. Ibargüengoitia mocks the privileged group that forms the conspiracy. For instance, the narrator rents a room from the Magistrates with a tree that produces rotten avocadoes, foreshadowing the bitter fruits of the conspiracy as does Periñón's sour wine. Furthermore, in a scene of class parody, Carmelita, the Magistrate's wife, looks down from her comfortable home at the poor neighborhood below where children are playing in the mud and exclaims: "¡Qué dignidad hay en la pobreza!" (16). [There's such dignity in poverty!] Most significantly, in *Los pasos* there is no Spanish mistreatment of the white *criollos* in power who initiate the revolution. In a somewhat reductionist view of history, the indigenous workers in the mines are the only oppressed people in the novel.

As Castañeda Iturbide asserts, there are devastating implications that the fathers of Mexican independence were misguided members of the upper class who were little concerned with whether their plan would help or harm the subaltern groups they claimed to represent. Unlike the revolution one hundred years later, "Los iniciadores de la Independencia de México no fueron los de abajo, sino los de arriba, pero aún éstos no tenían claros sus propósitos" (59) [the initiators of Mexican independence were not the underdogs but rather the upper class, but even they did not have their objectives clear]. Beginning with the narrator's name, Chambón, *Los pasos* indicates that the privileged conspirators planned the independence movement poorly. The narrator acknowledges that he has joined the conspirators not so much from convictions as from peer pressure. Furthermore, the group's argument of Spanish injustice toward *criollos* is unconvincing; when Chandón competes with a better-qualified Spaniard for a military post, Periñón and the Magistrate stack the odds by giving the narrator the answers to the written test and packing the Spaniard's cannon with mud so that it misfires. And while the Magistrate wants to invite Fernando VII to rule as king of an independent Mexico, Periñón shows no interest in whether the nation will be a monarchy or a republic; he knows he will not live to see the end of the revolution. Frye describes such an ironic approach as "Sparagmos, or the sense that heroism and effective action are absent, disorganized or doomed to defeat, and that confusion and anarchy reign over the world" (192). Rather than making history, the conspirators set off a chain of events that resemble an arbitrary accident of chance. They do not foresee the consequences of their game and precipitate a series of battles with tremendous human losses and no final success.

Lucas Alamán corroborates the lack of organization and planning in the historical record. Insurgent soldiers eagerly go about attacking, robbing, and killing Europeans without foresight; for Alamán, Hidalgo thoughtlessly guides his soldiers into arbitrary violence, chaos, and defeat. This again feeds into *Los pasos de López*' depiction of the independence revolution as an accident of history. Periñón reveals to Chandón that he has not foreseen the long-range consequences of his movement:

> Me le quedé mirando y comprendí que estaba decidido a matar al que comprometiera sus planes. Más tarde me di cuenta de que también estaba dispuesto a morir. Le pregunté qué forma de gobierno iba a tener la Nueva España después de la revolución, y él dijo:—Puede ser una república como tienen en el Norte o bien un imperio como tienen los franceses, pero es cuestión que francamente no me preocupa, porque sería raro que llegáramos a ver el final de esto que estamos comenzando. (76)

[I kept looking at him and realized that he was determined to kill anyone who jeopardized his plans. Later I realized that he was also prepared to die. I asked him what form of government New Spain would have after the revolution, and he said:—It could be a republic like they have up north or it could be an empire like the French have, but it's a matter that frankly doesn't concern me, because it would be unusual for us to survive to see the end of what we are unleashing.]

Ibargüengoitia reveals his skepticism of the motives of the conspirators in *Estas ruinas que ves* (1975), a satirical novel about a professor in the backward town of Cuévano (Guanajuato). The novel briefly refers to a local historian who believes that the Independence movement began as a parlor game: "autor de la más lúcida interpretación que por desgracia ha quedado relegado al olvido por no coincidir con la versión aprobada por la Secretaría de Educación Pública, debido a que don Benjamín considera que la Independencia de México se debe a un juego de salón que acabó en desastre nacional" (16) [author of the most lucid interpretation who unfortunately has been banished from memory for not agreeing with the version approved by the Secretary of Public Education, since don Benjamin considers that Mexican independence came about from a parlor game that ended in national disaster]. This perspective challenges official versions of a series of heroic acts planned prophetically. In Ibargüengoitia's novel, the conspirators are merely playing a game that they take too far.

In stark contrast to the novel's lack of sympathy for the privileged *criollos* who organize the uprising, the narrator describes with empathy the inhumane treatment of indigenous workers in the mines. *Los pasos* indicates how poorly armed and trained indigenous masses were cannon fodder in the criollo power struggle with the Spaniards. Chandón dryly notes the abrupt end that awaits Periñón's followers, impassioned by his speeches. When the hero releases the prisoners from the Cuévano jail:

Entonces oí a Periñón decir su primer discurso revolucionario:

—Libertad os doy—dijo a los presos—porque habéis sido víctimas de un gobierno injusto.

—¡Viva el señor cura Periñón—gritaron los presos.

Lo siguieron lealmente en su aventura. Todos murieron. (108)

[Then I heard Periñón give his first revolutionary speech:

"I give you liberty," he told the prisoners, "because you have been victims of an injust government."

"Long live Father Periñón," shouted the prisoners.

They loyally followed him in his adventure. Every last one of them died.]

The narrator also witnesses the virtual slavery of the indigenous laborers who work under abominable conditions in the mines of Cuévano. They suffer under Spanish rule much more than the *criollos*:

Nunca he pasado un rato tan malo: sudaba, casi no veía, me costaba trabajo respirar, escurría agua del techo, en el piso había un lodazal, pero lo que más me inquietaba es que hubiera hombres que casi vivieran allí adentro....Eran flacos, tristes, amarillos y estaban casi desnudos.

—Como tú comprenderás—me dijo Periñón—nadie está aquí por su gusto. (82)

[I've never had such an awful time; I sweated, I could barely see, I had trouble breathing, water trickled from the ceiling, there was a mudbath on the floor, but what disturbed me the most was that there were men who practically lived in there....They were skinny, sad, sallow and they were nearly nude.

—As you can see, Periñón told me—no one is here because he wants to be.]

Such scenes in the novel indicate Periñón's sense of social justice. After defeating the Spaniards in Cuévano (Guanajuato), he frees all of the mules who worked trampling the separation mixture that ate through their hooves. He then calls for the workers to come out.

Cuando por fin salieron todos los que habían estado abajo, cansados, embarrados, casi encuerados, Periñón les dijo:

—Con estas palabras que oyen queda abolida la esclavitud en América.

Esta declaración solemne fue recibida en silencio. Los que oyeron no entendían. Eran indios a quienes sus amos compraban y vendían y hacían bajar a la mina a fuerzas, pero como no eran negros creían que no podían ser esclavos. Periñón comprendió su azoro y explicó: Quiero decir que ahora en adelante bajará a la mina el que quiera, porque convenga el sueldo y el que no, no. (127)

[When all who had been down there finally came out, tired, muddied, practically naked, Periñón told them:

"With these words that you hear slavery is hereby abolished in América."

The solemn declaration was received with silence. Those that heard didn't understand. They were Indians whose masters bought and sold them and forced them to go down to the mine, but since they weren't black they thought they couldn't be slaves. Periñón understood their alarm and explained: "I mean that from now on whoever wants to go to the mine because the salary is agreeable can do so, and if not, he won't."]

Nevertheless, this righteous image of the hero deflates immediately thereafter, when Chandón and the priest hear the news of a junta that has formed in Bogotá. The narrator reacts with pleasure to the news that they have proclaimed independence in Nueva Granada. Periñón, however, is furious that someone else beat them to it. Thus, *Los pasos* juxtaposes Periñón´s shadow side of pride and envy together with his nobler sense of egalitarianism.

Ibargüengoitia also reduces Riaño, the Spanish lieutenant in Guanajuato. While Mateos and Castillo Ledón depict him as a worthy rival, *Los pasos* simply emphasizes his humanity as a gracious host. According to Castillo Ledón, Hidalgo obtained his information on how to make cannons while visiting Riaño, whose neighbor lent him an encyclopedia that included an article on cannon and artillery manufacture. Riaño later dies in Guanajuato defending the Alhóndiga de Granaditas from Hidalgo's forces. *Los pasos de López* heightens the pathos of Riaño's death by having the lieutenant himself (Pablo Berreteaga in the novel) lend Periñón the encyclopedia while warmly receiving the priest and Chandón in his home and treating them like family. Periñón explains to Berreteaga that he needs to borrow the C volume to look up how to plant cherry trees. This lie about cherry trees is a comic reminder of another American father of Independence: George Washington, who, according to legend, never told a lie, admitting to his mother that he had chopped down the cherry tree. Ibargüengoitia's collapsing technique creates greater poetic resonance when the narrator breaks down the door to the Alhóndiga (here the Requina) with the very cannon that Berreteaga unknowingly helps them to build. The narrator later learns that don Pablo Berreteaga did not turn them in when he received reports on the conspiracy. Chandón laments: "Cuando supe esto más agradecimiento sentí hacia don Pablo y más pena me dio lo que ocurrió después" (83). [When I found this out I felt more grateful to don Pablo and I was sorrier about what happened afterwards.] This deepens the tragedy of his death.

The narrator also regrets the carnage in this incident, in which revolutionary forces massacred the Spaniards fortressed in the Alhóndiga:

Si yo hubiera tenido entonces la experiencia que tengo ahora, hubiera aconsejado sitiar la troje y esperar a que buenamente los que estaban adentro se cansaran de estar encerrados y se rindieran. La ciudad estaba en nuestras manos y eran pocos los que nos estorbaban. Pero en nuestros ardores de insurrectos nuevos los cuatro estuvimos de acuerdo en que había que acabar con la resistencia. (120)

[If I'd had the experience then that I have now, I would have recommended surrounding them and waiting for those inside to get tired of being closed in and surrender. The city was in our hands and there were few impeding us. But in our ardor of new insurrectionists the four of us agreed that we had to finish off the resistance.]

As history tells it, once within the building the insurgent masses mercilessly slaughtered both the Spaniards who resisted as well as those who surrendered. Like Mateos in his novel *Sacerdote y caudillo* and Castillo Ledón in his biography *Hidalgo: La vida del héroe*, Chandón debates with critical accounts such as Lucas Alamán's *Historia de México*, although he does accept some responsibility:

Desde entonces hasta la fecha muchos nos han acusado a los jefes insurgentes de sanguinarios. ¿Que por qué no evitamos la matanza de la Requina? Porque no pudimos. Tratamos de detener a la gente pero no nos obedecieron. No era un ejército, era un gentío, habían tenido muchas bajas, la resistencia había sido tenaz.... ¿Que fue culpa de los jefes? En parte. Pero también fue, en parte, culpa de los que resistieron y, en parte, de los que los mataron. (122)

[Since then many have accused us, the insurgent leaders, as being bloodthirsty.

Why didn't we avoid the slaughter at the Requina? Because we couldn't. We tried to stop the people but they didn't obey us. It wasn't an army, it was a mob, they had taken many losses, the resistance had been tenacious.... Was it the leaders' fault? In part. But it was also, in part, the fault of those who resisted and, in part, of those who killed.]

Following this first pivotal battle, the denouement occurs in *Los pasos*. The priest converts into a commander and calls for his white horse in order to parade around the plaza. Periñón reveals that power has changed him; "el primer indicio del cambio que había ocurrido en su carácter a consecuencia del Grito: para ir a la plaza, que estaba a cincuenta pasos, hizo que Cleto le ensillara su caballo blanco" (109). [The first sign of the change that had taken place in his character as a consequence of the Shout: he had Cleto saddle his white horse to get to the plaza that was just fifty steps away.] The priest exalts in the role of the hero on his white horse, and when the leaders meet and agree to give themselves higher ranks, "No se habló de qué grado debería tener Periñón, pero a partir de ese momento actuó como si fuera el único jefe" (115) [what rank Periñón should have was not discussed, but from that moment on he acted as though he were the only leader]. Periñón takes over.

After the triumph in Guanajuato, Periñón's actions are questionable. Following mass, he is ready to celebrate and chaos ensues when he takes money from the bank and throws it from a balcony to the crowds below. Chandón declares with irony that Periñón's delight inspires "un ambiente festivo" in which "hubo borracheras, comercios saqueados, mujeres violadas, incendios, robos, pleitos a puñaladas" (127) [a party atmosphere of drunkenness, sacked businesses, raped women, fires, robberies, knife fights]. The narrator also takes an ironic perspective on the town's reaction; he asks whether they would have shouted "Viva la Independencia" if the insurgents had lost, and finds their enthusiasm naive: "Me di cuenta de que aquella gente creía nomás porque habíamos tomado Cuévano [Guanajuato], que habíamos acabado con el Imperio Español" (124) [I realized those people believed that just because we had taken Cuévano we had finished off the Spanish Empire].

The novel also refuses to commemorate early battles as great events of history. Under Periñón's leadership, chaos erupts as the troops increase. The narrator addresses the issue of violence to civilians with humor. He notes that towns greet the vanguard with flowers but by the time he arrives at the tail end of the army, they receive him with bills for damages. Chandón further comments that he and the other generals wanted to discipline soldiers who razed towns and ranches but Periñón prohibited punishment. *Los pasos* also turns its wry gaze to Hidalgo's military prowess. Periñón is not a great war hero; instead he is ineffectual as a military strategist. The cannon he builds is so disproportionate and heavy that the artillery man, the narrator Chandón, cannot keep up with the army. In the final battle in *Los pasos* Periñón commits a grave error; all goes well in the fighting until he gives the order to charge; his soldiers go forth into enemy lines to be slaughtered. The priest later recognizes his mistake before the other leaders: "—Ya sé que metí la pata. No les pido perdón porque no lo merezco" (150). [I know I stuck my foot in my mouth. I don't ask for forgiveness because I don't deserve it.] In addition, the narrator recognizes Periñón's idea to retreat after winning the battle on the Monte de las Cruces (here, El Cerro de los Tostones) as a major mistake in military strategy. There are no forces protecting Mexico City, he observes.

Los pasos also overlooks some of the hero's more disturbing military acts, including cutting the throats of Spanish prisoners in Guadalajara. Notwithstanding such notable deeds as declaring the abolition of slavery and the restoration of land rights to indigenous peoples, Hidalgo falters in his democratic ideals. Alamán wrote, "Nada influyó tanto en el descrédito de la revolución, como la pompa regia que desplegó en Guadalajara el cura generalísimo" (216). [Nothing had as much influence in discrediting the revolution as the regal pomp that he unfurled in Guadalajara as the most excellent priest-general.]. As "Alteza Serenísima" in Guadalajara, the historical figure Hidalgo ordered large-scale, daily killings of Spanish prisoners. His soldiers took them to the countryside late at night and slit their throats. Castillo Ledón does not cover up the bloodshed in Hidalgo's adventures; like Mateos, he justifies it in the name of war. He further maintains that Hidalgo was merciful with his enemies: "Era Hidalgo un espíritu lleno de piedad para sus semejantes, debido a su alta ilustración" (II 272). [Hidalgo was a spirit full of mercy for his neighbors, due to his enlightenment.] In Mateos's novel, the killings are the job of a character whose lust for blood arises from his victimization by the Inquisition; as a child, this character had witnessed the horrific torment of his father.

Whereas Mateos depicts not only battles but also torture in gory detail, Ibargüengoitia omits bloody scenes from the novel. As Ibargüengoitia paints it, "la época colonial parece menos opresiva, incluso la Inquisición...resulta, por incompetente, mucho menos siniestra" (Barrientos 19). [The colonial period seems less oppressive; even the Inquisition...turns out to be less sinister by virtue of being incompetent.] Barrientos deplores how the novel cleans up Hidalgo's image as it omits the priest's crimes in Guadalajara, crimes that even Mateos and Castillo Ledón did not overlook and that Alamán repudiated as bestial: "*Los pasos* puede parecer un relato expurgado debido a que se omiten algunos crímenes de que se acusó a Hidalgo, es decir las matanzas de Valladolid y Guadalajara, donde los españoles de esas ciudades que se encontraban detenidos por los rebeldes murieron degollados" (19). [*Los pasos* can seem like an expurgated account because some of the crimes Hidalgo was accused of are omitted, that is, the slaughters of Valladolid and Guadalajara, where the Spaniards detained by the rebels had their throats slit.] Although it could be argued that through the elimination of the killings Ibargüengoitia trivializes the magnitude of the war's human destruction, I believe that this expurgation occurs so that not only Hidalgo's greatest deeds are reduced but also his worst deeds, thereby making him appear more commonplace in the novel. A hero's evils are as magnificent as his virtues; *Los pasos* reduces Hidalgo to a human being with lesser merits and lesser faults.

Soon after these bloody incidents in Guadalajara, the counterinsurgent Elizondo tricks and captures the revolutionaries in the northern desert. *Los pasos* conflates Elizondo and Arias into Adarviles, a traitor twice over who turns in the conspiracy, returns to their ranks, then betrays them again. When Adarviles sends a letter inviting them to join him in the Ojo Seco ranch in the north, the narrator lives on to tell the tale only because he has never trusted him. He goes his own way:

> Adarviles nos traicionó una vez y volverá a traicionarnos—dije—a esa hacienda no voy.
>
> No pudieron convencerme ni pude convencerlos, optamos por separarnos....Periñón me confesó: Voy a la hacienda del Ojo Seco porque ya quiero que acabe pronto esta historia. (153)
>
> ["Adarviles betrayed us once and he'll betray us again," I said, "I'm not going to that ranch." They couldn't convince me nor could I convince them; we opted for separating. Periñón confided to me: "I'm going to the Dry Eye Ranch because I want this story to end soon."]

Chandón never sees his comrades again. They are caught, tried, and put to death.

Before his execution, the historical figure Hidalgo signed a retractation of his mistakes against God and king, asking for forgiveness and urging others to cease fighting. We can recall that in *Los pasos de López*, Periñón signs his confession with a pseudonym, "López." In *Sacerdote y caudillo* the confession is a forgery. Mateos proclaims: "Los enemigos de nuestra nacionalidad han acogido esas calumnias como un documento histórico, y las han publicado para desconceptuar a los héroes de 1810" (495). [The enemies of our nationality have accepted those calumnies like a historical document, and they have published them to discredit the heroes of 1810.]. On the other hand

Hidalgo: La vida del héroe postulates that although the hero did not write the confession himself, he signed it willingly. Denying Alamán's report that Hidalgo attempted to save his skin by laying the blame on Allende, the biographer commends the priest for declaring responsibility for his acts.

In Mateos's impassioned version of the execution that follows, Hidalgo resembles the Messiah on Calvary, sacrificing himself for the salvation of the Mexican people: "La patria, que parece haberte abandonado como Dios a su hijo en las horas solemnes de la redención humana, te abre el cielo del porvenir, levanta altares a tu gloria y prosternada ante tus plantas te saluda con el incienso de la gratitud y con los cantos inmortales de la libertad! ¡Hosanna! ¡hosanna! ¡hosanna!" (520). [The fatherland, which seems to have abandoned you as God did to his son in the solemn hours of human redemption, opens the heavens of the future, raises altars to your glory and, prostrated before the soles of your feet, greets you with the incense of gratitude and the immortal songs of freedom! Hosanna! Hosanna! Hosanna!] In contrast, *Los pasos* treats the hero's death much more lightly. Periñón confronts his end with a sense of humor; after stubbornly playing cards for months with his jailers, he finally agrees to sign an act of contrition so that they will proceed with his execution. "Dieciséis años pasaron antes de que alguien se diera cuenta de que, en el acto de contrición que le llevaron, Periñón, en vez de firmar, escribió nomás 'López'" (154). [Sixteen years went by before anyone realized that, in the statement of contrition that they took, instead of signing Periñón just wrote "López."]. His last laugh is to sign with his theatrical nickname, his pet name at the brothel, a name without historical value.

As Fernando Aínsa writes, Ibargüengoitia's parody of such exaltation of the hero makes Hidalgo a more authentic human being: "Su figura, usada y abusada en manuales escolares y en la utilización acartonada, y, por lo tanto, irreal en discursos y emblemas oficiales, se recupera efectivamente, al despojarse de la imagen de mármol y bronce con la que aparece generalmente envuelta, es decir, se humaniza a través de la ficción" (9). [His figure, used and abused in school manuals and in cardboard and thus unreal utilization in official speeches and emblems, is recovered upon stripping him of the image of marble and bronze that he usually appears wrapped in; that is, he is humanized through fiction.] Ibargüengoitia addresses his characters informally as contemporaries and peers, disassembling the myths built around Hidalgo's image. Rather than amplifying Hidalgo's virtues as do Mateos and Castillo Ledón, or hyperbolizing his evils as does Alamán, Ibargüengoitia cuts down the dimensions of his character and the narrative itself, diminishing to a trifle the heroic greatness of both the priest's accomplishments and his flaws. *Los pasos de López* thereby releases Hidalgo from the pedestals of official history, humanizing him and making him more accessible to the contemporary reader.

2

Highlighting Women in History: Rosa Beltrán's *La corte de los ilusos* and Brianda Domecq's *La insólita historia de la Santa de Cabora*

Courage, humor, cunning, and fortitude] have retroactive force and will constantly call in question every victory, past and present, of the rulers.

—Walter Benjamin, "Theses on the Philosophy of History," 254

Although the retroactive force that Benjamin refers to in the epigraph is inspired by class struggle, his idea reasonably applies to other struggles as well, such as those based on ethnicity and gender. In historical novels from the 1980s to the present, these issues have begun to move from the periphery to the center, calling victorious histories into question by presenting an alternate perspective of the events at hand. In this chapter I grapple with the readings of two novels that illustrate, in very different ways, one example of this retroactive force: highlighting women who were previously on the margins of recorded history. I begin with Rosa Beltrán's domestic narrative of an empire, *La corte de los ilusos* [*Court of the Deluded*], and conclude with Brianda Domecq's desert novel about a rebel mystic, *La vida insólita de Santa Teresa de Cabora* [*The Astonishing Story of the Saint of Cabora*].

La corte de los ilusos

Rosa Beltrán's novel *La corte de los ilusos* (1995), winner of the prestigious Premio Planeta, traces the brief reign (1822–1823) of Agustín de Iturbide, controversial liberator and emperor of newly independent Mexico.[1] Rather than building upon recognized historical sources as writers such as Fuentes, Solares, and Ibargüengoitia have done, Beltrán quotes marginal texts from the period in order to give precedence to the domestic side of history. In accordance with Josefina Ludmer's classic article on Sor Juana, "Las tretas del débil" [Tricks of the Weak], minor genres such as letters and recipes can speak eloquently to power from the margins. *La corte* does this by quoting etiquette guides, prayer manuals, and popular refrains; the novel also centers domesticity by giving voice to several women from Iturbide's court, figures previously relegated to the feminine periphery of history. Clothing forms an integral part of this focus on the private daily life behind the monumental events. In this section of the chapter I explore the motif of costume to examine history as seen from the hearth and to consider the ways in which Iturbide's sister, Princess Nicolasa, uses camp to parody both gender roles and the fashionable court.

Agustín Iturbide (1783–1824), whom one critic calls "el personaje más contradictorio de la vida nacional"(Armenta 5) [the most contradictory character of national life], was the son of noble Spaniards. He fought mercilessly against pro-independence insurgents in New Spain until 1821, when he unexpectedly shifted alliances and formulated the Plan of Iguala. Iturbide's shrewd strategy made consensus possible between the rebels, the wealthy *criollos*, the Church, and Spaniards residing in the colonies. Within the year Agustín Iturbide became emperor of the newly independent Mexico. His reign was brief, however, lasting only ten months. From the start, a Congress ready for democracy endeavored to wrest power from Iturbide. When he responded by dissolving the legislative body and arresting several deputies from the opposition, even his principal military officers turned against him. Reinstating Congress was too little too late, and Iturbide was obliged to resign and leave Mexico for Europe. When he returned from exile in disguise a year later, he was promptly recognized and was executed for treason.

Because of his previous status as a royalist and his attempts to consolidate imperial power, national history does not celebrate Iturbide as a liberator, despite his fundamental role in Mexico's achievement of independence. Instead, he shifted between hero and villain status in the nineteenth century and settled into the role of an object of ridicule in the twentieth century. Given that official historical versions of both defenders and detractors of Iturbide's reign were contradictory,

Beltrán explains that she turned instead to unofficial perspectives to construct an alternate history, representing women's experiences of the period:

> Me intrigó el hecho de que las mujeres en la historia siempre ocuparan un papel no sólo secundario, sino a veces inexistente; eso provocó el deseo de buscar cuál había sido la participación de las mujeres de esa época. Todo ese material decidí meterlo en una novela que permitiera imaginar cómo pudo haber sido la historia al margen de los documentos oficiales. ("Con el virus" 7)
>
> [I was intrigued by the fact that women in history always occupied a role that was not only secondary, but at times inexistent; this provoked the desire to seek out what had been the participation of the women of that period. I decided to put all of that material into a novel that would permit one to imagine how history could have been, at the margins of the official documents.][2]

Beltrán's historical narrative, then, questions the concept that the hearth is a trivial space while the battlefield or the courtroom are places of consequence. Just as women could produce art with a clay jug or a quilt just as well as a painting destined for a museum, they could make history in the home as well as in the public sphere.

Critic María Cristina Pons poses an intriguing related question in her study of the new historical novel that she does not subsequently explore, but that is worthy of further investigation; she observes that even today there are few historical novels written by women, and few historical novels can be found that recognize the fundamental roles of women in the construction of history: "siempre queda abierto el gran interrogante de por qué uno de los agentes sociales más importantes en la construcción de la historia, la mujer, es casi invisible, aún en el momento actual, en lo que respecta a la escritura y reescritura de la historia" (13). [The big question always remains open as to why one of the most important social agents in the construction of history, women, are almost invisible, even at present, in terms of the writing and rewriting of history.] However, although male historical figures still tend to occupy center stage, there are notable novels today that give women a focal place, such as Fernando del Paso's vivid characterization of the mad Empress Carlota in *Noticias del Imperio* (1987) (as seen in chapter 3 of this book) and Elena Poniatowska's daring interpretation of photographer and activist Tina Modotti's life in *Tinísima* (1992).[3] Beltrán turns this dilemma on its head by focusing not on a prominent woman but rather on the women in the domestic world that surround a well-known man of history. This act is appropriate in a novel that mocks a court styled after a European empire, as the rearrangement of center and periphery is a significant political gesture in postcolonial theory.

In addition, Beltrán's treatment of such seemingly trivial "feminine" matters as clothing and her incorporation of a pastiche of minor literatures together render a send-up of "literatura light," a label that a number of critics have employed to dismiss the popular success of women writers from the mid-1980s to the present in Latin America. These critics denounce best-selling works by novelists such as Laura Esquivel (*Como agua para chocolate*) and Isabel Allende (*La casa de los espíritus*) as simplistic and formulaic. Beltrán's novel responds to this censure by playing with the idea of the triviality of women's writing. However, rather than producing a work vulnerable to accusations of "literatura light," this technique conversely creates what Roland Barthes would call a challenging, "writerly" narrative that invites the reader to participate in interpreting the work.[4] Beltrán's novel thereby makes the outer peel of the peripheral, "feminine" domestic side of history to be equally nutritious (and intellectually satisfying) as the central core.

La corte finds this side of history in the ephimera, creating, in the Bakhtinian tradition, a hybrid, carnivalized collage of marginal sources and intimate perspectives combined with official references from the period. The novel incorporates the emperor's memoirs and the histories written by contemporaries Carlos María Bustamante and Lucas Alamán, and adapts juicy episodes from an early anonymous biography of Antonio López de Santa Anna (1794–1876), the opportunistic general who later became president, and from Artemio del Valle Arizpe's gossipy novel about Iturbide's lover, *La güera Rodríguez* [*Blondie Rodriguez*] (1945). *La corte* also turns to folklore, making visible such minor printed matter as recipes, letters, satirical verse, catechisms, ballroom dance instructions, and etiquette tips. The first of these minor texts appears on the inside cover, with illustrations from the traditional card game *lotería*. The colorful figures include common images such as Death and The Boot; Beltrán has also playfully added to the traditional Barrel card the addendum "sin fondo (las arcas del Imperio)" [bottomless (the chests of the Empire)], a reference to the excessive spending of Iturbide's government, and has stamped on the Temptation card the image of the seductive Güera Rodríguez. Epigraphs are popular refrains such as "Del plato a la boca, cae la sopa" [from the dish to the mouth, falls the broth], and the chapters often begin with short minor texts from the period. In one example of the humorous inclusion of popular culture, a section from an etiquette manual instructs the reader to refrain from making animal noises or bell sounds when dealing with social superiors.

In the tradition of Menippean satire, the use of extraliterary genres not only uncovers the domestic side of history, but also serves a critical purpose; these seemingly playful citations often illustrate sociopolitical problems (see Bakhtin 26). For instance, one fragment, the "Tratado de las obligaciones del hombre en sociedad" [Treatise on a Gentleman's Social Obligations], demonstrates a throwback to feudalism, as the etiquette guide instructs subjects to gladly submit to rulers:

> Después de Dios no hay obligación más estrecha que la que tenemos a nuestra patria, a nuestros gobernantes y a nuestros padres. Debemos tener por ellos un amor sincero, un agradecimiento eterno y una absoluta sumisión. Asimismo debemos ejecutar pronta y alegremente lo que ellos nos manden, abstenernos de toda actividad o palabra que pueda ofenderlos y aun sufrir con gusto los castigos que nos impongan para corregir nuestros vicios y defectos. (43)[5]

> [After God there is no closer obligation than that which we have toward our fatherland, our rulers and our parents. We should have sincere love, eternal gratitude and absolute submission for them. Likewise we should carry out quickly and joyfully what they command us to do, abstain from any activity or word that may offend them and even suffer with pleasure the punishments that they may impose to correct our vices and defects.]

When Iturbide suspects conspiracies against him, he complains that dissidents are breaking this rule of submission: "se habían olvidado de los preceptos morales incluidos en el *Tratado de las obligaciones del hombre en sociedad*: cuidado de conspirar contra el prójimo, cuidado de ofender al soberano, cuidado, cuidado, que Dios te ve" (145) [They had forgotten the moral precepts included in the *Treatise* ... careful not to conspire against your neighbor, careful not to offend the sovereign power, careful, careful, God is watching you.]

Beltrán's domestic critique of the emperor's reign goes beyond employing popular refrains to also draw attention to minor women characters who surround the emperor: the pretentious seamstress Madame Henriette, the ever-pregnant wife Ana María, the rebellious cousin Rafaela, and the senile older sister Nicolasa. Significantly, Madame Henriette's domestic perspective of the empire begins and ends the narrative. A designer who creates the lavish displays of the mock court, she is a Parisian with an attitude. It is this haughty demeanor that first prompts Iturbide's mother to hire her; Madame Henriette simulates aristocracy with her proud manners, as she loudly glorifies France and denigrates Mexico:

> Antes de ser contratada, se sintió en obligación de decir:
>
> —*Madame, Monsieur*: no tengo ninguna preferencia por quedarme aquí.
>
> La insolencia del tono bastó para que la modista fuera contratada de inmediato. La mujer de don Joaquín la aceptó al instante, convencida de que la altanería y el acento francés eran síntoma inequívoco de superioridad y experiencia. (9)
>
> [Before being hired, she felt obliged to say:
>
> —*Madame, Monsieur*, I'm not the least interested in remaining here.
>
> The insolence of her tone was enough for the dressmaker to be hired immediately. Don Joaquín's wife accepted her instantly, convinced that the haughtiness and the French accent were unequivocal symptoms of superiority and experience.]

Madame Henriette dresses Agustín from infancy in ornate outfits: "Por órdenes expresas de Doña Josefa, la modista se esmeró en cubrirlo con trajes llenos de lazos y primores, como si estuviera vistiendo al niño Jesús en el pesebre" (10). [By Doña Josefa's express orders, the dressmaker took great care in covering him in outfits full of ribbons and lovely things, as though she were dressing baby Jesus in the manger.] Already she is costuming the young Iturbide for his theatrical role-playing.

It is also significant that it is a Frenchwoman who determines the Mexican court's dress. Toward the end of the eighteenth century and continuing into the nineteenth, France strongly influenced clothing styles of the white upper classes in New Spain. Textile historian Chloe Sayer notes the efforts that *criollos* made to imitate French fashion: "France, which had taken over from Spain as the source of costume inspiration, led women to favor tightly waisted conical skirts.... Hair was piled high with ribbons, while men either wore wigs or powdered their hair" (91). Men and women displayed "a truly astonishing quantity of jewelry," including as many as seven gold watches at a time for the women and diamond buttons and shoe buckles for the men. This Francophile fashion trend is notable for its political repercussions; the *criollo* elite, frustrated with limited opportunities for those born in the New World, was distancing itself from Spain and turning to the forbidden writings of French philosophers of liberty Voltaire and Rousseau. Adhering to French rather than Spanish fashion was a way for the privileged classes in Mexico to assert cultural independence from the fatherland.

Furthermore, the upper echelons of society in New Spain continued to use wealth and ornamentation to mark their status as linked with European "whiteness" and "civilization." During the colonial period the Spanish court published decrees that attempted to control dress in order to keep certain groups from claiming higher status. Sayer explains, "Dress was seen as a way of reinforcing the caste system, which comprised many categories beyond that of the *peninsulares* and the Indians" (91). For instance, a 1623 decree prohibited lace ruffs for *criollo* subjects, and a 1571 law barred women of African descent from wearing such finery as gold, pearls, or silk. Madame Henriette inherits the legacy of clothing as a vexed issue in Mexican history, a legacy that she contends with as royal seamstress.

Madame Henriette dresses Agustín in French-styled finery in order to make him resemble a European emperor. Unlike the sly tailors in Hans Christian Andersen's "The Emperor's New Clothes" who fool the king with nonexistent garments, she fashions real clothes that Iturbide wears to fool the people. Rather than peeling off layers to reveal the emperor's weaknesses, the seamstress covers his defects with ornamentation, as a curling baroque grapevine disguises a column. Style takes precedence over substance. In this sense, the seamstress herself builds the simulacrum of an empire by dressing Iturbide for the show, creating an imperial performance. For the coronation, the Frenchwoman dresses her Mexican mock emperor as Napoleon.[6] She designs the garments with a clear purpose in mind—to mimic the grandeur of the French emperor: "todo era cosa de estudiar cuidadosamente los grabados y reproducir, palmo a palmo, los trajes de Napoleón y Josefina. Si querían que el gobierno que iba a estrenarse dentro de poco tuviera algún lucimiento había que copiar adornos, modales y el ejemplo de un verdadero Imperio" (14). [It was all about studying carefully the etchings and reproducing, inch by inch, Napoleon and Josephine's costumes. If they wanted the government on the verge of its debut to have some splendor, then the adornments, manners, and example of a true empire must be copied.] Beltrán thereby gives a minor figure, Madame Henriette, a pronounced role as designer of the empire through her cloth confections.

Beltrán's fiction reflects the historical record, in which witnesses of Iturbide's coronation summarize the event as all pomp and show. Historian (and enemy of the emperor) Carlos María Bustamante describes the ceremony as a farcical spectacle of theatrical adulation. Bustamante links the ridiculous excess of pageantry with the tyranny of an absolute ruler: "En el acto de su inauguración imperial, al verlo con la corona en la cabeza y el cetro en una mano, limpiándose el sudor y abrumado de fatiga con el peso de las vestiduras y arreos, temblé, y presumí que en breve pesaría su autoridad sobre el pueblo que lo observaba, y también sobre mí" (22) [In the imperial inauguration, upon seeing him with the crown upon his head and scepter in hand, wiping off sweat and overwhelmed with fatigue from the weight of the garments and adornments, I trembled, and I presumed that soon his authority would weigh over the people that observed him, and over me as well.] Unable to create a new paradigm of leadership for the emerging independent nation of Mexico, Iturbide mimics Napoleon and the Spanish colonial viceroys. While leaving judgment to the reader, Beltrán's depiction seems to concur with Bustamante that Iturbide's decision to reject Mexican traditions and blindly copy European ones will only lead to ruin.

A number of signs in Beltrán's novel indicate that the newly crowned Mexican emperor is a cheap imitation destined to fail. The Empress Ana María shows off the flashes of gold insignia for the coronation; nevertheless, she confides to a cousin that the glittering baubles are not real gold but tinsel. The relative responds with shock that the empire would use such shoddy, inauthentic materials: "—Cómo!— dijo Joaquinita sorprendida– ¡Un imperio de pacotilla!" (47). ["How could it be!" Joaquinita said, surprised, "A shoddy empire!"] Significantly, at the end of the coronation ceremony, the bishop notes that Iturbide's crown is tilted. He warns him, "—Que no se le caiga la corona, Señor Emperador" (55). [Watch out or your crown will fall, Lord Emperor.] The burlesque continues as the court proceeds through the filthy streets of Mexico City, and the empress trips, providing easy fodder for another political joke: "Un lépero gritó que el Imperio apenas comenzaba y la Emperatriz ya estaba dando malos pasos" [A low-class person shouted that the empire was barely beginning and the empress was already taking bad steps]. Like the boy who cries out that the emperor has no clothes, here it is a lowly man on the street who calls attention to the empire's faults. The historian Lucas Alamán wrote of such occurrences: "Fue como si a despecho de la pompa y circunstancia, los asistentes y el emperador se hubiesen sabido marionetas de una representación teatral, de una parodia en la que, inútilmente, se pretendía transplantar a América instituciones y ceremonias, cuya veneración en otras partes no puede venir sino de la tradición y de la historia" (qtd. in Krauze, *Siglo* 107). [It was as if, despite the pomp and circumstance, the assistants and the emperor had been puppets in a play, a parody in which institutions and ceremonies whose veneration in other places could only come from tradition and history were being uselessly transplanted to America.] Such strange incidents seem to proclaim that the empire is a farce, a shoddy imitation of European monarchy instead of a bright new republic shaped in the Americas.[7]

The royal vestments, then, appear as an extended metaphor throughout the novel for the illusory nature of Iturbide's empire. Friar Servando Teresa de Mier also plays the role of the child who cries out that the emperor is in the buff. The insurgent monk indicates that the pomp and splendor of an emperor's robes do not fit in the context of an independent Mexico and will quickly slip from Iturbide's shoulders, leaving him exposed. Mier responds to a coquettish poetry recital by Nicolasa, "—El candor de este poema—dijo—me recuerda un bello cuento popular con el que fui arrullado cuando niño. Se llama *El traje nuevo del Emperador*, y tiene una bonita moraleja" (131). [The candor of this poem, he said, reminds me of a lovely folk tale that lulled me to sleep when I was a boy. It's called *The Emperor's New Clothes* and it has a nice moral.] Andersen's fairy tale comes to mind again at the end of the novel, as the seamstress dresses the emperor's cadaver in the robes of Saint Francis and closes the circle of the narrative by relating the tale as it begins, with the emperor trying on his new garments. At first Iturbide seems to be in on the joke: the clothes exist to fool the public rather than to cheat the emperor by leaving him naked. Nevertheless, when Andersen's emperor realizes the trick, he walks on, whereas Iturbide does not save face when he returns. Thinking that he is covered by disguise, he is revealed and executed.

Just as the emperor's ministers in the fable uphold the illusion of the imperial vestments, Iturbide's court likewise is blinded by trivialities. For instance, the headline in the *Gaceta Imperial* tells the most pressing story of the day: a velvet cape is missing. The long-titled names of court members attest to their social advantage: Doña Ana María Josefa Ramona Huarte Muños y Sánchez de Tagle, Emperatriz de México; Don Pedro Jesús María Romero de Terreros y Rodríguez de Pedroso, Tercer Conde de Regla y Caballerizo Mayor, and so on. As critic and novelist Jorge Volpi observes, "En cierto sentido, un emperador sólo vive para su corte; su destino ineluctable es ser admirado y vituperado por ella.... Un título nobiliario podía transformar al peor palurdo en un refinado caballero" (75). [In a certain sense, an emperor lives only for his court; his inevitable destiny is to be admired and vituperated by it.... A noble title could transform the worst boor into a refined gentleman.] Beltrán's inclusion of these lengthy invented titles illustrates the illusory nature of the aristocratic pretensions of the empire.

The superficiality of the ruling elite in *La corte* also shows in its lack of interest in social problems, favoring instead an obsession with consumption and appearances. In one scene, the emperor's cousin Rafaela attempts to initiate a conversation in court. She asks the others whether they agree with Mier; is independence meaningless if the government is not truly free? No one responds to her trenchant question; instead, the court is distracted from pressing issues by its interest in keeping up ornamented appearances, in imitation of European royalty:

Los miembros de la Corte estaban atados sin remedio a los grilletes de sus larguísimos apellidos y a su obsecada necesidad de ver en estos un Imperio. Para ellos el país no sería el mismo sin una Corte y esta no sería la que era sin los retablos, las jofaínas, las cómodas, las trinqueras, los aguamaniles, los baúles y los ramilletes de calamina en plata, esa plata del Imperio que emitía destellos alegres como carcajadas ante las posibles amenazas del infortunio. (38)

[The members of the Court were irremediably tied to the shackles of their very long last names and their obstinate need to see an empire in that. For them the country would not be the same without a Court and the Court would not be what it was without the altarpieces, the bureaus, the carving boards, the wash basins, the trunks, and the dessert platters of silver, that imperial silver that emitted happy sparkles like giggles before the possible threats of misfortune.]

They prefer to polish their titles, dress in fashion, and collect luxurious objects rather than build political substance. This use of luxury to mark social distinction is a manifestation of the system of monarchy that was becoming outdated in Iturbide's time. As historian Remy

Saisselin points out, "Luxury was also inextricably linked to the monarchical regime; as Montesquieu explains in the Esprit de lois, it is the spring or motive of monarchy. The striving for luxury is a drive for distinction" (33). For Beltrán, the emperor and his court must stand out; the gaze of their subjects affirms their nobility, as the emperor in Andersen's tale dons an elegant new "suit" to seek the gaze of his people.

In its parody of Iturbide's 1821 reign, Beltrán's novel also defies present-day Mexican politics and societal mores. As one critic affirms, "Todos sus gestos alevosos se vuelven guiño y esa saña subversiva con que se remueve la historia (que se ha vuelto marca registrada y tradición en las letras mexicanas) nos ofrece—de nueva cuenta—un espejo de nuestras dolencias y excesos" (Pohlenz 7). [All of its treacherous gestures turn into a wink, and that subversive rage with which it stirs up history (which has become a registered trademark and a tradition in Mexican letters) offers anew a mirror of our ailments and excesses.] When the novel was published in 1995, its parody of Iturbide resonated with readers in Mexico who were experiencing the fallout from the end of the Carlos Salinas de Gortari presidency; the peso fell drastically, the new *zapatistas* rose up in arms in Chiapas in response to the passage of NAFTA, relatives and colleagues of the former president were arrested for a variety of crimes, and Colosio, the PRI-designated candidate for president, was assassinated. The class pretensions in the novel also echo in the late twentieth- and early twenty-first centuries; certain family names in Mexico still carry weight, and certain families still travel out of the country—now to Miami rather than to Paris—to purchase the latest fashions. Beltrán amplifies her parody of Mexican social mores in Iturbide's time and her own time as a paradoxical wish for both independence and imitation; the result is a lifestyle as performance.

As Iturbide's sister Nicolasa acts out her own theatrical dreams of passion, she goes beyond the costumery of her brother to embody a camp performance. She personifies camp excess. Writers have availed themselves of camp as a means to subvert social and political models; both Judith Butler and Susan Sontag provide theoretical tools for exploring Nicolasa's camp, as the princess parodies both gender portrayals and class emblems. In Butler's theory of gender as performance, camp draws attention to the artifice of femininity. On the other hand, Sontag's earlier understanding of camp places little emphasis on sexual identity; Sontag instead sees camp as a burlesque of the way superfluous objects are used as markers of social class.

Iturbide's decrepit sister dresses extravagantly, behaves coquettishly, steals trinkets, and fantasizes about upstart Santa Anna: "Está sentado junto a ella, hablándole al oído, sin embargo ella lo imagina de pie, con las piernas abiertas delante de su Alteza Nicolasa, desafiando cualquier avance de las enjoyadas manos" (76). [He's seated next to her, talking into her ear; nevertheless she imagines him standing, with his legs apart before her Highness Nicolasa, challenging any advance of her jeweled hands.] The princess's campiness is a parody of feminine sexual wiles, a travesty, like that of an aging drag queen.

Camp makes details the center of the world, like the baubles that Nicolasa steals from the neighbors and hides in her skirts. Sontag describes camp as a sensibility in which aestheticization and style take precedence over substance, often elevating banal content to extravagant levels; "the essence of Camp is its love of the unnatural: of artifice and exaggeration" (105). Priorities are skewed; what is important is trivialized and insignificant trifles are aggrandized. Witness this love of artifice in the antics of the elderly Princess Nicolasa, as she designs for herself a scandalously youthful and flirtatious dress for the coronation:

> Estaba empeñada en llevar un vestido amarillo con volandas y una corona de flores en el pelo a la ceremonia de coronación....Había cuidado todos los detalles: los pliegues que caían desde abajo del pecho, el bies ligeramente arriba del empeine. E1 escote, un dedo más abajo de lo usual, imitando el estilo que inmortalizara Josefina. Tanto se entusiasmó la Princesa con el diseño del ajuar que en el camino se olvidó de un mínimo detalle, el paso del tiempo sobre su persona. Siempre había ignorado a ese molestoso visitante, pensando que de este modo él se retrasaría en llegar. Pero el intruso se había metido por la puerta trasera y ahora estaba frente a ella, instalado en medio de sus senos marchitos, de la boca sin dientes, dispuesto a pedirle cuentas. (25)

> [She was determined to wear a yellow dress with ruffles and a crown of flowers in her hair at the coronation ceremony....She had taken care of all the details: the folds that fell from beneath her chest, the bias slightly above the instep. The cleavage, a bit lower than usual, imitating the style that Josephine would immortalize. The Princess was so enthused by the design of her trousseau that along the way she forgot a minor detail: the passage of time over her person. She had always ignored that bothersome visitor, thinking that then he would arrive late. But the intruder had come in through the back door and now he stood before her, installed between her wilted breasts and her toothless mouth, prepared to call her to account.]

The description of Nicolasa's aging body in the novel is merciless, a Bakhtinian carnivalization that crudely and comically degrades the lofty figure of a princess.

However, under her brother's watchful gaze, campiness may also be Nicolasa's method of subversion. Whereas Madame Henriette's clothing carefully constructs the artifice of an emperor, Nicolasa insists upon designing her own apparel. In contrast with the other characters, she does not dress in accordance with the court's wish for decorum, and her use of clothing goes beyond even the immoderation of her peers in the novel. While her cousin Rafaela rebels secretly by aiding Fray Servando Teresa de Mier, Nicolasa's politics are a play of clothes, trinkets, and melodrama. According to Butler, transvestism reveals the gender role that it mimics as an artificial construction; likewise, Nicolasa simulates and subverts both femininity and nobility. In Bakhtinian fashion, Nicolasa's physical appearance hovers between laughter and death as it burlesques the very image of a delicate and regal princess. If the feminine role is a theatrical performance, then the transvestite, like Nicolasa, overemphasizes these qualities, thereby making them visible. Butler suggests, "In imitating gender, drag implicitly reveals the imitative structure of gender itself—as well as the contingency" (137). She adds that a drag queen "implicitly suggests that gender is a kind of persistent impersonation that passes as the real" (x). Transvestites inscribe the feminine sign upon their bodies with makeup, wigs, and clothing. Similarly, the elderly Princess Nicolasa impersonates the image of youthful feminine beauty, displaying her cleavage with a low-cut dress and flashing a coquettish smile from behind a fluttering fan.

Nicolasa exaggerates gender markers in accordance with Butler's theory, but these markers are tied in with class roles; the dress is made with yards of expensive cloth, and the elegant fan is also an emblem of social prestige. The princess mocks not only gender but also social class by illustrating that they are both products of role-playing. Nicolasa is a *mujer producida*, an overproduced woman, with her excess of makeup and clothing. As Sontag observes, "The whole point of Camp is to dethrone the serious.... Camp introduces a new standard: artifice as an ideal, theatricality" (116). In the aesthetics of camp, what is in bad taste, what is awful, becomes tasteful. Critics have denounced campiness as immoral, a nonutilitarian extravagance, a novelty. Camp resembles nonproductive eroticism, sexuality for mere play and pleasure. Princess Nicolasa's sexual fantasies are scandalously nonproductive, as she is too far beyond menopause to reproduce for the Iturbide family line, which Ana María does so thoroughly.

The constantly pregnant Ana María attempts to live up to both Agustín's pressures, convent teachings, and her own internalized model of how to be a perfect *"ángel del hogar"* [domestic angel], suffering silently through Agustín's affair with La Güera Rodríguez while managing the household. When Agustín sends her to a convent "for her safety," their carriage passes through popular neighborhoods where her "fine nostrils" are offended by the odor of pulque (cactus liquor), while women undeserving of the "eyes of an empress" thrust themselves into her line of sight. Ana María is both titillated and horrified at the open sexuality of the women in her path as they show their bare feet and bare their teeth with laughter; "Era que la llamaban desde fuera y al saludarla y al agitar los brazos repletos de pulseras la acariciaban con sus gestos indecentes" (167) [it was that they called her from out there, and upon greeting her and waving their arms replete with bracelets, they caressed her with their indecent gestures]. Like the plebeian women in the street, Nicolasa also offers no excuses for a sexuality that is not pretty. She simply revels in the joy of the touch, the wink, and the fantasy, and in this way she subverts her gender role and her royal status. By the end of the novel Ana María has come to envy Nicolasa's madness, a madness that allows her to escape from the hypocrisies of her brother's game of empire.

Described in the narrative as a chubby bumblebee (46) and a carnival queen (47), the rebellious princess illustrates through her own dress and behavior that the royal empire is a performance. She performs an extemporaneous version of both nobility and femininity, swelling the stereotype until it explodes. As Toril Moi comments, "Anger is not the only revolutionary attitude available to us. The power of laughter can be just as subversive, erasing old differences, producing new and unstable ones" (40). Through the absurdity of Nicolasa's camp, Beltrán's novel brings to light the excesses of the character's sociopolitical surroundings.

The fragmented narrative and the extravagance of the characters in *La corte* together signal the insanity of Iturbide's ephemeral reign. Agustín's meditations on the obliteration of his empire again remind the reader of how today he has nearly been effaced from the pages of Mexican history. Like the emperor of the folktale who was tricked into parading naked around the town, Iturbide finds himself undressed, his regal robes made invisible. The fallen emperor ponders the erasure of his empire and perhaps of his very existence: "Desmontar un Imperio puede tomar solo un minuto. No hay más que oír al Congreso notificar que la elección del pueblo fue ilícita, que el aplauso y las juras de la plebe son nulas y que por tanto no hay ni hubo jamás Imperio" (218). [It only takes a minute to dismantle an empire. You just have to hear Congress notify you that the people's election was illicit, that the applause and vows of the masses are null, and that therefore there is no empire, nor was there ever.] Now the emperor himself must become invisible, like the imaginary ermine robes that were never there. To add insult to injury, the fancy objects symbolic of his court continue to disappear when he is compelled to sell them in exile in Italy in order to cover his family's expenses. He must sacrifice the luxury that had marked his imperial status. In Iturbide's time, the worldview is changing and political power is evolving. As Bustamante concludes upon Iturbide's downfall, "bien sabido es que el espíritu del siglo detesta a los reyes" (85) [It is well known that the spirit of the age detests kings]. Iturbide's subjects are no longer willing to see the emperor as a divine instrument of God, despite his title "Varón de Dios" [Man of God].

It is fitting that Madame Henriette close the narrative. She dresses Iturbide for his burial, this time not in shiny raiments but in the coarse robe of Saint Francis. The seamstress's thoughts turn to Iturbide's reign, which she sums up from the perspective of a woman's domestic sphere:

> había pasado la vida exigiendo, obligando, forzando a otros a hacer las cosas por él. Tenía inclinación por las familias grandes, ahí esta, que Ana María tuviera los hijos, los cuidara y les enseñara a conducirse frente al padre con admiración y respeto. Había tenido el capricho de portar el uniforme de generalísimo y sentarse con él en un palio imperial, muy bien, se había hecho montar el número y luego había llevado a todos a inmiscuirse en la representación de la famosa corte. Y cuando ya no quiso jugar más se fue, simplemente, dejando al resto con un palmo de narices. Un año después había decidido volver, sin importarle que los demás se hubieran fastidiado de jugar el mismo juego. (257)

> [He had spent his life demanding, obliging, forcing others to do things for him. He preferred big families, that was it, that Ana María have the children, take care of them and teach them to conduct themselves with admiration and respect in front of their father. He had had the capriciousness to wear the uniform of the *generalísimo* and sit with it on in the imperial pallium, very well, he had made them put on the show and then he had gotten them all involved in the theatrical representation of the famous court. And when he did not want to play anymore he simply

left and blew them off. A year later he had decided to return, without caring about whether the others had tired of playing the same game.]

For Madame Henriette, Iturbide's incumbency was merely the dress-up game of a vain and capricious boy. Through her eyes, *La corte* compels the reader to question Mexican history, politics, and societal mores, both past and present. By focusing upon clothing the emperor and his court, Beltrán unclothes the pretentions of an empire and provides an alternative reading of history. The result is a novel that opens a new dialogue both on women's place and on Iturbide's place in Mexican history.

The Astonishing Story of the Saint of Cabora

In the novel *The Astonishing Story of the Saint of Cabora* (1990), Mexican writer Brianda Domecq also recenters women, here by revisiting the tale of Teresa Urrea, or Saint Teresa of Cabora (1873–1906), a Sonoran mystic and anti-Porfirian activist whose life ended in exile in the United States. Domecq revives Teresa Urrea in light of new history and feminist theory to forge a new kind of protagonist who diverges from her depiction in the primary sources. In the prerevolutionary novel that first inspired Domecq, *Tomochic* (1893, revised 1906) by Heriberto Frías, Teresa is an exploited hysteric, but *The Astonishing Story* draws a complex portrait of a rebel, a flawed human being, and a healer of both mystical and political wounds. Just as Teresa is a *curandera*, or healer, *The Astonishing Story* serves as what activist historian Aurora Levins Morales calls history as *curandera*, a healing history.

Levins Morales advocates the role of historians as *curanderos*, healers who tell the tales of those who are most forgotten or most overlooked. She explains, "My interest in history lies in its medicinal uses, in the power of history to provide those healing stories that can restore the humanity of the traumatized" (25). In "The Historian as Curandera," Levins Morales describes the set of fifteen guidelines she followed in *Remedios* (1998), a history of Puerto Rican women. Although she designed these specifications for historical research and writing, most of them are applicable to Domecq's fictionalized account of Urrea's life. *The Astonishing Story* puts into practice a number of Levins Morales's observations, such as telling untold or undertold stories, centering women to change the landscape, identifying and contradicting strategic pieces of misinformation, showing agency rather than passive victimization, and embracing complexity and ambiguity.

The Astonishing Story divides into three long narrative sections. The first of these sections alternates between Teresa's experiences growing up on a ranch and the adventures of a woman a century later who takes a trip to Cabora to research Teresa. A nameless figure, the researcher's identity gradually blends with Teresa's until she falls down a hill in Cabora and Teresa falls off of her horse. The second part of the novel tells of Teresa's subsequent three-month trance (her first "death") and transformation into a popular healer on the ranch, while the third part narrates Teresa's life from exile in Arizona and Texas until her "second" and final death. An epilogue concludes the novel with the apparent reappearance of the researcher, who has resuscitated from a coma and now claims to be Teresa.

Telling Untold or Undertold Histories

Domecq's narrative follows closely Levins Morales's first instruction to tell untold or undertold histories such as those of women of color, rural women, or emigrant women. A rural mestiza who emigrated from Mexico to the United States, Teresa Urrea's story has been little told until recently. While she appeared briefly a century ago in Heriberto Frías's *Tomochic*, today the desert mystic is undergoing a revival. During key years of the civil rights movement in the United States in the late 1960s and 1970s, Urrea's story reappeared briefly as that of a vital Chicana predecessor. Richard and Gloria Rodríguez published an article in *El Grito* providing background on her life and her influence on the U.S.-Mexico Frontier; they describe her not as a revolutionary but as a healer whose "part in the history of Aztlán should be known" (179). While Alfredo Mirandé and Evangelina Enríquez in turn view Urrea more as a revolutionary advocate for indigenous groups, they also agree with the Rodríguezes in claiming her as a significant Chicana forerunner: "Teresa Urrea served as a precursor not only of the Mexican Revolution but of Chicano political movements and remains a symbol of resistance for contemporary Chicanos" (86).

More recently on both sides of the border, both Domecq's novel and recent historical studies have once again resuscitated Teresa de Cabora as a complex agent of history.[8] In *Tomochic*, Frías, a government soldier, gives an account of a series of three battles that took place in 1891 and 1892 in a small (population 300) Tarahumara town in the desert state of Chihuahua. In contrast with the revisionist histories written in the 1990s, in his 1890s account Frías only briefly mentions the political motives of the rebels, which include obligatory and poorly paid labor in a nearby mine and other abuses by local authorities. Instead, in Frías's version, the people of Tomochic are ignorant messianists fighting under the banner of the illusory Saint Teresa of Cabora. In later editions of the novel, Frías further develops the mysticism of Teresa as a tragic figure whose deluded followers have been mysteriously manipulated into believing that her hysteria is saintliness.

Despite this depiction of Teresa as a spellbound and spellbinding beauty exploited for profit and violence, the contradictory footnotes to the 1906 edition caught Domecq's attention. Perhaps because of the impending revolution, the editor's footnotes describe Teresa as a militant activist and leader of a resistance movement. These footnotes acknowledge that in addition to selling relics and earth with curative powers, Teresa militantly opposed the Porfirio Díaz regime, encouraging the uprisings of Tomochic and Tomosochic. The editor also observes that she continued her insurgent activities in exile, when she was directly implicated in the failed customs house attack in 1893 in Nogales, Arizona; the plan was to rob funds to finance the revolution. In response to these contradictory versions in Tomochic and in newspaper accounts of the period, Domecq's novel confronts these discrepancies from the past.

Centering Women to Change the Landscape

Levins Morales explains that once a writer has decided to tell such undotold stories, this alters the questions that she or he asks. For example, the tale of Teresa de Cabora raises questions about the predecessors of the Mexican Revolution. In addition to such well-known figures as the brothers Flores Magón, in Domecq's novel indigenous groups such as the Yaqui and Mayo also appear as important forerunners of the revolution. *The Astonishing Story* focuses not upon generals or presidents but rather upon a woman who works as a healer, a popular leader who nevertheless has no *corridos* sung about her exploits and who does not appear in national history textbooks. Teresa de Cabora particularly stands out as a woman leader because of her epoch, a paternalistic period under the presidency of Porfirio Díaz. Jean Franco explains that "although traditionally strong in times of war and strife [during the Porfiriato], Mexican women were slow to challenge the domestication of women and often fearful of taking a step into areas where their decency would be put into question" (93). The historical figure and the fictional character Teresa de Urrea ventures into forbidden political territory and takes on a leadership role, thereby transcending the paradigm of women's domestic passivity during Porfirio Díaz's rule. The character in the novel who researches Teresa's life does so in part because she realizes that, unlike Teresa, the "great men" of history such as Porfirio Díaz and Francisco I. Madero will not be forgotten: "A don Porfirio nadie lo olvidaría. Como fuera, estaba sólidamente instalado en la Historia…El milagro había sido Díaz; el milagro había sido Madero. Inacabables en su permanencia, en su historia, en su recuerdo. Salvados para siempre del olvido" (29). ["Nobody would forget Don Porfirio. No matter what happened, he was firmly installed in history….The miracle had been Díaz; the miracle had been Madero. Everlasting, with their permanent place in history" (24).] The researcher hopes to restore Teresa de Cabora into the national memory, giving her a place of prominence alongside already well-documented figures.

Identifying and Contradicting Strategic Pieces of Information

In addition to recentering women in the narrative, Levins Morales suggests pointing out inconsistencies in the historical record. An example of this strategy would be to note the erasure of a people from the annals of history, often due to ideas of national or cultural purity. As mentioned earlier, in *The Astonishing Story* indigenous rebels are given new importance as precursors of the Mexican Revolution. In addition, Teresa is neither nationally nor culturally "pure" as honorary "Queen of the Yaquis" and an expatriot in exile. She does not fit into any previous paradigm of a national hero. Domecq juxtaposes conflicting news accounts to demonstrate the contrasting interpretations of Teresa Urrea's life and work.[9] For example, the investigator in the novel who is researching Teresa's life cites Frías and then explains that the incongruities in *Tomochic* inspire her to learn more about Teresa Urrea:

> Una figura amarga y fascinante se le materializaba a través de las frases: "¿No era acaso un instrumento finísimo, un cristal, manejado en la sombra por ocultas manos?, para que a través de sus facetas y de sus aristas los hombres incultos y fuertes perpetuasen en los baluartes

inexpugnables de sus montes una guerra horrenda de mexicanos contra mexicanos, en el santo nombre de Dios?" ¿Cómo compaginar esas
descripciones excelsas con frases como "aquella pobre muchacha histé-
rica," "epilepsia pacífica," "aquella criatura ilusa toda nervios?" Desde
ese momento se sintió poseída por una curiosidad malsana que le
comía las entrañas. (11)

[An amorphous and fascinating figure arose from the impassioned
descriptions in the book: "Was she perhaps a fine instrument, a crystal
controlled in the shadows by hidden hands so that, inspired by her fac-
ets and sparkling edges, strong, rough men would, from their impreg-
nable mountain strongholds, perpetrate a horrendous war of Mexicans
against Mexicans, in the sacred name of God?" How was it possible to
reconcile such sublime descriptions with phrases such as "that poor
hysterical girl," "a victim of passive epilepsy," and "that deluded, high-
strung creature"? From that moment on she felt possessed by a cantan-
kerous curiosity that gnawed at her peace of mind (5).]

While traveling to Urrea's birthplace, the researcher recalls the contradictory documentation she had collected from Mexican and U.S.
newspapers, from activist Lauro Aguirre's publications, and from
Porfirio Díaz's letters. One account embellishes her: "la joven Teresa
era de una belleza imponente, con largos cabellos negros que caían
hasta la rodilla, ojos luminosos y claros y amplia sonrisa" (46)
["Young Teresa was of imposing beauty, with long black hair and
clear, luminous eyes" (37)], while another account describes her as
unappealing, "analfabeta, ignorante, y sucia" (48) ["illiterate, ignorant,
and dirty" (40)]. Others portray Teresa Urrea as a saintly pacifist on
one hand or as a fanatical warrior on the other. In this example she
incites violence: "La señorita Urrea, con todo conocimiento y malicia,
planeó y encabezó levantamientos contra el legítimo gobierno" (44).
["Miss Urrea, with complete knowledge and malice, planned and led
uprisings against the legitimate government" (36).] And yet in another
account she is a gentle figure who bears no responsibility for politics
or rebellion: "esta joven dulce, fina y hermosa predicaba sólo la paz,
la meditación, la paciencia como forma de conquistar una mayor justicia" (48). ["Refined and beautiful, she preached only peace, medita-
tion, and patience as a means to achieve justice" (38).] Teresa Urrea
appears alternatively as a heretic: "la joven fanática usurpa los
derechos sacramentales de la verdadera religión" (48) ["The young
fanatic is usurping the sacramental rights of the true religion" (38)] or
as a saint: "¿no era más satisfactorio recibir los sacramentos de manos
de una virgen inspirada y no de las de un sacerdocio explotador,

ambicioso y pérfido?" (49) ["Wasn't it more rewarding to receive the sacraments from the hands of a lovely young virgin than from those of an exploitative, ambitious, and treacherous priesthood?" (38)]. Once living in exile, Teresa notes that U.S. newspapers would also print paradoxical and sensationalist news about her:

> Un día la ensalzaban describiéndola como la joven valiente que se había enfrentado al ogro de México; otro, decían que era injustamente perseguida por el dictador, y al siguiente, la acusaban de ser una mujer ignorante y analfabeta…que todavía se daba el lujo de fanatizar a los ignorantes mexicanos con supersticiones absurdas. (295)

> [One day they exalted her, describing her as the brave young woman who had stood up to the ogre of Mexico; the next day they said she was unjustly persecuted by the dictator, and on the following day they accused her of being an ignorant, illiterate woman who had never attended school, who lacked any sign of culture, and who still had the nerve to preach about good and evil and to fanaticize the ignorant Mexicans with absurd superstitions (280)].

On both sides of the border, Cabora is one day a hero, one day a fool, one day a victim and the other a victimizer. Through juxtaposing these contradictions in the historical record, Domecq's novel suggests that Teresa's story deserves a sophisticated analysis that recognizes complexity in the tale of the "Saint of Cabora."

Showing Agency

One method of replacing binary thinking with a more complex analysis is to show agency. In other words, as Levins Morales suggests, rather than portraying subaltern communities as victims, one must also demonstrate their strategies of resistance, even if their tactics are less than heroic, involving betrayal or resulting in failure. In the novel Teresa makes conscious decisions about her role as healer and leader; for example, when her father orders her to turn people away, she refuses and instead arranges for a separate area of his property where she can receive the multitudes of impoverished and desperate patients. Upon her exile in the United States, she becomes even more politically active, allowing her photograph to be sold to raise funds for the resistance movement and signing an anti-Porfirian constitution written by activist Lauro Aguirre. Furthermore, in Domecq's narrative, Cabora's followers are not deluded victims; the indigenous groups who rebel in

Teresa de Cabora's name employ her as a banner to support their political cause against Porfirio Díaz, a president who forced recalcitrant Yaquis and Mayos to work virtually as slaves in mines and remote plantations. Most of these workers died within a few years of being sent to such locations as the National Valley.

In exile in Nogales, Arizona, Teresa treats the most miserable indigenous people, the uprooted who search for a history after they have left their homelands to escape from the Díaz government: "Sólo venían los más desahuciados, yaquis y mayos sucios, malolientes, con las ropas desgarradas, exudando miseria por cada poro" (294). ["Only the most destitute continued to arrive: foul-smelling Yaquis and Mayos covered with dirt, in ragged clothes, exuding misery through every pore" (278).] They ask her to perform baptisms and other ceremonies because, uprooted, they lack elders to pass on their customs and rituals: "Teresa comprendió que la mayoría no necesitaba alivio de males físicos, sino espirituales: querían identidad de pueblo, querían renovados mitos, querían reinventar tradiciones perdidas para sentir que pertenecían a algún lado, a alguna historia" (294). ["Teresa realized the majority didn't need relief from physical ailments but from spiritual ones; they wanted the identity of a community, they wanted renewed myths, they wanted to reinvent lost traditions in order to feel that they belonged to some place, to some history" (279).] In ministering to a people who suffer from the spiritual ill of a lack of cultural identity, Teresa attempts to treat what literary theorist Gay Wilentz calls "cultural illness." Wilentz describes a remedy in fiction writing that is similar to what Domecq has produced and what Levins Morales has outlined. The literary critic finds curative possibilities through "wellness narratives," novels by ethnic women writers in which the protagonist moves from illness to wellness through reconnection with ethnic cultural traditions and healing practices. Wilentz explains,

> These writers appear to be exploring a reexamination of women's traditional role of custodian of the culture in order to develop a community-based model for healing the culturally ill through their writings. They begin the process of a healing discourse to heal the culturally ill. For people from oppressed cultures, this means reclaiming personal wellness through self-esteem and the "discredited" (to quote Toni Morrison) knowledge of a culture's healing practices. (3)

The theorist claims that the novelistic genre, through its use of metaphorical language, displaces diseased polarities.

In *Borderlands/La Frontera: The New Mestiza*, Gloria Anzaldúa emphasizes the importance of displacing binary paradigms by crossing borders and making cross-cultural connections: "At some point, on our way to a new consciousness, we will have to leave the opposite bank, the split between two mortal combatants somehow healed so that we are on both shores at once" (79). This is especially true for figures such as Teresa. As the daughter of a white landowner and an indigenous peasant girl, and with her frontier-crossing role as an Arizonian of Mexican origin, Teresa Urrea is a precursor for the "new *mestiza*." Indeed, it is when working together with the local physician, who regards her as a normal human being and as a professional equal, that Teresa is most satisfied in her work. Here she is neither glorified nor denigrated for her healing powers. She is able to practice in peace and to work as a team partner together with the physician as they raise funds for a community hospital. This practice of overcoming polar oppositions resembles that of the "wellness narratives" that Wilentz describes, in that they respect modern medicine but also work to overcome its practice of fragmentation in a tradition that tends to neglect the emotional, social, and spiritual aspects of disease and wellness. In *The Astonishing Story*, Teresa works toward this goal by treating not only physical ailments but also cultural or political wounds in her patients.

Examples of Embracing Complexity and Ambiguity

While Teresa is a hero in the novel, *The Astonishing Story* portrays her character as an individual with human frailties, a trait we have seen in other new historical novels such as *Madero, el otro* and *Los pasos de López* featured in chapter 1. Levins Morales writes that rather than simplifying historical figures into absolute heroes or absolute villains, "it is in many ways more empowering when we show our heroic figures as contradictory characters full of weaknesses and failures of insight. Looking at those contradictions enables us to see our own choices more clearly and to understand that imperfect people can have a powerful, liberating effect on the world" (31). There are a number of instances in the novel that show Teresa as a flawed character. For example, she makes errors of judgment, choosing as a mate first a man who wants to kill her, then her best friend's son. Before awakening from the trance that precedes her rebirth as a healer, her process of recovery takes life from others, as all of the babies in the area die in utero. When she begins to cure clients, she neglects her own hygiene, and when Teresa first becomes conscious of her healing abilities she finds herself wishing calamities upon others in order to have more opportunities to feel the surge of power that comes with treating their illnesses:

> Empezó a padecer hambre de lo maravilloso. Nada de lo que conocía era comparable con las vibraciones del misterio que ella experimentaba. Llegó a fastidiarse de lo rutinario y se sorprendía deseándoles enfermedades terribles a las personas para poder ejercer de nuevo el milagro y sentir aquello que la trascendía pero, también, la elevaba por encima de los demás (185).

> [She began to crave the miraculous experience and hunger for the high it gave her. Anything routine began to bore her, and she was surprised to find herself actually wishing that the people who came would be struck with terrible diseases so she could perform a miracle again and feel the force that transcended her but that also elevated her above the rest (175).]

Moreover, at times Teresa's powers falter, and their nature is unclear. She often feels responsible for sending others to their death when rebellions or attacks fail. In sum, Domecq has created a flawed character in Teresa Urrea, bringing her to the level of the reader as neither a saint nor a mysterious guru. As Marina Pérez de Mendiola points out, the lengthy and detailed descriptions of Teresa's healings enable the reader to conceptualize and accept her ministrations as ordinary: "At first surprising and mysterious, they become natural; we are in the presence of Teresa no longer a mystic healer but rather a person who, like anyone else, uses her skill in the service of others" (64). As a human who works to transcend her faults and aid the community, Teresa becomes more inspiring to the reader, who can identify with her earthly qualities and struggles.

Make the Work Accessible; Cross Borders

In addition to making the hero more accessible to the public by pointing out her contradictions and complexities, Levins Morales also suggests using familiar language and easily obtainable media. This technique makes the work available not only to other scholars but also to the communities involved in the story. Levins Morales also advises crossing borders, delving into a variety of disciplines and geographical spaces as Domecq did, crossing the borders of her training as novelist and essayist to devote several years to historical investigation and crossing the U.S.-Mexico border to complete research for her novel. A further suggestion for accessibility that Levins Morales makes is to share work through "theater, murals, historical novels, posters, films, children's books or a hundred other art forms" (37). Though not a best seller, Domecq's novel has been widely read in both Spanish and English, thereby making Urrea's tale accessible to people on both sides of the border who would not have otherwise become familiar with her story. Indeed, it was the reading of the novel that inspired a citizen of Clifton, Arizona, to organize a public history project in the town to commemorate Teresa Urrea (see Vanderwood 323–329).

Making Absences Visible; Personalizing

In addition to Urrea, *The Astonishing Story* also revives the character Huila, the practitioner of a vital indigenous healing tradition. To make absences visible, Levins Morales recommends attempting to trace those that are missing from the record, as historical evidence is sometimes incomplete in these areas. To personalize this missing information, the historian further suggests using the names of freed slave women or indigenous women whenever possible, writing a personal narrative of an individual life. In this case, Huila takes on a bigger role in the novel than in the historical record, in which she merits a scarce mention as María (a colonized name), the indigenous woman who dwelled on Teresa's father's property and who may have taught Teresa about herbal remedies. Levins Morales suggests that a fictional character can be created if necessary to highlight an absence, "as Virginia Woolf does in *A Room of One's Own* when she speaks of Shakespeare's talented and fictitious sister, for whom no opportunities were open" (28). The genre of fiction provides Domecq with the opportunity to fill in the scarce tracings of Teresa's mentor that she found in the historical record.

Huila is an indispensable figure in Teresa's formation. In contrast with the patriarchal law of Porfirio Díaz's modernizing State that sacrifices the poor, Huila's law rejects both weapons and words to serve and heal the poor by means of senses and perceptions that precede the word. As Aralia López González affirms, Huila "organiza la conciencia de Teresa dentro de una lógica de servicio comunitario en contraste con la lógica de poder patriarcal de don Tomás, revinculándola así con su cultura de origen" [organizes Teresa's consciousness within a logic of community service in contrast with don Tomas's logic of patriarchal power, thereby reconnecting her with her culture of origin (502)].

Huila teaches beyond the logic of language, explaining to her pupil that words fragment the world; naming separates that which was unified: "El problema, Niña, son las palabras: el lenguaje no nos acerca a la realidad sino que la esconde. Fíjate: tomamos el 'maíz' y el 'metate' y la 'mano' y el 'agua' y la 'cal' y los juntamos bien mezcladitos. ¿Tenemos maizmetate-manoaguacal? No. Tenemos 'tortilla,' otro pedacito huérfano, desprendido de su origen" (133). [The problem, child, is words: language doesn't bring us nearer to reality, it hides it. Just look: we take "corn" and "grinding stone" and "hand" and "water" and "limestone" and we mix them all up. Do we have corngrindingstonehandwaterlimestone? No. We have "tortilla," another little orphaned piece detached from its origin (124).] Teresa applies this lesson in her practice, entering a wordless trance and reaching beyond language for comprehension: "Aprendió a mirar detrás de los nombres de las cosas, buscarles los hilos que las unían con el resto de la vida, descubrir sentidos ocultos para darle la vuelta al intelecto, esquivar la razón, liberarse del lenguaje y ver aquel indivisible fluir" (134). [She learned to look behind the names of things, to look for the threads that joined them with the rest of life, and to discover hidden meanings in order to turn around the intellect, evade reason, free herself from language, and see that indivisible flowing (134).]

However, although her initial rejection of language verges on mysticism, Teresa does not weaken her position as an irrational, silent woman spiritualist as Jean Franco warns: "By subordinating women on the grounds of their lesser rationality and relegating them to the domains of feeling, the clergy unwittingly created a space for female empowerment.... [However,] in accepting silence and self-obliteration, the mystics legitimized the institution's separation of male rationality from female feeling and the exclusion of women from the public domains of discourse" (xiv–xv).

While the label of irrationality provided mystics with a powerful space of their own, it also denied them the possibility of alternative forms of reason and access to public discourse. Teresa, however, breaks the binary oppositions of reason versus mysticism, transcending language to heal but also using words to foment revolution and to sign a constitution that challenges the Porfiriato.[10]

Aguirre's constitutional reform plan of 1896 attempted to create new political options for women in Mexico, denouncing Díaz and including surprisingly feminist elements such as granting women the right to vote and to be elected president. Likewise, writers such as Domecq today are producing new possibilities. Forging an identity as mother, healer, and insurgent, Teresa of Cabora stirs up the dust, asserting her presence in a desert parched for women of resistance. It is thus that *The Astonishing Story* offers a healing contribution to Mexican letters.

Together, works such as Domecq's *The Astonishing Story* and Beltrán's *La corte de los ilusos* move women from the margins to the center of historical debates. As Josefina Ludmer observes, "It is always possible to take a space where one can practice what is forbidden in other spaces; it is always possible to annex other fields and institute other territorialities" ("Las tretas" 76). *La corte* annexes private, daily, minor genres and reconstitutes them as part of a broader political discourse; likewise, *The Astonishing Story* provides an alternative reading of history that brings power to the peripheral space inhabited by a female historical figure. As a reader, I look forward to encountering further unexpected literary representations of formerly untold stories and previously marginalized figures in history.

3

Mourning the European Legacy: Homero Aridjis's *1492: Vida y tiempos de Juan Cabezón de Castilla* and *Memorias del Nuevo Mundo*, and Fernando del Paso's *Noticias del Imperio*

> *There is no document of civilization which is not at the same time a document of barbarism.*
>
> —Walter Benjamin, "Theses on the Philosophy of History," 256

For Walter Benjamin, the documents of civilization correspond with the records of barbarism, a reminder of how sovereign power is indissolubly linked with violence. This phenomenon extends from the consolidation of a modern Spanish state in 1492 to the totalitarian states of the twentieth century seen in chapter 2. During the colonial period the Black Legend, or *leyenda negra*, of Spain took root in Protestant Northern Europe. The Dutch and English, though responsible for atrocities of their own, cited the cruelties of the Inquisition and the Conquest as evidence of the brutality and regression of their imperialist rival.[1] However, my analysis of Homero Aridjis's narrative in this chapter will indicate how the violence of the Inquisition was not an ancient form of barbarism incomprehensible to the modern observer; on the contrary, in its very brutality administered through bureaucracy, the Holy Office was a sign of the future, the biopolitical tool of a modern state. We shall see how in Aridjis's novels, this synthesis of violence and power is manifested in the Inquisition's punishment of the body and censorship of thought. Then in the second part of this chapter I explore a later phase of mourning for the European legacy of imperialism as seen in Maximilian's rule (1864–1867) in del Paso's novel *Noticias del Imperio*.

As we have seen in the introduction to this book, restoring the Americas' fertile but sometimes noxious European roots is a key tendency in many recent historical novels of the hemisphere. In particular, the 500th anniversary of the Spanish conquest (1492–1521) provided rich ground for revisitations such as Libertad Demitrópulos's *El río de las congojas* (Argentina, 1981), Juan José Saer's *El entenado* (Argentina, 1983), Herminio Martínez's *Diario maldito de Nuño de Guzmán* (Mexico, 1990), Abel Posse's *El largo atardecer del caminante* (Argentina, 1992), and Alicia Freilich's *Colombina descubierta* (Venezuela, 1991), to name a few. Mexican poet and ecological activist Homero Aridjis is one of the many writers who have grappled with the 500th anniversary of the conquest. However, he takes the conflictive European inheritance back even further, focusing on the violent legacy of Spain's *leyenda negra*: the Spanish Inquisition, in his novel *1492: Vida y tiempos de Juan Cabezón de Castilla* (1985); and the conquest, in the New World sequel, *Memorias del Nuevo Mundo* (winner of the International Novedades-Diana prize, 1988). In narratives such as Aridjis's, history tells a tale not of triumph but of peril and loss. Aridjis's storytelling responds to Walter Benjamin's warning that one has a responsibility to tell history as an act of resistance against totalitarianism, to "seize hold of a memory as it flashes up at a moment of danger" ("Theses" 255). The particular moment of danger that Aridjis's narrative seizes is a key point in European, American, Muslim, Jewish, and Christian history: the apocalyptic memory of 1492.

1492 was a landmark year. On this date three major empire-building events took place that changed the course of history: under the sponsorship of the Catholic sovereigns of Castile and Aragón, Isabel and Fernando, Columbus sailed to the Americas; after 800 years of flourishing Islamic reign in the southern portion of the peninsula, the Catholic sovereigns conquered the last remaining Moorish stronghold, the magnificent Andalusian city of Granada; and the Crown further enforced religious uniformity by expelling all remaining unconverted Jews from the kingdoms. As Aridjis's novels register, these events of the Inquisition and Conquest were intimately intertwined as part of the modernizing project of state formation.

In *1492: Vida y tiempos de Juan Cabezón de Castilla*, the title character, a *converso* born in Madrid, tells the story of his childhood in picaresque style, making lively use of period language and refrains to narrate a hungry youth, loss of family, and apprenticeship with a blind beggar.[2] However, beyond this recreation of the picaresque genre, the narrative is framed by a greater concern: the increasing persecution of the Jews, which culminates at the end of the novel with the 1492 expulsion. Mid-novel, Juan Cabezón meets Isabel de la Vega and her brother Gonzalo, who have been accused of being cryptic Jews and have escaped from the Inquisition. In a series of passages that alternate between lyrical eroticism and nightmarish paranoia, Juan loves and shelters his new wife Isabel until she suddenly flees from a prying familiar of the Holy Office. The protagonist pursues her through several cities until he finally finds her with their young son boarding a ship to Portugal. Inquisitorial guards bar him from accompanying her, so he instead joins Columbus in his first voyage. Aridjis adheres closely to historical events as chronicled in the sources that he cites at the beginning of the text. Historically documented figures, events, and descriptive particulars turn up throughout *1492*; for instance, the narrative mentions such historical details as the assassination of inquisitor Canon Pedro Arbués, the 250 armed familiars that accompany the unyielding Torquemada at all times, and the telling scent of Jewish cooking of the period when onions are fried with olive oil instead of lard.

The second novel, *Memorias del Mundo Nuevo*, also relies heavily on extensive research from both primary and secondary sources on the inquisition and the conquest; Aridjis lists these in a note at the end of the text (391–396). *Memorias* takes Juan Cabezón to the Americas, where he survives as a healer in the Caribbean, participates in the conquest and colonization of Mexico, witnesses the continuation of state-sponsored religious violence on the part of both Mexicans and Spaniards, and finally, in his old age, reunites with two compassionate hybrids of Judaism and Catholicism who have left the Old World for the New. The first is Juan Cabezón's blind cohort's son, Pánfilo Meñique, a naturalist who studies the abundant flora and fauna of New Spain and dies administering to smallpox sufferers. His appreciation for the region's natural resources has continued relevance; Aridjis, who grew up in Michoacán amidst the monarch butterfly migrations, founded in 1985 the Grupo de los Cien (Group of 100), intellectuals and artists who act on behalf of ecological concerns such as deforestation, dams, and the protection of whales, turtles, and butterflies in Mexico.[3] Aridjis's environmental interests are linked with his long-running concern with Sephardic history and with biological forms of repression in this history (see, e.g., his poem "Sepharad" in Stavans). The second compassionate hybrid of Judaism, Catholicism, the Old World, and the New is Juan Cabezón and his wife Isabel's own son, Juan de Flandes, a man of the cloth who dies a hermit. Both are sons of victims of the Inquisition, an agent of state power that continues to pursue and burn suspected heretics in the New World.

1492: Vida y tiempos de Juan Cabezón de Castilla

In 1478 King Ferdinand pressured the Pope for permission to revive the Inquisition. His goal was to unify and control religious practice by cracking down on converts to Christianity who still privately kept Jewish customs. Conversion had its advantages, which included access to professions prohibited to Jews, and, more urgently, protection from murderous anti-semitic riots. However, conversion also had its risks; Catholic doctrine maintains that baptism marks an individual as the church's possession, so a subsequent renunciation of the Catholic faith is considered apostasy, a grave offense.

Although the three major religious communities of Muslims, Jews, and Christians had lived in relative peace for several centuries in the peninsula, the hardships of the plague and other catastrophes in the fourteenth century led to a sharpening of hostilities against Jews. Preaching monks inflamed Christian crowds by classifying Jews as the crucifiers of Jesus and rumors spread that they were poisoning the wells in order to propagate the plague. Massacres broke out, the first in Toledo in 1355, followed by another in Seville in 1391.

The novel 1492 begins with the birth of the narrator's grandfather during the Sevillian riot of 1391, in which the historical figure Ferrán Martínez, a virulently anti-semitic preacher, induces Christian peasants to ransack the *aljama*, or Jewish quarter, "dejando tras su paso fuego y sangre, saqueo y muerte" (11) [leaving fire and blood, looting and death in his wake (13)]. In response to the pillage, rape, and murder, the narrator's grandfather vows never to bring another baby into such a world, where "el mal recorre las aldeas, las ciudades y los reinos para destruir los setos de las criaturas justas" (12) [evil advances through villages, cities and kingdoms to destroy the crops of the righteous (14)]. In both the novel and in the historical record, scenes of looting and murder explode throughout the peninsula, and thousands convert.[4] Working compatibly with the upper classes, many of these *conversos* soon take on prominent roles in society, achieving positions prohibited to Jews but available to them as New Christians.[5] However, this rising middle class inspires envy, and the riots begin once again, in Toledo in 1449 and in Córdoba in 1473, now targeting converts to Christianity, seen as "false Christians." Popular prejudice becomes legislation, and "blood purity" (*limpieza de sangre*) laws appear, whereby anyone with a Jewish ancestor is to be excluded from privileged posts. Soon after, in 1480, the Inquisition is revived, and the final blow falls with the expulsion of 1492.

Violence and Power

This use of legislative bureaucracy to control religious orthodoxy was key in the state modernizing project. Indeed, so successful was this project that the modern Spanish state continues to incorporate Catholic doctrine in the public school curriculum and subsidize Catholic schools. In contrast and in part because of its Spanish colonial—and inquisitorial—history, Mexico's public today, while predominantly Catholic, is wary of the convergence of Church and State. For instance, the influential 1917 Constitution prohibited the Church from owning property and required that priests register with the government. As historians Gilbert Joseph and Timothy Henderson note, "Anticlericalism was a major theme in the Mexican revolution. Modernizing elites blamed the Roman Catholic Church for inculcating superstition and ignorance among the masses, and of meddling repeatedly in politics on behalf of reactionary elements" (418). The Church was seen as an obstacle to progress.

This legacy of wariness toward state-sponsored religion continues in the twenty-first century. Witness, for example, the uproar that ensued when Vicente Fox (president 2000–2006) publicly kissed the Pope's ring. Mexican citizens today remain aware that the Holy Office was a state apparatus that reached into the New World. Under the *Ancien Régime*, individuals expressing religious differences were seen as rebels against the State. In his study of the sixteenth-century illuminist Erasmus, Marcel Bataillon notes that the Inquisition was unique in this bureaucratic function: "The Spanish repression was distinct not so much through its cruelty as through the power of the bureaucratic, policing, and judicial apparatus at its disposal. Its centralized organization covered the whole peninsula in a relatively tight network, and it even had antennae abroad" (qtd. in Pérez 174). The Holy Office was the Crown's principal tool for bringing about ideological uniformity. Historian Joseph Pérez astutely links this institutionalization of intolerance to modern totalitarianism:

> Everywhere else [in Europe during the Religious Wars], flare-ups of intolerance would produce thousands of victims—flare-ups that were preceded and followed by more or less long periods of peace. In Spain, one finds an intolerance admittedly less deadly, but institutionalised, organised and bureaucratised, which lasted far longer, from 1480 to 1820. The very formula of the Holy Office rendered it redoubtable. With its mixed jurisdiction, designed for religious purposes but placed under the authority of the State, it in some ways constituted an anticipation of modern totalitarianism. (175)

Italian philosopher Giorgio Agamben's analysis of biopolitics in the modern totalitarian state can aid us in understanding how these practices of the Inquisition, as depicted in Aridjis's novels, foreshadow the union of sovereign power and violence in modern times, as when, for example, the police use hot pepper spray when interrogating suspects in Mexico today.

Taking from Michel Foucault's concept of biopolitics, the politicization of bare life as seen in power's penetration of the human body in state institutions, Agamben readapts the ancient Roman term *homo sacer*, or sacred man, one who has been convicted of a crime and who can be killed with impunity but cannot be sacrificed. This contradictory condition, for Agamben, is symptomatic not only of the prison camps of modern fascism but also of modern democracy, in which the bare life of the *homo sacer* is constitutively intertwined with political life: "The entry of *zoê* into the sphere of the *polis*—the politicization of bare life as such—constitutes the decisive event of modernity and signals a radical transformation of the political-philosophical categories of classical thought" (4).[6] Similarly, the politicization of the human body in the spectacles of the Inquisition is an essential step in the formation of a modern state; as Agamben describes it, "Placing biological life at the center of its calculations, the modern State therefore does nothing other than bring to light the secret tie uniting power and bare life" (6).

In Aridjis's novels, the biopolitics of the state controlling the body appear in both the *auto de fe* and in Mexica sacrifice. Those who wait in the prisons of the Inquisition are neither fully alive nor fully dead, neither fully human nor animal; they submit to torture and to the Kafkian unfathomability of the mysterious investigation until the day they emerge for the *auto de fe*, whereupon their living bodies are exposed, stripped bare, and burned.[7] The *auto de fe*, with its procession, sermon, and pomp, stands in denial of the suffering and humanity of those processed. Juan Cabezón describes the ceremony with abject horror:

> Algunos herejes condenados anduvieron con gran dificultad, recién sacados de los calabozos del tormento, donde los habían sometido a la tortura de la cuerda y el agua. En sus rostros se veía el terror y en sus cuerpos las huellas del verdugo. Dos o tres hablaban solos, como si hubiesen perdido la razón, oraran o se contaran cosas para vencer el miedo. Otros, entre dientes, cantaban salmos. Los hombres primero, las mujeres atrás, por el orden de sus culpas....las víctimas no eran santos ni dioses sino hombres y mujeres comunes horrorizados ante ese monstruo de mil caras y dos mil puños que se llamaba multitud, azuzando al sacrificio humano a los sacerdotes sanguinarios, que habían transformado las parábolas de amor en instrucciones de muerte y el paraíso prometido en infierno terrestre. (*1492* 176–177)

> [Several of the condemned heretics staggered painfully, having only recently emerged from the torture chambers where they had been subjected to the pulleys and water torture. Terror was etched on their faces, and the torturer's marks, on their bodies. Two or three were talking to themselves, as if bereft of their reason, or praying, or reciting some charm to ward off fear. Others mumbled Psalms. The men went first, the women behind, in order of their crimes....The doomed were neither saints nor heroes, merely ordinary men and women aghast at that monster of a thousand faces and as many fists, that crowd which goaded on the ruthless priests who transformed parables of love into instructions for death, and the promised paradise into hell on earth (157–158).]

The legalized and bureaucratized inhumanity of this scene exemplifies the "state of exception," in which sovereign power can transgress its own laws. The Inquisition legislates but is also outside the law, controlling the body at the most basic level and thereby denying basic laws of human life. The Holy Office stands behind the laws it has created to cover up its crimes against humanity: causing unusual suffering through torturing, maiming, and killing. Juan Cabezón describes the inquisitor's blindness to ethical doubts thus: "Ciego a la humildad doliente de un hombre que muere mártir por otra religión, en la exaltación sincera de su Dios, seguía con cruel satisfacción los más mínimos detalles de la muerte en ese hombre, en la soledad extrema del crimen que se envuelve de legalidad para cometerse y no conoce otro perseguidor que la propia conciencia" (*1492* 178). [Blind to the harrowing humility of a man who dies martyred for his religion in the sincere exaltation of his own God, the inquisitor followed with cruel satisfaction the slightest details of that man's death in the exquisite loneliness of a crime cloaked in legality, whose only judge is the perpetrator's own conscience (159).] The Inquisitor exalts in his own moral superiority, blind to the immorality of legislating and condoning suffering.

Juan Cabezón displays the wariness provoked by this practice, which placed all individuals of Jewish origin under suspicion, and by which their lives, honor, and livelihoods were constantly at risk. *Conversos* who privately continued to observe Jewish rites were in greater danger than ever. Seemingly minor infractions such as those of Juan Cabezón's wife, Isabel, and her brother Gonzalo, were enough to be declared a "Judaizer" (*judaizante*), a heresy sufficient to merit death at the stake. Agamben describes the Kafkaesque meaningless and endless trials for minor infractions as a hint of the modern mass societies and totalitarian states that were to come: "For life under a law that is in force without signifying resembles life in the state of exception, in which the most innocent gesture or the smallest forgetfulness can have most extreme consequences" (52). Benjamin also foresaw these conditions in the developing fascist state of Germany between the two world wars: "The tradition of the oppressed teaches us that the 'state of emergency' in which we live is not the exception but the rule" ("Theses" 257). An example can also be found in Mexico's more recent history, when the government employed the pretext of a state of emergency to fire upon unarmed civilians in 1968 in a student protest at Mexico City's *Plaza de Tlatelolco*, the location of the Spanish slaying of Mexica in 1521.

In *1492*, the brother and sister's crimes against the State in a "state of exception" include such innocent acts as observing the Saturday sabbath, abstaining from pork and shellfish, praying the psalm of David, and washing their father before burial. Here is an excerpt from Aridjis's depiction of their Inquisitorial trial records, imitating the precise legal language of the genre:

> ... biviendo los dichos Isabel de la Vega y Gonzalo su hermano en nombre e posesión de christianos en ofensa de Nuestro Señor y de nuestra Santa Fee Cathólica, sin themor de las penas y censuras que por judaysar e guardar la ley de Muysén e rictos judaycos esperar deviera, los dichos Isabel de la Vega e su hermano judaysaron e hereticaron guardando la ley de Muysén en lo que sigue: Uno, que encendieron e fisieron

encender candiles linpios los viernes en la noche por honra e cerimonia del sábado, segund forma judayca. Iten, que guisaron e fisieron guisar viandas los biernes para los sábados a cabsa de non lo guisar en los sábados por fiesta, vistiéndose en ellos ropas linpias e de fiesta, más aquel día en que otros de la semana, de paño e de lino, como yéndose ellos a folgar en los tales días a casas de sus parientes. (303)

[...the said Isabel and Gonzalo de la Vega live under Christian names and enjoy the benefits of such, committing an offense against Our Lord and our Holy Catholic Faith, with no fear of the punishments and censures which, on account of Judaizing and keeping the Law of Moses and performing Jewish rites, they might well expect, practicing heresy in the following particulars: First, that they did kindle and caused to be kindled lights in clean lamps on Friday nights in honor of the Sabbath ceremony, in accordance with the Jewish custom. Item, that they did cook and caused to be cooked viands on Fridays to be eaten on Saturdays, to avoid cooking them on a Saturday, a feast day, arraying themselves in clean garments of fine cloth and linen more so that day than on any other during the week, and going to take their ease on such days in the houses of their kinsmen (272).]

The list of Isabel and Gonzalo's offenses continues; they have observed Jewish days of fasting, and have eaten only unleavened bread and meat prepared by a kosher butcher. The Inquisition employs the term *rebeldía*, rebellion, for suspect behavior such as that of Isabel and Gonzalo. It is a question of control, even in the most private sphere of the home, of what food one consumes and when, of how one prays and how one mourns. In sum, the state invades and attempts to dominate one's humanity at the most intimate spiritual level.[8]

Indeed, the Inquisition controls the body at such a private level in the novel (and historically) that it sends out inspectors, the quintessential agents of biopolitics, to examine men's penises for signs of circumcision:

Cuando hallan a un circunciso, invariablemente declaran que por el defecto del cuero en los miembros y pixas se demuestra la faba descubierta en alguna parte, pero como no pueden saber si el defecto viene por natura o por efecto de arte, dejan la respuesta en manos de los inquisidores, los que, invariablemente, se inclinan por el efecto de arte. (*1492* 169)

[And when they do discover a circumcised man, they invariably declare that owing to a defect common to the skin over members and penises, the head may be exposed in some measure, but as they cannot determine

whether the defect springs from nature or man's handiwork, they leave
the answer to the inquisitors, who invariably lean toward man's handiwork (151).]

For the inquisitors, this artful lack of foreskin is sufficient motive for
arrest; even the most private bodily choices are privy to the state. As
seen in *1492*, then, the Inquisition strives to erase from the citizenry
all vestiges of Jewish identity, of Jewish religious and cultural practices, in order to create a uniform modern state.

Memorias del Nuevo Mundo

After living on the run, in disguise, hiding and moving constantly
from one town to the next, Isabel and Gonzalo finally leave their
homeland upon the expulsion decree of 1492.[9] The brother and sister
flee to the havens of Portugal and Flanders, while Juan Cabezón leaves
for the Americas. With this voyage, undertaken the next day after the
final expulsion, the two novels trace the presence of the Holy Office
from the Old World to the New. Historically, Andalusia, launching
point of the conquest and primary beneficiary of the wealth of the
Indies, was also the most brutal Inquisitorial region, where hundreds
were burned at the stake in *autos de fe* during the cruelest period of
the Holy Office, the fourteen years leading up to 1492. The institution kept a direct hand in the Americas through the creation of branch
offices in Lima, New Spain (now Mexico), and Cartagena. Although
its reach could not extend to remote regions and natives were exempt
from prosecution, the Holy Office was able to pursue "judaizers" of
Portuguese origin, Protestants from England, and "witches" of
Spanish descent who employed indigenous herbs and incantations.[10]
While less active in later years, the Office was not abolished in New
Spain until 1819, just two years prior to Mexican independence.

In *1492* agents of the Holy Office are straightforwardly hateful
and narrow-minded, with ominous physical characteristics such as
claw-like hands or devouring mouths. On the other hand, Jews and
converts are agreeable characters throughout the novel. In contrast,
while Aridjis's portrayal of the Inquisition is similarly unsympathetic
in *Memorias*, the narrative complicates this polarity, as acts of brutality and bloodshed are propagated equally by Mexica and Spaniards.
In fact, in *Memorias* there is no clear victim or victimizer. Many
Spaniards in the novel are exposed as greedy for gold and guilty of
slaughter and enslavement of the natives, but the Aztec Empire is not

held up in contrast as a noble civilization. For both empires, violence and faith are intertwined.

Juan Cabezón is horrified by the ferocity of his fellow conquerors. During their bloody attack in Cholula, fighting behind the banner of moor-killer Santiago, "la furia de ellos era tan grande como su fe en la Virgen María y el verdadero Dios, Jesús" (75) [their fury was as great as their faith in the Virgin Mary and the true God, Jesus]. However, when he ascends the pyramids of the Sun and Moon in Tenochtitlán where prisoners are sacrificed to the war god Huitzilopochtli, he is equally frightened and repulsed: "Juan Cabezón y Gonzalo Dávila se acercaron al *tzompantli* y observaron con horror las paredes de cráneos, las hileras de cabezas conservadas después de los sacrificios, en diferentes estados de descomposición....

—Parece que estos naturales han puesto tienda de horrores— comentó Gonzalo Dávila" (80). [Juan Cabezón and Gonzalo Dávila approached the *tzompantli* and observed with horror the walls of skulls, the rows of heads conserved after the sacrifices in differing states of decomposition... "It seems that these natives have put up a horror show," Gonzalo Dávila commented.] As seen in *Memorias*, the spectacle of sacrifice is reminiscent of the *auto de fe*, a similarly violent display organized by the state and ostensibly aimed to appease a divinity. However, in the novel the Mexica captives' suffering is somewhat attentuated, as they are drugged into ecstasy, and their death, though bloody, is quick and is an honor rather than a black mark upon future generations.

Indeed, the irony inherent in Aridjis's comparison of the blood of sacrifice with the blood of the Inquisition and conquest is made apparent with Pedro de Alvarado. A historical figure known for his ruthlessness, as a character in the novel Alvarado slaps a passerby who offers him food, insults an old man, rapes young women, and slaughters native after native until only the bloody handle of his lance remains. Nevertheless, blind to his own cruelty, Alvarado critiques the brutality of Mexica sacrificial rites:

> —Doña Marina me ha contado que durante la dedicación del gran templo de Huitzilopochtli y Tláloc, el año 8 Acatl, año de Nuestro Redentor de 1487, veinte mil prisioneros fueron sacrificados, ¿habéis visto tal crueldad?—profirió Pedro de Alvarado, corriéndole la sangre al rostro, la espada salida un tercio de la vaina.
>
> —Qué estaba haciendo ese año nuestro piadoso Inquisidor General en toda España?—preguntó Juan Cabezón.

"—Sin duda, quemando herejes, mi viejo Juan—soltó una carcajada Pedro de Alvarado." (95)

["Doña Marina has told me that during the dedication of the great temple of Huitzilopochtli and Tláloc, year 8 Acatl, year of our Redeemer 1487, twenty thousand prisoners were sacrificed. Have you seen such cruelty?" proffered Pedro de Alvarado, blood rushing to his face, his sword pulled a third of the way out of the sheath.

"What was our pious Grand Inquisitor doing that year in all of Spain?" Juan Cabezón asked.

"Without a doubt, burning heretics, my old Juan," Pedro de Alvarado guffawed.]

Juan Cabezón's response to Alvarado voices the link between the viciousness of the conqueror and that of the Inquisition.

Conquistador Gonzalo Dávila is another brutal but complex character, a close friend of Juan Cabezón whose foul practices unite Spanish and Mexica violence. Guided by his avarice for gold and power, he descends to a cavern where Mictlantecuhtli, the god of the dead, dwells. There, his conqueror's greed and brutality merges with the strength and darkness of this god, as its gold mask is incrusted in his face. He lives a mysterious life with unlimited access to wealth and influence, until in old age he is captured and sacrificed high in the volcanic mountains. This deathly merging of the *conquistador* and the Aztec god, both equally cruel and powerful, is emblematic of the complexities of cultural transition in Mexico as depicted in the novel, in which both parties are at times honorable, at times guilty of villainy.

The Holy Office, on the other hand, appears consistently as an agent of villainy in *Memorias*. For example, the question of "blood purity" plagues the conquerors and colonizers from the start. Restless sailors on the first voyage, eager for an excuse for mutiny, contemplate the possibility of Columbus's *converso* lineage: "—Es un miembro apestado de la herética pravedad, la cual nuestro fray Tomás de Torquemada acuchilla con el puñal de la fe y abrasa con las llamas de la verdadera religión—" (15). [He is a pestilential member of heretical depravity, which our friar Tomás de Torquemada stabs with the dagger of faith and burns with the flames of the true religion.] Shortly thereafter, the fictional character Rodrigo Rodríguez, a familiar of the Inquisition from *1492*, appears in Santo Domingo to investigate the possibility of Columbus's *converso* background: "había venido con el comendador para saber si Cristóbal Colón era judío oculto"

(49). [He had come with the commander to find out whether
Christopher Columbus was a hidden jew.] Even at the early stages of
the conquest, when Columbus notes that the island natives are tame
and will easily obey and accept Christian conversion, Juan Cabezón
responds, "Queréis esclavizarlos presto?" [Do you want to promptly
enslave them?], and when Columbus lists the benefits of the Castilian
language and religion they will be given, the *converso* interpreter puts
the universal benefits of Spanish civilization into doubt, asking
whether the benefits will include "También la Santa Inquisición?"
(24) [The Holy Inquisition too?]. Despite these two voices of conscience, soon the first colonizers arrive, hungry for gold and oblivious
to moral concerns regarding treatment of the natives.

Following the conquest of Mexico in 1521 and before the official
establishment of the Inquisition there in 1571, monks took the liberty
of exercising inquisitorial powers. They thereby aimed to enforce
native conversion to Catholicism and also to control the new gold and
prestige-hungry colonizers, or *criollos* (Latin Americans of Spanish
descent). Bishop Zumárraga, a historical figure, appears in the novel
Memorias ready to prosecute both cryptic Jews and natives who
maintain their own religious customs. He also comes armed with the
Libro Verde de Aragón, a book that old Christians consulted to identify the last names of formerly Jewish families or families condemned
during the years under Torquemada, "para que los cristianos viejos
que no quisiesen mezclar su sangre con la de los cristianos nuevos,
tuviesen conocimiento de la genealogía de éstos" (215) [so that the old
Christians that did not wish to mix their blood with that of the new
Christians had knowledge of their geneology]. Zumárraga master-
minds the controversial execution of don Carlos Chichimecatecuhtli,
a Mexica nobleman who is burned alive at the stake for continuing to
practice idolatry following his Christian baptism and indoctrination.
In the novel, Juan Cabezón is obligated to witness this *auto de fe* just
as he had witnessed others back on the peninsula in *1492*:

En su posada, Juan Cabezón comprendió que por más que le repugnara
el espectáculo de la quema de un hombre, tenía que estar presente;
pues de lo contrario, se levantarían sospechas contra él, ya que había
tenido algunos tratos con Hernando Alonso, uno de los quemados del
auto de fe de 1528....Por no hablar de Diego de Ocaña, "viejo hombre
de negocios de pluma," que andaba públicamente con túnica muy
grande y sombrero redondo negro, muy ajudiado, que había sido rec-
onciliado y era amistad suya. (230)

[At his inn, Juan Cabezón understood that as much as the spectacle of burning a man at the stake repulsed him, he had to be present; if he were not, suspicions would be raised against him, since he had had some dealings with Hernando Alonso, one of those burned at the stake at the *auto de fe* of 1528 .... Not to mention Diego Ocaña, "old man of dealings of the pen," who went around in public with a very big tunic and a big black hat, very Jewish, who had been reconciled and was a friend of his.]

The New World is not the safe haven from the Inquisition that Juan Cabezón had hoped for, as the bodies of friends and acquaintances continue to be humiliated and burned at the stake.

Punishing the Body

Punishment of the body is an essential element of the biopolitical control exerted by the state: the body is dehumanized, its basic needs denied or denigrated as shameful, its capacity for pleasure "disciplined" with pain. In *1492*, the impassioned monk Friar Vicente Ferrer (historically, the promoter of doña Catalina's 1411 decree of enclosure of Jews), travels from town to town in the early 1400s to convert Jews to Christianity and work Christians into an anti-semitic fervor. He has his donkey castrated "para que no ofendiera con su miembro la vista de nadie" (15) [so that the sight of its member would offend no one (16)], grants himself only two sips of watered down wine, never sets his eyes upon his own body other than his hands, limits his sleep to five hours, and whips himself each night. In *Memorias* another particularly fervent friar, Bernardino de Mura, similarly punishes his body in the name of faith: he fasts three days a week, sleeps on a wooden board, and wears a hair shirt against his skin: "Tenía guerra declarada contra su cuerpo y lo trataba como a un enemigo, sentenciándolo a pan y agua" (143). [He had declared war against his body and he treated it like an enemy, sentencing it to bread and water.] The friar has hired two natives to pull him by a noose around his neck and to whip him strenuously:

> El varón de Dios, el cuerpo llagado, los ojos puestos en el polvo, los pasos cortos, los suspiros frecuentes y las lágrimas corriéndole por las mejillas, imitaba humildemente al Redentor, y recorría los cerros y los llanos soportando la afrenta de ser conducido como una bestia de carga. Al caerse la cruz al suelo y arrodillarse para recogerla y besarla, los indios le escupían en rostro, le daban de bofetadas, le desnudaban el hábito y lo golpeaban hasta sacarle la sangre. (174)

[The man of God, his body wounded, his eyes looking at the dust, his steps short, his sighs frequent and tears running down his cheeks, humbly imitated the Redeemer, and he traveled through the hills and plains enduring the affront of being led like a beast of burden. Upon the cross falling to the ground and kneeling to pick it up and kiss it, the Indians spat in his face, slapped him, denuded him of his habit and beat him bloody.]

While the priest endures his torment in an attempt to imitate the passion of Christ, an agent of the state, governor Nuño Beltrán de Guzmán, engages in the brutalization of others' bodies, torturing native leaders, burning their feet with oil and setting them on fire so that they disclose where their wealth is hidden.

The much more sympathetic character, Juan Cabezón's blind travel companion Pero Meñique, rejects the friars' corporal denial and punishment, complaining in *1492* of the cruelty of the monastic life he has abandoned: "De sólo acordarme de la vida monástica me despeluzo entero. Enflaquecía y enflaquecía, sin que nunca fuera bastante el ayuno: para sentirme verdaderamente virtuoso tenía que desaparecer mi cuerpo del mundo" (80). [The mere recollection of monastic life makes my hair stand on end. I grew thinner and thinner, but my fasting was never sufficient: to feel truly virtuous my body had to disappear entirely from the world (75).] While he slowly starves, a monk delights in whipping him with all of his might.

In contrast with these sufferings, the novel celebrates Pero Meñique's particular enjoyment of the pleasures of the flesh with a welcoming woman, the innkeeper Oroceti Lumbroso. In addition, Aridjis's scenes of lovemaking between Juan Cabezón and Isabel in *1492*, or between Juan Cabezón's son Juan de Flandes and Ramona in *Memorias*, are sensuous and lyrical. Although the latter, indoctrinated in Christianity, is tinged with guilt, the erotic relationship between Juan and Isabel is a struggle of life, friendship, and desire against the death, hatred, and fear in the streets outside, during the most fervent years of the Inquisition:

Siguieron mis ojos cada ondulación, cada cambio de luz de la candela sobre su cuerpo, como si mi agradecimiento a la vida se derramase en cada centímetro de su piel y en la abundancia de su vientre.

Con cruda franqueza me tendió en la cama, la cabeza inclinada sobre sus pechos como Leda que va a recibir el cisne entre sus piernas; los brazos extendidos a lo largo de sus caderas, la panza hundida en su centro.

Me absorbió, no sólo por su natura, en donde se concentraba la acción, sino por sus miradas, que registraban hasta el más mínimo gesto.

Nuestros cuerpos fueron así reconciliados, no por la Iglesia de los inquisidores, pero por el amor....

—Mil clérigos han muerto sin haber conocido la carne, y miles más morirán sin haberla siquiera imaginado; excitados solamente cuando un cuerpo se ha vuelto cenizas, está bañado en sangre o yace bajo una piedra—dije. (*1492* 132)

[My eyes followed her, attentive to every ondulation, every flicker of candlelight on her body, as if my gratitude to life would flood every inch of her skin and the open abundance of her belly. With artless candor she pulled me down to the bed, resting my head between her breasts, like Leda about to receive the swan between her legs, and extended her arms along her hips, her stomach sunken in the center. She engulfed me, not with her sex alone, but with her eyes as well, which took in my slightest movement.

And thus were our bodies reconciled, not in the church of the inquisitors but in love....

"A thousand monks have died without knowing the flesh, and thousands more will die without even imagining it, roused solely by a body that has turned to ashes, is bathed in blood or lies beneath a stone," I said (120).]

In this sense, the character Juan Cabezón advocates an acceptance of bodily pleasures, rather than a denial of basic bodily needs—food, water, rest, the touch of a loved one—and he laments the replacement of these desires with pain and punishment inflicted through the mechanisms of biopolitical power.

Compassionate Hybrids

Pánfilo Meñique in *Memorias* is the product of the love of the inn-keeper Orocetí Lunbroso and of Pero Meñique, Juan Cabezón's blind companion mentioned earlier who is killed in *1492* for attacking a member of the Inquisition. Hidden under his mother's table, Pánfilo hears New Christians' whispered conversations about the times when practicing Jews still lived in Castile, and he notes their admiration for his father's (foiled) plan to assassinate the Grand Inquisitor Torquemada. Well indoctrinated in Christianity but conscious of his Jewish heritage, he completes training as a naturalist and departs for the New World in defiance of the decree to deny passage to the children or grandchildren of condemned heretics. In New Spain two native guides teach him the Nahuatl language and show him the wonders of all manner of plants and animals of the region, discoveries that he then shares with his pupil (and love), Mariana Pizarro, Gonzalo Dávila's niece. Pánfilo Meñique's nightmare in New Spain of inquisitorial friars pursuing his mother and himself points toward the continuity of the Inquisition's deathly legacy. The friar that pursues him in the bad dream is a hybrid of a Dominican priest and a Mexica priest who leaves his most valuable possessions from both worlds in disarray, his collections of European books and of American plants and animals irrevocably disordered:

> El desorden parecía no tener arreglo, por ser un desorden de la historia, de la existencia misma, de la condición de la tierra y de las criaturas que en ella moraban. Una descompostura irremediable, heredada de los padres a los hijos, y que él heredaría a los suyos, si tenía descendencia. En suma, una descompostura que venía de generaciones atrás e iba a continuar para siempre. (*Memorias* 244)

> [The disorder seemed to have no remedy, because it was a disorder of history, of existence itself, of the condition of the earth and the creatures that dwelled upon it. An irremediable breakdown, inherited from parents to their children, and that they would bequeath to their own, if they had descendants. In sum, a breakdown that came from generations back and that was going to continue for evermore.]

What does this disorder, inherited from his history, mean for his future in Mexico both in the spiritual world and in the natural world?

Juan de Flandes, Juan Cabezón and Isabel's son, is another compassionate hybrid who struggles with the two worlds. Trained in a Franciscan monastery, despite his Catholic convictions, like Pánfilo Meñique he remains loyal to his *conversa* mother. While visiting a school funded by the wealth confiscated from *conversos* persecuted by the Inquisition, he becomes uneasy with the inconsistencies of a religious training that speaks of mercy and forgiveness. He decides to leave for the New World in search of his father Juan Cabezón.

> Mientras los frailes le explicaban las buenas obras del obispo de Palencia y las bellezas del colegio y del monasterio, cruzó por su mente la imagen de su madre perseguida por ellos y sintió la urgencia de entregarse a una religión de amor y no de terror, de amistad y no de odio entre los hombres (*Memorias* 253).

> [While the friars explained to him the good works of the Bishop of Palencia and the beauties of the school and the monastery, the image of

his mother persecuted by them passed through his mind and he felt the urgency to surrender himself to a religion of love and not of terror, of friendship and not of hate between men.]

Juan de Flandes pledges to seek out a more compassionate religious practice, and he impresses his peers with his quietly noble character, so much so that rather than questioning his old Christian origin, they imagine that he is of royal blood: "Todavía más se hubieran sorprendido al saber que en lo íntimo no había renunciado a [sus padres], sino, por el contrario, se había propuesto en cuanto la fortuna le fuese propicia pasar a las Indias, adonde suponía se encontraba su padre Juan Cabezón" (257). [They would have been even more surprised upon knowing that deep down he had not renounced his parents; on the contrary, he had decided as soon as the time was right to go to the Indies, where he supposed that his father Juan Cabezón would be found.] While preparing for the voyage to seek out his father, Juan de Flandes practices Illuminism, finding God not in church ritual but through an intimate relationship with the Divine. He also decides to take on a painful lesson about his history, reading anti-Jewish tracts in order to better understand his mother's experiences and to try to fathom the hatred toward her people:

Y como si fuera por un camino de zarzas y espinas que le hacían daño físico y moral, cogió en sus manos los panfletos llenos de odio y maldad como el *Puñal de judíos*...el *Azote de los hebreos*...*Contra los judíos*...y la *Fortaleza de la fe*...que atacaba a los herejes, a los musulmanes y a los demonios, pero en especial a los judíos, a los que acusaba del asesinato ritual de un niño cristiano cerca de Vallodolid, en 1454. También revisó el *Libro Verde de Aragón,* que revelaba las genealogías de los conversos de ese reino. Siguió con la Pragmática de la reina Catalina sobre el Encerramiento de los judíos de Castilla, pregonada en las plazas de Valladolid el mes de enero de 1412; con la Bula del antipapa Pedro de Luna, llamado Benedicto XIII, de 1415; y, finalmente, con el Edicto de Expulsión de los judíos de toda España, firmado por los Reyes Católicos en 1492. A libelos, a ordenanzas entregó días y noches, con el propósito de entender el odio contra los judíos, contra sus padres, pero aunque desbarataba las razones en las que estaban basados, no podía explicarse el rencor vicioso de esas almas fanáticas. (258)

[And as if he were going down a path of brambles and thorns that harmed him physically and morally, he took in his hands the pamphlets filled with hate and evil like the *Dagger of the Jews*...the *Whip of the Hebrews*...*Against the Jews*...and *The Fortress of Faith*...that attacked heretics, Muslims, and demons, but especially Jews, whom it accused of the ritual murder of a Christian child near Valladolid in 1454. He also looked over the *Green Book of Aragón*, that revealed the geneologies of the converts of that kingdom. He continued with the Pragmatic of Queen Catalina on the Enclosure of the Jews of Castile, announced in the plazas of Valladolid the month of January, 1412; with the Papal Bull of the anti-pope Pedro de Luna, named Benedict XIII, of 1415; and, finally, with the Edict of Expulsion of the Jews of all of Spain, signed by the Catholic sovereigns in 1492. He dedicated days and nights to libels and ordinances in order to understand the hatred against Jews, against his parents, but while he took apart the reasons on which they were based, he could not explain to himself the vicious rancor of those fanatical souls.]

In light of his desire to overcome a legacy of fanaticism and hatred, it is appropriate that Juan de Flandes's voyage to the Americas is on the ship of Bartolomé de las Casas, the friar who in the novel closely follows the trajectory of the historical figure who penned the *Brevísima relación de la destrucción de las Indias* [*Brief Account on the Destruction of the Indies*] in 1542, regarding "el trato cruel que los españoles daban a los naturales, exagerando el número de los diezmados para mover [a Carlos V] a abolir las encomiendas" (259) [the cruel treatment that the Spaniards gave the natives, exaggerating the number of the decimated to move Charles the Fifth to abolish the *encomiendas*]. Las Casas incurs the *criollos*' wrath in the New World by returning to declare the abolition of slavery of the natives. Despite the *encomenderos*' hostility toward him "como de hombre alborotador de la tierra, inquietador de los cristianos y su enemigo, y favorecedor y amparador de unos perros indios" [as an agitator of the land, disturber and enemy of Christians, supporter and shelterer of a bunch of Indian dogs], the friar stands firm and goes so far as to deny the landowners absolution as long as they hold slaves:

A pesar de todo, fray Bartolomé de las Casas les dio a conocer las Leyes Nuevas sobre la esclavitud, los señaló como a hombres de mal estado e incapaces de absolución por tener ánimas que eran libres como esclavas; por cargarlos de tributos insoportables y por destruirlos y matarlos a todos, y porque ni los justicias ni los particulares obedecían la ley de Dios ni de su rey, había mandado que ningún confesor los absolviera para no irse con ellos al infierno. (269)

[Despite everything, Friar Bartolomé de las Casas informed them of the New Laws on slavery, pointed them out as men in a bad state and incapable of absolution for holding free souls as slaves, for loading them with insufferable tributes, and for destroying and killing them all, and because neither the justice officials nor the private individuals obeyed the law of God nor of their king, he had commanded that no confessor absolve them so as to not go to hell with them.]

As described by las Casas, natives subsumed under the *encomienda* system of forced, unpaid labor and tribute—for all purposes, slavery— have become the *homo sacer* of the New World, bare bodies less than human, set apart from political life, freely available to use and even to kill with impunity.

Censoring the Mind

In ruling over the body, sovereign power attempts to subsume the mind as well. Historically, as it censors bodies, the Inquisition also censors books, particularly in the New World, in order to control uniformity of ideas. Spanish writer Miguel de Unamuno wrote in 1918 of this damaging anti-intellectual legacy, in which envious individuals denounce their neighbors and creative thought and expression are stifled. "People could not bear to see anyone distinguishing himself, not thinking as others did, standing out from the herd. They could not tolerate heresy, personal opinions, thinking for oneself. By the very force of things, one had to stick to orthodoxy, the central dogma, the general opinion" (qtd. in Pérez 141).[11] A tradition is established in which nonconformity is harshly censored, and this carries over into the New World, where the Inquisition's list of prohibited books included those associated with the French Revolution, the works of Rousseau, and fiction such as the picaresque novel *Lazarillo de Tormes*. Back on the peninsula, priceless books in Arabic and Hebrew were burned. Bartolomé de las Casas's tome *La destrucción de las Indias* mentioned earlier, deploring the mistreatment of natives in the Americas, also appears on the banned books list as of 1660, as it fuels Spain's bad reputation. As a result of the Index, it becomes a point of pride to be illiterate, proving one's Old Christian peasant heritage and saving one from suspicion of reading banned books.

Paradoxically, inquisitors in both the Old and New World were men of letters, both historically and as depicted in Aridjis's novels. Angel Rama describes the ideal "lettered city" of the elite political, ecclesiastical, and scholarly strata in Latin America: "The lettered city acted upon the order of signs.... This was the cultural dimension of the power structure" (17). In New Spain, commissaries and familiars came from elite families, and the seal of the inquisition awarded them prestige, confirming an old Christian heritage and granting them social powers and even immunity from persecution. "Socialmente constituyen, sin lugar a duda y salvo excepción, los sectores más relevantes del poder económico y social, y ningún humilde labrador parece haberse colado entre sus filas impresionantes si no respetables" (Alberro 54). [Socially they constitute, without a doubt and without exception, the most relevant sectors of economic and social power, and no humble laborer seems to have placed himself among their impressive if not respectable ranks.] It is ironic that these prestigious figures are aligned with the world of letters, as the institution they represent seeks to severely restrict access to published ideas. The inquisitorial class manipulated their command of the written word as a source of power rather than of enlightenment.

Gonzalito, Gonzalo Dávila's mestizo offspring engendered with an indigenous prostitute, employs brute force as his source of power, as he is illiterate. In the novel, Gonzalito represents the future of the Mexican state devastatingly; he is an idiot who sleeps and eats with the dogs, a large individual who delights in overpowering and harming others, and who takes special pleasure in viewing both *autos de fe* and Mexica sacrifices. Gonzalito aspires to become governor of New Spain and takes part in his father's sacrifice at the conclusion of the novel in order to attain his goal. How does this character, a hybrid not of the best but of the worst of both worlds, bode for the colonial years to come?

In raising such concerns, Aridjis's work plays a role in keeping alive the awareness of the machinations of biopolitics. In fact, there is a convergence in Aridjis's narrative of his eco-mindedness and his Sephardic concerns. His poem "Sepharad" aptly expresses his concern for the land and for the possible link today between state-sponsored abuse of the ecosystem and of the human body: "The exile comes not from God, but men—/neighbours, friends, your own kin./Vain words those of the prophet/who swore he'd lead us to a promised land,/lead us, rich and hugely honoured, out from Sepharad" (Stavans 56). Aridjis's work bears witness indirectly to the fragility of the human body not only in the time of the Inquisition and Conquest, but also in the modern state, a fragility seen for instance in the 1968 government shooting of student protesters in Tlatelolco.[12] The Spanish Inquisition is undoubtedly "una de las primeras máquinas represivas modernas" [one of the first modern repressive machines], and can be traced as a source of twentieth- and twenty-first-century forms of repression and control, whether insidious or brutal (Alberro 7). As Hannah Arendt testifies, "We can no longer afford to take that which was good in the past and simply call it our heritage, to discard the bad and simply think of it as a dead load which by itself time will bury in oblivion" (*The Origins of Totalitarianism* ix). These past events did occur and will rise to the surface, and they require examination as Benjamin has called us to do and as Aridjis has attempted in his work.

Fernando del Paso's *Noticias del Imperio*

Fernando del Paso's critically acclaimed novel *Noticias del Imperio* (1987) also entails mourning for tragic events from the European historical legacy. *Noticias* recounts the rise and fall of the French Empire of Maximilian and Charlotte in Mexico (1864–1867). Del Paso's encyclopedic novel is a landmark text, marking important Spanish American literary trends of recent decades that appear in the "new historical novels" examined throughout this book; it celebrates postmodern fragmentation with contradictory voices that question Mexico's "grand narratives," critiques Mexico's relations with Europe and the United States through the lens of postcolonial theory, and questions and reshapes historiography.

As an exemplary model of this genre, *Noticias del Imperio* has merited studies by prominent Hispanic literary theorists such as Seymour Menton, Juan José Barrientos, and Robin Fiddian. Menton has explored the 900-page novel as a Bakhtinian symphony of voices that merits "instant canonization," while Barrientos has emphasized the postmodern problematization of historiography in the novel. Fiddian, in turn, has interpreted del Paso's historical narrative as a critique of imperialism. In relation to this focus on imperialism, I delve into the theme of mourning as a trope in the novel that mediates the uneasy alliance between tradition and modernity[13] as well as the association between Europe and the Americas. While depicting the process of mourning for Maximilian and Charlotte, *Noticias del Imperio* moves toward resolving two pressing questions that are key to this book: How do we define Mexico's uneasy relationship with the colonial powers of Europe and the United States? How does Mexico reconcile its desire to maintain its autonomous traditions while embracing modernity? Charlotte ("Carlota"), the most fascinating voice in the novel, responds to these two questions as she mourns for the losses brought about by the encounter between Mexico and Europe, arbitrates the debate between them, serves as a diplomat of transculturation, and moderates modernity from both shores.[14]

Mourning for Europe and Mexico

Noticias del Imperio is not an elegiac novel of grief and abjection; rather, del Paso's narrative utilizes mourning to explore Maximilian and Charlotte as representative of Mexico's contentious relationship with the imperial powers of Europe and, later, the United States. Mourning is a crucial means for negotiating the losses entailed both personally, for Charlotte, and collectively, for Mexico and Europe. As we shall see, storytelling is coextensive with mourning. Furthermore, transculturation, both on the part of the characters Maximilian and Charlotte and as seen in the novel as a whole, represents the ways that Mexico comes to terms with its mourning in relation to Europe.

Del Paso's novel reveals the task of transculturation: while colonialism is to be discarded and not "incorporated," to use the psychoanalytical term for unhealthy mourning, the colonial heritage is to be owned and transformed, or to be "introjected," to use the term for healthy mourning, which will be addressed shortly. Transculturation is thus a tool to be used in this process of mourning, as it provides a means of negotiating Mexico's relationship with modernity as well as its relations with Europe, associations that del Paso claims as Mexico's birthright.[15] *Noticias del Imperio* seeks to critique the errors of European imperialism but also to understand and to recognize the European legacy in the Americas. As prominent intellectuals from José Vasconcelos and Alfonso Reyes to Carlos Fuentes and Héctor Aguilar Camín have reminded us, it is essential to recognize that Mexico's roots are not only Aztec but also Spanish. The *mestizo* nation has proactively selected and incorporated European traditions over the years. For example, cultural critic Néstor García Canclini has signaled how, in negotiating modernity, Mexican indigenous artisans sell tapestries with designs copied from Picasso paintings alongside weavings with native patterns. By incorporating both Mexican and European narrative voices to address the French legacy in Mexico, *Noticias del Imperio* also produces a work of transculturation.

In del Paso's configuration, the colonized subjects responding to European influence are not the only agents of transculturation. While the power relations are frequently and undeniably uneven, the process is nevertheless reciprocal, as the colonizers Maximilian and Charlotte also undergo transformation in response to Mexican cultural influence. This is the novel aspect of del Paso's version of transculturation, a version built upon the ideas of such predecessors as Alfonso Reyes, who, in his 1936 lecture "Notas sobre la inteligencia americana" [Notes on American Intelligence] demanded recognition of the Latin American right to citizenship of the world (15). Fiddian measures del Paso's writing against the intellectual paradigm of another groundbreaking Mexican philosopher, Leopoldo Zea, whose later work (in the 1970s and 1980s), informed by the postcolonial theory of Frantz Fanon, reverses the dichotomies civilization/barbarism; Europe/Americas. For Zea, the process of cultural *mestizaje* in Latin America, as in the African diaspora, should entail assimilating the colonial legacy without being assimilated (73). This active, not passive, integration is the task of transculturation seen in process in del Paso's novel.

Furthermore, in a more recent study of transculturation, Silvia Spitta provides a definition that allows for transculturation on the part of the colonizer as well, a definition that is appropriate for this innovative aspect of del Paso's epistemology. For Spitta, transculturation encompasses the "complex processes of adjustment and re-creation—cultural, literary, linguistic and personal—that allow for new, vital and viable configurations to arise out of the clash of cultures and the violence of colonial and neo-colonial appropriations" (2). The "transculturated subject," in turn, is someone who mediates between the two worlds, cultures, languages, and subjectivities (24). Following Spitta's paradigm, the transculturated subject can come from the dominant culture as well (the shipwrecked Spanish colonist Cabeza de Vaca in *Naufragios*, for example). Her assertion allows us to see the literary characters Maximilian and Charlotte not as simply appropriators and impostors, but rather as complex transculturated subjects transformed by their experiences in Mexico.

Storytelling as Mourning

In addition to transculturation, storytelling is another healthy means of negotiating personal and collective losses. Mourning is coextensive with telling. The mourner must tell stories of the loved one over and over to complete the task of grieving. As part of this practice, Charlotte attempts to tell Maximilian's story as she continues to struggle with the process of mourning sixty years after his death. She will tell the story of the Second Empire, to understand the good and the ill of

Maximilian and his memory: "Con tu lengua y tus ojos, tú y yo juntos vamos a inventar de nuevo la historia" (97). [With your tongue and your eyes, you and I together will invent history all over again.] This passage reveals the relation between the body itself and the story that the body—the tongue, the eyes—creates.

Charlotte's conflicting desires represent healthy and unhealthy aspects of the mourning process, as she aims to tell the history of her deceased husband and yet also retain his corporal presence. Sigmund Freud began his exploration of the task of mourning in his essay, "Mourning and Melancholia" (1917). According to Freud, mourning is a gradual and necessary process, in which the grieving individual must recognize the finality of death and loss to release the psychic energy (libido) invested in the loved one. This process is much like storytelling, as it is a painful struggle that requires retrieving, one by one, the memories and hopes that bind the mourner to the lost object:

> The task is now carried through bit by bit, under great expense of time and cathectic energy, while all the time the existence of the lost object is continued in the mind. Each single one of the memories and hopes which bound the libido to the object is brought up and hyper-cathe-cted, and the detachment of the libido from it accomplished....When the work of mourning is completed the ego becomes free and uninhib-ited again. (154)[16]

Two inventive aspects of this storytelling in the novel involve what psychoanalysts would call introjection, a healthy grieving process, and incorporation, an insalubrious fantasy of incorporating the departed into one's own body. "So in order not to have to 'swallow' a loss, we fantasize swallowing that which has been lost" (Abraham and Torok 126). Through incorporation, or a refusal to mourn, one ingests the love object, entombing it within in a psychic crypt.

Incorporation can be seen in the novel when the mad Empress Charlotte grotesquely longs for Maximilian's lost body parts. In one passage, the empress claims to hold a rosewood box with a piece of Maximilian's heart and the bullet that killed him; not for a moment will she release the box (12). Not only will she not let go of his heart, but Charlotte also asks that Max's eyes and ears be reawakened so that she can recover her own sight and hearing: "si estoy ciega, es porque me quitaron tus ojos...me quitaron todo lo que yo veía a través de ellos, porque fue con tus ojos que aprendí a ver" (87). [If I'm blind, it is because they took your eyes from me...they took from me everything I saw through them, because it was with your eyes that I learned to see.] This impossible relationship is seen most clearly in her desire for sex with the absent lover, as Charlotte copulates with a Maximilian doll she has fabricated. "Yo me propuse no olvidarte nunca y que nadie, jamás, te olvide de nuevo. Es por eso que decidí quedarme en un sueño con los ojos abiertos" (153). [I decided to never forget you and that no one would ever forget you again. That is why I decided to remain in a dream with my eyes open.] The sex with the imagined and remembered body represents an emphasis on the immediate, since pleasure reaffirms the moment, but it also represents the regenerative possibilities for a future existence, one that is possible only in fantasy.

Her madness, then, is the product of her decision to remain in a world that has passed, a world when Maximilian lived: "Porque si es mi condena, también es mi privilegio, el privilegio de los sueños y de los locos, inventar, si quiero, un inmenso castillo de palabras" (154). [Because if it is my downfall, it is also my privilege, the privilege of dreams and of the mad, to invent, if I wish, an immense castle of words.] With these words, she models him, shapes him, creates him, gives birth to him, all functions of her fantasy of reviving Maximilian:

Ándale, Maximiliano, atrévete tú también a volver a ser todos los Maximilianos que fuiste alguna vez.... Ándale, Maximiliano, quítate los algodones que tienes en la nariz, y que no te dejan respirar.... Ándale, Maximiliano, quítate la esponja empapada en vinos egipcios y sangre de dragón con la que te rellenaron la boca y diles a los doctores que te pongan de nuevo la lengua y la campanilla para que vuelvas a hablar conmigo.... Ándale, dime cómo has pasado tú tu vida entre tus sábanas de plomo, y yo te contaré cómo ha pasado la mía. (234–237)

[Come on, Maximilian, dare to be once again all of the Maximilians that you once were.... Come on, Maximilian, take the cotton out of your nose that will not let you breathe.... Come on, Maximilian, take out the sponge soaked in Egyptian wines and dragon blood that they filled your mouth with and tell the doctors to put your tongue and uvula back in so that you can talk to me again.... Come on, tell me how you've spent your life between sheets of lead, and I'll tell you how I've spent mine.]

In sum, this grotesque desire to revive the deceased's body parts represents her symptom of incorporation in wanting to retain his presence in her life. Because he represents both Mexico and Europe for her, she must make him exist in order to continue her own existence.

The process of mourning is also incomplete because Charlotte not only wishes for Maximilian's return but also refuses to weep for his absence: "yo era una princesa que había aprendido a estar triste sin aparecerlo. A parecer alegre sin estarlo....Desde entonces no he vuelto a llorar, y no quiero hacerlo por nadie, ni siquiera por ti" (407). [I was a princess who had learned to be sad without appearing so. To seem happy without being so....I haven't cried since, and I don't want to do it for anyone, not even for you.] Her training in the dissimulation of emotions is highly internalized. Charlotte can only complete the process of mourning by telling Maximilian's story:

> Creí o quise creer que el planeta entero te iba a llorar, pero cuando llegué a la calle y me encontré a un florista...y le dije con el telegrama en la mano Maximiliano, mi adorado Maximiliano el rey del universo ha muerto y me preguntó con ojos asombrados Maximiliano, ¿quién es Maximiliano?, me di cuenta que si yo no le decía al mundo quién eres tú, Maximiliano, el mundo jamás sabrá quién fuiste. (663)

> [I believed or wanted to believe that the entire planet was going to cry for you, but when I got to the street and ran into a florist...and I told him with the telegram in my hand Maximilian, my beloved Maximilian the king of the universe has died and he asked me with astonished eyes, Maximilian, who's Maximilian? I realized that if I didn't tell the world who you are, Maximilian, the world will never know who you were.]

This step of telling the world is essential, as Charlotte, at first unable to accept Maximilian's absence, comes to terms with his demise through telling his tale. Furthermore, her mourning is not merely personal, but must be a public act of storytelling, so that together with the community she can process the emperor's role in Mexico and his death.

From Individual to Collective Mourning

Charlotte's mourning for Maximilian in the novel illuminates the need for Mexico to collectively process its history of the French Intervention. In *The Untimely Present*, a study of post-dictatorial novels from the Southern Cone, Idelber Avelar defines mourning as active, not passive, forgetting. Following Walter Benjamin, these works respond to loss and defeat by showing allegorical ruins. Avelar employs the term "affects" to distinguish between individual feeling or emotion (interiority, self), and the social aspects of mourning that he wishes to emphasize in the writings of Diamela Eltit and others. He aims to desubjectivize mourning and memory and study them not as the psychology of a nation but rather to "delimit them as immanent to the social field" (23). Following Avelar's distinction between social affects and individual subjectivities, we can then approach Charlotte's symptoms of incorporation or introjection as symptoms of a greater national mourning that must be completed.

Despite Charlotte's symptoms of incorporation mentioned earlier, the empress also has moments of lucidity, perhaps in part because she employs language as part of the process of collective mourning. The act of storytelling enables her to come to terms with the errors of the Second Empire and with the death of Maximilian. The use of language is an integral means of addressing unresolved issues of grieving, as incorporation results when one is unable to articulate certain words and to acknowledge loss, perhaps due to an unnamable trauma regarding the deceased: "The words that cannot be uttered, the scenes that cannot be recalled, the tears that cannot be shed—everything will be swallowed along with the trauma that led to the loss. Swallowed and preserved" (Abraham and Torok 130). The lost love object is protected, its shameful secret covered up in order to maintain the object as an ego ideal:

> The primary aim of the fantasy life born of incorporation is to repair—in the realm of the imaginary—the injury that really occurred and really affected the ideal object. The fantasy of incorporation reveals a utopian wish that the memory of the affliction had never existed or, on a deeper level, that the affliction had had nothing to inflict. (134)

The mourner's melancholic tendency is to idealize the deceased, remembering his best qualities while taking on his failings as the mourner's own. Moral self-condemnation disguises the flaws of the object by incorporating them into the subject.

Despite her symptoms of incorporation, Charlotte eventually moves beyond suppressing Maximilian's failures and projecting them onto herself; instead, she engages in introjection through telling his story. With introjection, the mourner does not swallow what is lost but rather works through the loss by filling the mouth with language (and with food, important in wakes and Day of the Dead practices) in an effort to communicate and manage the loss.[17] Charlotte moves toward this process as she tells of Maximilian, releasing the deceased

by naming his faults as well as his virtues. To remember him for
herself and for the history of Mexico, she enumerates his virtues and
vices; he is a martyr but also a usurper, generous yet unforgiving,
noble yet foolish (821–843).

No fuiste, tampoco, otro Iván el Terrible: no hubo en las calles de
México gente que fuera destazada o asada viva. Fuiste Maximiliano el
bondadoso. ¿Pero te acuerdas que a García Cano lo ejecutaron porque
le negaste la gracia?...por más baños de pureza que quieras darte tienes
que saber que también fuiste, también, Maximiliano el sordo,
Maximiliano el inmisericorde...y Maximiliano el ciego porque le escri-
biste a Napoleón diciéndole que en México había sólo tres clases de
hombres: los viejos testarudos, los jóvenes ignorantes y los extranjeros
mediocres o aventureros sin porvenir en Europa, y no supiste ver que tú
reunías, en una sola persona, los defectos de los tres. (822–823)

[You weren't another Ivan the Terrible either; in the streets of Mexico
there weren't people hacked into pieces or roasted alive. You were
Maximilian the good. But do you remember that they executed García
Cano because you denied him a pardon?...As much as you may play
innocent you have to know that you were also Maximilian the deaf,
Maximilian the merciless...and Maximilian the blind because you
wrote to Napoleon telling him that in Mexico there were only three
kinds of men: stubborn old men, ignorant youth, and mediocre or mer-
cenary foreigners without a future in Europe, and you didn't know
how to see that in yourself, as one person, you brought together the
defects of all three.]

Charlotte wavers back and forth, then, in the process between
introjection and incorporation. Only in 1927, after witnessing sixty
years of change, can she complete the mourning process, permitting
herself anger in order to give up the lost object while allowing comforting fantasies to endure. She must accomplish this not only in order
to reclaim her lucidity and welcome death (like don Quijote), but also
in order to mourn on behalf of Mexico, ask for Mexico's forgiveness,
and ask to be welcomed in the Mexican pantheon.

Del Paso's novel thereby works toward transferring fantasies of
incorporation into introjection, giving way to the painful but beneficial process of mourning so that the memory of Maximilian and his
ill-fated empire may be articulated and finally buried in Mexican soil.
Language gives figurative shape to presence and is shared among a
community.[18] Charlotte directs her words to the imagined listener
Maximilian and also to the reader; this act moves toward communal

mourning for the losses caused by the French Intervention as well as for the deleterious effects of other instances of colonialism and imperialism in Mexico. In this way, Maximilian's death in the novel marks the path to collective recovery for Mexico.

In his study *La jaula de la melancolía*, [*The Cage of Melancholy*] Roger Bartra explores how the concepts of mourning and Mexican cultural identity are linked; he sets out to dispel myths of Mexican character (such as the listless *pelado*), and turns to the *axolotl*, perhaps facetiously, as a new metaphor. The *axolotl* is a curious aquatic animal that reproduces in its larval stage and never completes the process of development that would turn it into a salamander. For Bartra, this creature represents the mythical Mexican, strange and melancholic, never undergoing metamorphosis. Bartra argues that Mexico must escape from this cage of misery and free itself from the legacy of the image of the Mexican "type" that intellectuals such as Samuel Ramos (*El perfil del hombre y la cultura en México*, 1934) and Octavio Paz (*El laberinto de la soledad*, 1950) sketched in their work. Del Paso creates a variety of alternatives with the Mexican characters in the novel, and generously creates a noble death for Maximilian by formulating a dignified protocol for his execution in the chapter "Ceremonial para el fusilamiento de un Emperador" (884–899):

> Si el emperador se encuentra aún vivo, el Médico de la Corte así lo comunicará al Gran Maestro de Ceremonias, para que éste a su vez, se lo comunique al Gran Canciller de las Órdenes del Imperio. El Gran Canciller presentará entonces, en un cojín de terciopelo negro, la bala destinada al tiro de gracia. Esta bala será de plomo, con cabeza de plata. Los asistentes, mientras tanto, deberán guardar un silencio absoluto. (895)

> [If the emperor is still alive, the Court Physician will inform the Grand Master of Ceremonies, so that he in turn may inform the Grand Chancellor of the Imperial Order. The Grand Chancellor will then, on a black velvet cushion, present the bullet destined for the final shot. This bullet will be lead, with a silver head. The assistants, meanwhile, should maintain absolute silence.]

In del Paso's ceremony, formulated as Maximilian may have wished it, the firing squad is dressed formally in black with white sashes, and they are all the same height. The instructions also stipulate that before firing, they will ask, and be granted, the emperor's pardon.

In accordance with this social protocol for Maximilian's final moments, Bartra also recognizes that collective mourning is a necessary process, and that the practice of communal grieving (the Day of the Dead, for instance) disproves the stereotype of Mexican indifference to death. "Toda cultura, dada la inevitabilidad de la muerte individual, necesita crear rituales y símbolos que permitan que los muertos comiencen a morir en nosotros...para no correr el riesgo de morir con ellos" (78). [Every culture, given the inevitability of individual death, needs to create rituals and symbols that permit our dead to begin to die within us...in order to not run the risk of dying with them.] Bartra further argues that the Mexican apparent disdain for death is a strategy to provide ritual control over suffering, "un rito colectivo que le da sentido a la vida" [a collective ritual that gives meaning to life], and should not be confused with apathy toward the loss of life (78). This seeming fatalism or disdain for death was resurrected by intellectuals and artists during the Mexican Revolution as they dealt with the violence of the period. Through the etchings of José Guadalupe Posada, for instance, death was elevated to a heroic gesture: "morir fácilmente, como sólo los miserables saben hacerlo" (Bartra 79) [to die easily, as only the wretched know how to do]. With this death, there is not only storytelling and remembering; there also must be forgiving and releasing, a result of the mourning process that Charlotte embodies.

As part of the collective mourning process of together releasing the lost object of desire, the mourner must ask others for forgiveness, pardon the vanished object, and forgive all those involved in his demise. This Charlotte does early in the novel: "no hay noche en que no me dedique a ordenar mi casa y mi conciencia" (14). [There is not a night in which I don't devote myself to straightening out my house and my conscience.] She clears her conscience and also forgives Maximilian and Mexico: "y así como te perdono todo lo que me hiciste, perdono a todos nuestros enemigos y perdono a México" (14). [And as I forgive you for everything you did to me, I forgive all of our enemies and I forgive Mexico.] While she undergoes this process, her narrative is again often contradictory; here she speaks of the forgiveness necessary on her part and on the part of the Mexican people:

Tendrás tú, tendrán los mexicanos que entender que cuando hablo de mi rencor por ti y por ellos, puedo estar hablando, en realidad, de mi ternura. Cuando escribo sobre mi odio, puedo estar escribiendo, en realidad, sobre mi amor por ti, mi amor por México, por lo que fuiste tú, por lo que será mi Imperio. Mi Imperio, Maximiliano, sólo se levantará sobre el olvido: necesitamos olvidar lo que nos hicieron. Necesitan olvidar ellos, los mexicanos, lo que les hicimos. (671)

[You will have to understand, the Mexicans will have to understand, that when I speak of my rancor for you and for them, I could really be speaking of my tenderness. When I write about my hate, I could really be writing about my love for you, my love for Mexico, for what you were, for what my Empire will be. My empire, Maximilian, alone will rise from oblivion; we need to forget what they did to us. They, the Mexicans, need to forget what we did to them.]

To show her continued affection for Mexico, Charlotte claims that she regularly plays the Mexican national hymn and washes and lovingly displays the Mexican flag: "la cuelgo a secar en la punta de la torre más alta, y la plancho después, Maximiliano, la acaricio, la doblo, la guardo y le prometo que mañana, de nuevo, la sacaré a ondear para que la vea Europa entera" (15). [I hang it out to dry at the top of the highest tower, and then I iron it, Maximilian, I caress it, I fold it, I put it away and I promise it that tomorrow, once again, I'll take it out to wave so that all of Europe sees it.] She also specifies that, in her fidelity to Mexico, though she will weep for the death of Maximilian she will not weep for the death of the Second Empire.

Mourning Past and Future

The novel acknowledges that Charlotte has outlived all of the players in the history not only of the Second Empire but far beyond into the modern era: the Mexican Revolution of 1910, World War I, the Marxist Revolution. "Yo enterré al General Porfirio Díaz con la tierra del Cementerio de Montparnasse y con la tierra del Cementerio de Highgate enterré a Carlos Marx." [I buried General Porfirio Díaz in the soil of Montparnasse Cemetery and in the soil of Highgate Cemetery I buried Carlos Marx.] Now she aims to bury Maximilian in a less renowned cemetery, with the flowers, mud and dust of Mexico:

con un costal lleno de la tierra mojada de Orizaba y de la tierra del Valle de México donde se derramaban como lava ardiente las flores amarillas del acahualillo cuando ibas camino a Cuernavaca y del polvo de los llanos de Apam donde cabalgabas todas las mañanas, y con ellas y mis propias manos te voy a enterrar, Maximiliano, para ver si así, tú que nunca aprendiste a vivir en esas tierras que dijiste que amabas tanto, para ver, te decía, si de una vez por todas aprendes a estar muerto bajo esas tierras donde nunca te quisieron. (94)

[In a sack filled with the wet earth of Orizaba and with the soil of the Mexican Valley where the yellow *acahualillo* flowers spilled over like burning lava when you used to go to Cuernavaca and with the dust of the Apam plains where you used to ride every morning, and with it and my own hands I'm going to bury you, Maximilian, to see if, you who never learned to live in those lands that you said you loved so, to see, I was saying, if at last you will learn to be dead beneath that soil that never loved you.]

Burial is a fundamental final step in the process of mourning. It provides the conviction that the individual is truly dead and at rest. It is at that point that the former empress dares to chastise Maximilian for his mistakes—and for dying:

¿De qué hechizo, Maximiliano, dime, de qué sortilegio fuiste víctima que no fuera la hipocresía y la mentira? Morir, claro, es más fácil que seguir vivo. Estar muerto y cubierto de gloria es mejor que estar viva y sepultada en el olvido. Por eso, nada más, y para echarte en cara todas tus mentiras, es que cada noche viajo hacia atrás en el tiempo. (248)

[Of what spell, Maximilian, tell me, of what hex were you a victim that wasn't hypocrisy and lies? Dying, of course, is easier than remaining alive. To be dead and covered with glory is better than being alive like me and buried in forgetting. That's why, just to throw all of your lies in your face, every night I travel back in time.]

Charlotte's narrative journey from past to present completes her acceptance of loss and her negotiation with the memories of Maximilian and of Mexico.

Del Paso's construction of this narrative journey calls attention to the vital role that the historical figures Maximilian and Charlotte played in consolidating Mexican modernity. As historian Daniel Cosío Villegas asserts, "El México moderno se consolida en dos grandes caídas: la caída de Maximiliano y la de Porfirio Díaz" (qtd. in Krauze, *Siglo* 17). [Modern Mexico is consolidated in two great falls: the fall of Maximilian and that of Porfirio Díaz.] In del Paso's novel the character of Charlotte mediates this transition, as she narrates from the perspective of the modern era that came about for Mexico in part as a result of the demise of the Second Empire. Her

present-day view destroys the epic distance of time that would otherwise separate the reader from national history. She speaks from the
voice of the present, sixty years beyond the events of the Intervention:
"¿te dijo alguien, Maximiliano, que inventaron el teléfono? ¿que
inventaron el gas neón? ¿el automóvil, Max? ... ¿y también que inventaron el fonógrafo?" (17). [Maximilian, did someone tell you they
invented the telephone? That they invented neon gas? The automo-
bile, Max? And that they also invented the phonograph?] She has
witnessed moments that mark the modern era: the invention of the
telephone, flight, cars, typewriters, film, the x-ray, as well as the tre-
mendously influential thought of Marx, Einstein, and Freud.

Charlotte's view from her immediate present brings history closer
to the reader; she plays the pivotal role of the fool or clown, who, as
described by Bakhtin, has "the right not to understand, the right to
confuse, to tease, to hyperbolize life, the right to parody others, the
right to rage at others with a primeval rage—and finally, the right to
betray to the public a personal life, down to its most private and pru-
rient little secrets" (163). These private secrets include, for example, a
passage in which she claims to coat her erogenous zones with honey
in order to attract the quivering sips of the houseflies. Such passages
humanize the royals, destroying the respectful distance of an anti-
quated period much as in Ibargüengoitia's and Madero's demonumentalization of the hero seen in chapter one of this book.

As mentioned earlier, an essential step in the mourning process is
not simply to venerate those who are gone but rather to acknowledge
disappointment and anger for the errors of the past. *Noticias del
Imperio* utilizes irony to offer a clear critique of the imperialist agenda
of Emperor Maximilian and Empress Charlotte and to undermine
European claims of civilized supremacy. For instance, in one particularly memorable passage, the sadistic Coronel du Pin tortures a
Mexican messenger in order to obtain military secrets for the forces
of occupation. Du Pin praises the greatness of French civilization and
celebrates cosmopolitan Paris as he instructs his soldiers to thrust
pins into his prisoner's testicles; later, he compares fine French wine
to "nasty" Mexican *pulque* as he commands his soldiers to thrust
pins into the prisoner's eyelids. In the novel, the character of Benito
Juárez also voices an anti-imperialist assessment: "Ah, vientos de libertad corren en Europa, Señor Secretario, pero aquí en México esa
misma Europa quiere revivir la Edad Media, el oscurantismo" (437).
[Ah, the winds of liberty run through Europe, Mister Secretary, but
here in Mexico that same Europe wants to revive the Middle Ages, the

Dark Ages.] Juárez notes the irony of Europe's claims to progress and liberty when France's military forces are occupying Mexico and brutalizing Mexican soldiers.

A Mexican Burial

Despite Maximilian and Charlotte's grave error of spilling Mexican blood for the sake of their dream of a "liberal empire," Maximilian's last words in the novel (as adapted from the historical records) declare his love for Mexico and his identity as Mexican. As del Paso notes, Mexico's villains as well as its heroes must be buried in Mexican soil. They all belong to Mexico—the European Maximilian, the indigenous Benito Juárez—they are all part of the history that defines Mexican modernity today. Maximilian and Charlotte may not have been ideal precursors or ones that Mexico would have chosen for itself, but in the novel's depiction they are an important set of Mexico's predecessors that should not be forgotten. *Noticias del Imperio* takes a step toward acknowledging the importance of Maximilian's empire and his execution as a key moment in the construction of Mexican national identity. Playwright Rodolfo Usigli called the rise and fall of Maximilian one of the "tres elementos básicos de nuestra soberanía" (qtd. in Beardsell 86) [three basic elements of our sovereignty]. The European invader diverted internal hostilities as Mexicans united against a common imperialist enemy; in Maximilian's death is born a sense of national identity.

Nevertheless, in the novel Charlotte perceives Maximilian's last words with the irony of her knowledge of later events such as the Revolution that began in 1910: "¿Te acuerdas, Maximiliano, que en el discurso que pronunciaste ante el pelotón de fusilamiento pediste que fuera tuya la última sangre que se derramara en México? Bastante, sí, bastante sangre mexicana se había derramado ya por nuestra culpa, pero mucha sangre más habría de derramarse en México" (751). [Do you remember, Maximilian, that in the speech you gave before the firing squad you asked that your blood be the last spilled in Mexico? Enough, yes, enough Mexican blood had already been spilled because of you, but much more blood was going to spill in Mexico.] Despite his responsibility for the spilling of Mexican blood, Charlotte again insists on a proper burial in Mexican soil for Maximilian:

> Pero de todos esos mexicanos muertos sus huesos volvieron al polvo del que habían salido y su sangre tiñó la tierra que alimentó su carne, para fecundar una historia bárbara de traiciones y mentiras, una historia

bella de triunfos y heroísmos, una historia triste de humillaciones y
fracasos pero al fin y al cabo su historia, la de un pueblo que jamás fue
el tuyo ni el mío por más que lo quisiste y que lo quise yo. (752)

[But of all those dead Mexicans their bones went back to the dust they
had come from and their blood stained the earth that fed their flesh, to
fertilize a barbarous history of betrayals and lies, a beautiful story of
triumphs and heroisms, a sad story of humiliations and failures but
finally their history, that of a people that was never yours nor mine no
matter how much you wanted it and I wanted it.]

Charlotte shows her ambivalence as she acknowledges that she must
bear the weight of the death of the Mexicans who died during the
intervention, yet she persists in claiming the right for Maximilian to
be buried beside them: "Ay, Maximiliano, si pudieras venir a Querétaro
verías que de esa tu sangre, la que tú querrías que no fuera la última
que se derramara en tu nueva patria, no quedó huella, nada quedó en
el polvo o en las piedras, nada fecundó tu sangre…se la llevó el viento,
la barrió de la historia, la olvidó México" (752). [Oh, Maximilian, if
you could come to Querétaro you would see that from your blood
that you wanted to be the last spilled in your new land, not a trace
remained, nothing remained in the dust nor in the stones, your blood
fertilized nothing…the wind carried it away, it swept it from history,
Mexico forgot it.] Charlotte advocates for the blood of Maximilian to
be recovered and redeemed in order to enrich Mexican soil, and for
the two of them to be remembered despite their role as invaders.

In this sense, despite the novel's clear anti-imperialist stance,
Noticias del Imperio aims in part to collapse the distance between
Europe and Latin America just as Charlotte's voice destroys the distances of history. Del Paso points out the artifice of such historical
and geographical distances in a controversial 1991 speech at the
Sorbonne in Paris at an event honoring Mexican literature. The writer
responds to an epigraph in the program quoting Mexican intellectual
Octavio Paz, who describes Mexico as a nation on the periphery of
the world and in the margins of modernity. In contrast with Paz, del
Paso's speech makes three assertions that are implicit in the novel as
well: Mexico merits a place on the center stage of time and space; it
does not enter Europe through the back door; and likewise it is not
entering modernity through the tradesmen's entrance. Expressing his
disagreement with the quote from Paz, he states at the Sorbonne:

Yo, que de niño me nutrí con Jules Verne, Alexandre Dumas, Walter
Scott, y que después alimenté mi educación sentimental con Flaubert,

Marcel Proust, André Gide, y William Faulkner, de ninguna manera
me siento gente de la periferia, ni habitante de los arrabales de la historia, ni comensal no invitado. No he entrado a la cultura occidental por
la puerta de servicio, ni de ninguna forma me siento intruso en ella.
(qtd. in Mergier 46)

[I, who as a boy fed myself on Jules Verne, Alexandre Dumas, Walter
Scott, and afterward fed my sentimental education on Flaubert, Marcel
Proust, André Gide, and William Faulkner, in no way do I feel a peripheral person, nor an inhabitant of the outskirts of history, nor an unin-
vited guest. I have not entered Western culture by the back door, nor in
any way do I consider myself an intruder there.]

As a Mexican intellectual, Del Paso firmly asserts his right of access to
the European and American historical and literary traditions as part
of his own heritage. Furthermore, he contends that Mexico is not on
the periphery of modernity; rather, his novel shows that Mexico is
fully engaged with the dilemmas of negotiating long-held customs with
technical innovations and ontological transformations. To give one
example, President Benito Juárez, a noble yet human figure throughout the novel, embodies this melding of cultures as he balances his
indigenous (Zapotec) roots with his European-style formal education
and his reading of progressive French thinkers such as Rousseau.

Rather than claiming Mexico for the colonial powers of Europe, del
Paso's depiction of Charlotte and Maximilian reclaims the Europe that
belongs to Mexico and Spanish America and has belonged to them for
more than 500 years. As seen through the lens of mourning, del Paso's
novel denounces imperialism and recognizes that Mexico's relationship
with Maximilian and Charlotte is contentious. Nevertheless, del Paso
also acknowledges that Mexico's European patrimony cannot be denied
and must instead be explored with a critical eye so that it may be rein-
tegrated. Thus, while del Paso's novel offers an anti-imperialist critique
of Maximilian and Charlotte's paternalism and claims of manifest destiny, it avoids rejecting the European legacy in Mexico. In his speech at
the Sorbonne, del Paso makes an additional comment that merits mention here, as it further illuminates the writer's treatment of transculturation as a mourning tool in *Noticias del Imperio*. Unintimidated by
myths of European cultural superiority and Latin American exoticism,
the writer further claims Europe not only as part of his own literary
formation but as part of every individual's heritage in Latin America:

Como resultado principal del mestizaje, de la transculturación, hoy, y
desde hace cinco siglos, el hombre latinoamericano se ha transformado

> en copropietario de todos los valores de la historia y de la tradición que Shakespeare, Ucello, Bergson, y Mahler, para mencionar sólo algunos nombres, nos pertenecen en la misma medida y con el mismo derecho que pertenecen a los propios europeos. (qtd. in Mergier 46)

> [As a principal result of *mestizaje*, of transculturation, today, and for five centuries, the Latin American man has been transformed into coproprietor of all the values of history and of tradition that Shakespeare, Ucello, Bergson, and Mahler, to mention just a few names, belong to us to the same degree and with the same right that they belong to the Europeans themselves.]

In the same spirit in which he claims the European literary tradition, del Paso also understands that, for good or for ill, Maximilian and Charlotte are undeniably part of a European heritage that extends back to the Spanish conquest. German accordions play Mexican *corridos* and *música norteña*, French and Aztec cuisines blend to produce the celebrated dish *chiles en nogada*, and Italian fresco techniques applied by Diego Rivera's hand produce murals that commemorate Mexico's indigenous legacy. Del Paso's novel implies that such products of transculturation, with their mix of European and native traditions, play an indisputable role in the formation of Mexican national identity.

Del Paso's narrative project for Mexico relates Charlotte's process of mourning as a means to suggest the reconciliation of Mexico with the colonial powers of Europe and the United States. Del Paso's vision for Mexico rejects imperial domination, but in embracing modernity it does not deny the influence of intervening cultures and figures. Instead, del Paso's Mexico accepts, but does not ingest, the memory of Charlotte and Maximilian, in a process similar to the introjection of healthy mourning. Del Paso's novel asserts that Charlotte and Maximilian deserve to finally be buried in the Mexican pantheon, thereby bringing to closure the process of mourning and merging the two figures with the Mexican tradition. Such a completion secures redemption for all of the parties involved, Charlotte, Maximilian, Juárez, the Mexican people—a topic that I explore further in chapter 4, in which redemption for the main character and for the nation is made possible by means other than mourning.

4

Redemption of the Present: Carlos Fuentes's *Los años con Laura Díaz*

Our image of happiness is indissolubly linked with the image of redemption. The same applies to our view of the past, which is the concern of history.

—Walter Benjamin, "Theses on the Philosophy of History," 254

Despite the travails of the times, recent historical narratives throughout Latin America tend to balance a critique of past and present societal ills with some possibilities for redemption. In this study we have seen in a series of Mexican novels the redemptive powers of laughter at human folly, in *La corte de los ilusos, Los pasos de López,* and *Madero el otro,* of the inclusion of previously marginalized figures, in *La vida insólita de la Santa de Cabora, Noticias del Imperio,* and *1492,* and of the vigor of artistic production, in the novel at question in this chapter, *Los años con Laura Díaz.* Throughout his career, leading Mexican intellectual Carlos Fuentes (1928–) has grappled with Mexico's place in the world. The cosmopolitan son of a diplomat, Fuentes interprets Mexico's past and present in novels and essays written for an international public. *Los años con Laura Díaz* (1999) spans the twentieth century, attempting to come to terms with its wars and its miseries while considering promising possibilities for the twenty-first century. In the narrative, Fuentes provides a counterpoint to his oft-seen cyclical, mythical view of history with a newly progressive outlook that offers the possibility of change and even redemption.

The two angels mentioned in the Introduction, one Mexican and one European, provide the theoretical framework for my analysis. In the wake of destruction, Walter Benjamin's Angel of History[1] is hurled backwards into the future as it looks upon the ruins of the past. We can imagine the Angel of History gazing upon the remains of the Ángel de la Independencia, a towering monument built in Mexico City at the beginning of the twentieth century to celebrate the centenary of independence, toppled and broken in the 1957 earthquake, and raised again to become what is now a gathering place for jubilant soccer fans and for vexed political protestors. Looking back from the twenty-first century upon the horrors of the twentieth, we will ask whether Wilhelm Friedrich Hegel's early nineteenth-century optimistic representation of historical progress is still credible. Benjamin's twentieth-century Angel of History may offer the possibility of redemption and yet despairs for what lies ahead; in contrast, in Fuentes's work the possibility of redemption is linked to creation rather than destruction. The "everywoman" protagonist of Fuentes's novel, Laura Díaz, is rebuilt and redeemed like the Angel of Independence—in her case, through artistic production.

The awareness of historical temporality seen in *Los años con Laura Díaz* is not unexpected; such an awareness is the most prominent feature throughout Fuentes's several decades of work. The writer continuously bends concepts of time—spiraling, returning, moving forward, mutating backward. Indeed, in 1981 he gave his narrative series the title of "La edad del tiempo" [The Age of Time] to point out the overarching temporal theme, and he continues to organize his oeuvre in different categories subsumed under this general heading. Because Fuentes's understanding of Mexican history often appears to be mythical and cyclical, prominent critics such as Christopher Domínguez Michael and Ilan Stavans have described his later novels as retrograde, deterministic fiction in which pre-Colombian and colonial failings lead to Mexico's repeated demise in the present.[2] Nevertheless, in *Los años con Laura Díaz* (1999), while Fuentes shows the past as part of the present and therefore worthy of examination, he does not frame what went before as inescapably determining what happens today. Instead, despite the present consequences of the errors of history, the future still holds possibilities.

The narrative begins with Laura Díaz's great-grandson Santiago's contemplation of a mural famous for both its striking visual impact and for its political implications. He is in Detroit in 1999 to make a television documentary about the Diego Rivera mural as symbol of the industrial ruins of the century: "Quería fotografiar la ruina de la gran urbe industrial como digno epitafio a nuestro terrible siglo veinte" (11). [I wanted to photograph the ruin of a great industrial center as a worthy epitaph for our terrible twentieth century (7).] Santiago laughs at the naiveté of Rivera's Marxist faith in technology and progress as seen in the mural. Nevertheless, despite the character's reference to the ruins of a "terrible century," his very focus on the artistic contributions of the period and on his own artistic discoveries belies his pessimism. As he gazes at the workers in the mural, he discovers the (fictional) presence of his own grandmother, Laura Díaz, standing tall next to Frida Kahlo: "Tuve una sensación desplazada y excitante, de descubrimiento creativo, tan rara en tareas de televisión" (16). [I had a displaced and exciting sensation of creative discovery—very rare in television work (7).] He then walks alone in the dark, shooting photo after photo of the decaying city and its people. Despite the desolation of the landscape and even his being assaulted on the way back to the hotel, through the very act of photography he is uplifted in his thoughts of his photographer grandmother and of the century that her life has encompassed.

The great-grandson takes center stage again at the end of the novel, at the close of the century in 2000, when he reports on the restoration of the Siqueiros mural in Los Angeles and completes the remembrances of Laura Díaz that he had begun in Detroit. This framing of Mexico between Detroit and Los Angeles is significant, as the novel addresses major events of the century not only in Mexico but also within its sphere of influence. Fuentes has emphasized throughout his work that Mexico does not stand intellectually isolated from the rest of the world; for instance, *La frontera de cristal* (1995) tackles Mexican relations with the United States, while *Terra Nostra* (1975) links Mexico with Spain's El Escorial (Phillip II's castle, built in the sixteenth century). In accordance with Fuentes's global mind-set, *Los años con Laura Díaz* similarly establishes connections between Mexico, Europe, and the United States. Not only do the murals in Detroit and Los Angeles play a prominent role; the Spanish civil war, the Holocaust of World War II, and the McCarthy hearings of the Cold War era merit careful attention in the novel.[3]

Since a woman of Laura Díaz's generation was not likely to have the opportunity to study under the cream of Spanish intelligentsia at the university or to live the life of a diplomat in Europe, Fuentes uses Laura's lovers as a narrative device to connect her with these overseas concerns. Her great loves are, respectively, a Spanish exile from the civil war and an American exile from the McCarthy hearings. In 1939 Laura falls in love with Jorge Maura, a Spanish republican. Her response to him underscores the vital intellectual contributions of some 200,000 Spanish exiles in Mexico; for Laura, the exiles are the cream of Spanish academic, literary, artistic, and scientific circles, valuable immigrants who revive Mexico from provincial nationalisms with a transfusion of worldly ideas.

Later in Laura Díaz's life, she completes a photographic series that honors some of these prominent historical figures, including philosopher José Gaos, poet Luis Cernuda, filmmaker Luis Buñuel, and, in a nod to Carlos Fuentes's own international law professor who came from Seville, Manuel Pedroso. To further emphasize the importance of the link between Spain and Mexico, the narrative reads: "Laura se dio cuenta de que la guerra de España había sido, durante muchos años, el epicentro de su vida histórica más que la Revolución Mexicana" (520). [Laura now realized that for years the Spanish Civil War had been the epicenter of her historical life, not the Mexican Revolution (445).] And so, for the protagonist, the historical impact of the Spanish civil war took precedence over that of the Mexican Revolution itself. While this point may be questionable for many Mexican citizens of the period, it is in accordance with Fuentes's recurring emphasis on the Spain-Mexico connection, from his documentary series *The Buried Mirror* (1992) to his acceptance speech for the Cervantes prize, in which he proclaimed:

Mi país le abrió los brazos a la España peregrina que en México encontró refugio para restañar las heridas de una guerra dolorosa. La emigración española compartió con nosotros algunos de los frutos más brillantes del arte, de la poesía, de la música, de la filosofía y del derecho modernos de España.

Muchos mexicanos somos los que somos, y sin duda somos un poco mejores, porque nos acercamos a esos peregrinos y ellos nos ayudaron a ver mejor -Luis Buñuel-, a pensar mejor -José Gaos-, a oír mejor -Adolfo Salazar-, a escribir mejor -Emilio Prados, Luis Cernuda- y a concebir mejor la unión de la lengua y de la justicia, de las palabras y los hechos. (http://www.terra.es/cultura/premiocervantes/ceremonia/ceremonia87.htm)

[My country opened its arms to the pilgrim Spain that found refuge in Mexico to stanch the wounds of a painful war. The Spanish emigration shared with us some of the most brilliant fruits of art, of poetry, of music, of philosophy and of modern law from Spain.

Many Mexicans are who we are, and with doubt we are a little better, because we approached those pilgrims and they helped us to see better— Luis Buñuel, to think better—José Gaos, to hear better—Adolfo

Salazar, to write better—Emilio Prados, Luis Cernuda, and to better conceive the union of language and justice, of words and deeds.]

For Fuentes, Spanish exiles vividly shaped the intellectual life of his generation in Mexico.

The narrative links Mexican history with that of other European countries as well, particularly Germany. Germany is acknowledged for positive contributions, as seen in German phenomenologist Edmund Husserl's role as a brilliant teacher of philosophy in the novel, but the nation also functions in the narrative as a perpetrator of genocide during the holocaust of World War II. In one thread of the story, Laura's friend Baltasar tells the tale of his former lover Raquel, a German Jew (and converted Catholic) who disappears after she and her shipmates are denied landing permits in Cuba and Florida; he anguishes over her throughout the novel, until she reappears, in shambles but alive, at the end.

Finally, Fuentes incorporates the influence of the U.S.-Soviet Cold War in the novel through the tale of Laura's next lover, Harry Jaffe, an American filmmaker who has retreated to Mexico after enduring Senator Joseph McCarthy's red scare trials. Through Harry, Laura develops a more sophisticated awareness of the damages done by McCarthy's Cold War persecutions: fear, betrayal, careers ruined, even lives lost. In this way, Fuentes consistently reminds the reader of Mexico's links with humanitarian concerns overseas as well as of the contributions of European and U.S. intellectuals exiled in Mexico. Although Fuentes's primary focus throughout his oeuvre is Mexico, his proposal for redemption reaches across national barriers, reminding the reader of overarching connections in both the struggle for human rights and in cultural production, the two principal means of redemption featured in the novel.

Given, then, the twentieth-century crises that Fuentes includes in the narrative, such as World Wars I and II and the Cold War, would the novel be in accordance with Francis Fukuyama's controversial neo-Hegelian thesis in *The End of History* (1990), that history reached its culmination at the turn of the twentieth century with the crumbling of the Soviet Union and the fall of the Berlin Wall? To respond to that question, let us return briefly to Benjamin's *Angelus Novus* of history. In his writings completed earlier in the twentieth century, Benjamin would appear to have disagreed with Fukuyama; in his post–World War I "Theologico-political fragment" (1920), the German-Jewish philosopher sharply divides profane history from the sacred, maintaining that only divine violence could bring history to its conclusion: "Only the Messiah himself consummates all history, in the sense that he alone redeems, completes, creates its relation to the messianic" (312). While Fukuyama saw the end of the political cold war as the end of history, for Benjamin, in contrast, it would be nihilistic for humans to strive to achieve such an end through political means.[4]

Although *Los años* does not share completely in Benjamin's messianic vision of divine destruction, it does put Fukuyama's "end of history" triumphalism into question. The Spanish exile character Jorge Maura sums up his generation's disillusionment with progress after witnessing the horrors of the first half of the twentieth century, a century proposed as a "paradise of progress" that was instead an "inferno of degradation":

> No sólo el siglo del horror fascista y estalinista; siglo de horror del que no se salvaron los que lucharon contra el mal, ¡nadie se salvó, Laura! no se salvaron los ingleses que le escondieron el arroz a los bengalíes para que no tuvieran la voluntad de rebelarse y unirse a Japón durante la guerra, ni los mercaderes musulmanes que colaboraron con ellos; no se salvaron los ingleses que en la India le quebraron las piernas a los rebeldes que querían la independencia de su patria y no permitieron que los curaran; no se salvaron los franceses que colaboraron con el genocidio nazi o que clamaron contra la ocupación alemana de su patria pero consideraron derecho divino de Francia ocupar Argelia, Indochina, Senegal; no se salvaron los americanos que mantuvieron en el poder a todos los dictadores del Caribe y de Centroamérica con sus cárceles repletas y sus mendigos en la calle, con tal de que apoyaran a los Estados Unidos; ¿quién se salva...? (408)

> [Not only the age of fascist and Stalinist horror but of the horror that those who fought against evil could not save themselves from, no one was exempted, Laura! not the English who hid rice from the Bengalis so they wouldn't have the will to revolt and join Japan during the war, not the Islamic merchants who collaborated with them, not the English who broke the legs of rebels who wanted national independence and were refused medical care, not the French who collaborated in Nazi genocide or who cried out against the German occupation but considered the French occupation of Algeria, of Indochina, of Senegal a divine right, not the Americans who kept all the Caribbean and Central American dictators in power with their jails overflowing and their beggars in the streets as long as they supported the United States. Who was saved? (349)]

The character Jorge Maura's summary of inhumanities across the globe during the first half of the century provides little hope for the second half nor for the approaching twenty-first century. Still, while Laura Díaz would appear to disagree with Fukuyama that with the end of the Cold War and the prevalence of liberal democracy the big questions had been settled, her story is nevertheless more optimistic than Jorge Maura's—perhaps even Hegelian in its faith in art as a means of communion with the Absolute.

During the early nineteenth century, Georg Wilhelm Friedrich Hegel conceived of a time when human history would complete its inevitable progress and reach its apex, an end of history in philosophical terms.[5] In the *Philosophy of History*, he sanguinely wrote, "The history of the world is none other than the progress of the consciousness of freedom" (Intro 19). For Hegel, history was not a series of random events but rather a process that evolved and developed over time, from ancient civilizations of China, Persia, and India, through the classical periods of Greece and Rome, to the development of Christianity, the Protestant Reformation, and his own place and time, the Prussian state during the Enlightenment. For Hegel, the culmination of this historical process would be an "organic" state in which individuals used their faculties of reason and conscience to think critically and independently, thereby achieving "freedom" even while making individual sacrifices to serve the best interests of the state.

A key element in Hegel's analysis is the idea that the subject in this model state requires acknowledgment by the other of one's humanity and worth. This is a vital factor in the ability for human society to move toward this ideal state: "Self-consciousness exists in and for itself when, and by the fact that, it so exists for another; that is, it exists only in being acknowledged [*als ein Anerkanntes*]" ("Phenomenology of Spirit" 92). Although initially, conservative Hegelians interpreted his work from a Christian perspective, Hegel's legacy today derives primarily from leftist Hegelians such as Marx (with of course a few exceptions such as the former neoconservative Fukuyama). Marx made use of Hegel's formulations regarding the need for acknowledgment by the other, the "unhappy consciousness" and the "master and slave," to formulate his concept of historical materialism. It is through this lineage that Benjamin derived his progressive thought. What is unique about his view of history is that he combines Jewish mysticism with Marx's interpretation of historical change as the struggle between socioeconomic classes; Benjamin's concept of history is embodied in the *angelus novus*, an idea that takes up Hegel's philosophy of religion as a path to the Absolute; however, for Benjamin, the divine path through history is one of destruction.

In accordance with Benjamin's refusal to align himself clearly with either orthodox Marxist thought or Judeo-Christian religious credence, *Los años* likewise points to the failure—and the brutality—of inflexible loyalty to any ideology on either side of the political spectrum. In the novel, the failure of communism is embodied in Stalinism, the failure of liberal democracy in McCarthyism. Accordingly, the character Laura Díaz rejects both Christian and communist ideologies for the damage done under their banners; indeed, she appears to go so far as to perceive both dogmas as immoral. For example, when her husband dies she causes a scandal by refusing both the communist flag and the cross that his friends and colleagues try to place on the coffin. In another instance, the priest that raised her spouse (a morally complicated cleric who had stolen, though later returned, valuable church artifacts) explains why her husband had turned in a nun to the anticlerical Plutarco Calles (president 1924–1928) government authorities, who shot her:

> La política de entonces era acabar con el clericalismo que en México había explotado a los pobres y apoyado a los explotadores. No dudó en entregarla. Era su deber.... No medimos las consecuencias morales de nuestros actos. Creemos cumplir con la ideología, revolucionarios, clericales, liberales, conservadores, cristeros, y se nos va entre las manos el líquido precioso que llamamos, a falta de palabra mejor, "el alma." (432)

> [The policy then was to extinguish the clericalism that in Mexico had exploited the poor and supported the exploiters. He didn't hesitate to turn her in: it was his obligation.... We never measure the moral consequences of our acts. We think we're obeying the mandates of ideology, whether we're revolutionaries, clericalists, liberals, conservatives, Cristeros, and what slips through our fingers is the precious liquid we call, for lack of a better word, "the soul." (370)]

In the novel, figures such as Díaz's husband's "souls slip through their fingers," their humanitarian ethics compromised when they bow to an extremist ideology.

To further illustrate this point in the narrative, during the violent government repression of the 1968 student protest at Tlatelolco in Mexico City, Laura reflects upon the damage done by both political and religious dogma not only at that time but also extending from the beginning of her century: Por su memoria pasaron los dogmas que había escuchado durante su vida, desde las posiciones antagónicas, casi prehistóricas, entre los aliados franco-británicos y los poderes centrales en la guerra de 1914, la fe comunista de Vidal y la fe anarquista de Basilio, la fe republicana de Maura y la fe franquista de Pilar, la fe judeo-cristiana de Raquel... " (553). [Through her memory passed the dogmas she'd listened to all her life—the almost prehistoric antagonisms between the Franco-British allies and the Central Powers in the 1914 war, Vidal's Communist faith and Basilio's anarchist faith, Raquel's Judeo-Christian faith... (474).]

In Mexico, in the United States, in Spain, and throughout Europe, Laura has seen the impasses between extremist ideologies that, for her, lead to tragedy and loss.

In accordance with this resistance to dogma, Fuentes's version of redemption is unorthodox, as Benjaminian as it is Catholic. Despite the failures of the twentieth century, even in his scathing political novel *La silla del águila* (2003), the dedication is sanguine: "A los compañeros de la Generación ´Medio Siglo,´ Facultad de Derecho de la UNAM: La esperanza de un México mejor... " (n.p.). [To my comrades from the "Half Century" Generation, UNAM School of Law: Hope for a better Mexico....] Perhaps in accordance with Fuentes's future hopes for Mexico, while in *Los años* the protagonist is not a particularly empathetic character for much of her adult life, she blossoms late as a loving mother and grandmother, a talented artist, and an engaged contributor to civil society.

The maturation process slowly begins when, after eight years of "hearing the same sermon" from her husband, a labor activist, and of being shooed off when she asks to participate in his work, Laura Díaz grows disillusioned: "me hice chiquita, en vez de crecer me fui haciendo enanita" (157). [I've shrunk instead of growing, I've been turning into a little dwarf (130).] When her husband betrays the nun she herself had sheltered from the anticlerical government of the period, Díaz leaves him. However, she does so not merely for the sake of ideals; she also heads off in pursuit of pleasure. She leaves her two sons in the care of their aunts in the countryside for several years and goes to the capital to live off of a friend's expense account with a decadent lover, Orlando,[6] despite her aunt's plea, "Nos haces falta, hija. Les haces falta a tus hijos" (207). [We need you, daughter. Your sons need you (173).] To further demonstrate her self-absorption, when her lover ends the relationship and the protagonist returns to her husband and sons, she reminds herself how noble she is for her sacrifice and how much easier life would be without them, and she continues to disappear from home periodically with her new lover, the Spanish exile Jorge Maura. Late in maturing, only when her sons are twenty and twenty-one does she recognize that she had opted for personal fulfillment at the expense of her relationship with her children; the change in them that she has missed "reveló, obligó a Laura a darse cuenta de que ella se había ido, había vuelto y no había mirado en verdad a sus hijos, con razón ellos no la miraban a ella" (338) [forced Laura to realize she'd gone, returned, and hadn't really looked at her sons (287)]. In this sense, she is not a particularly redeemable protagonist at this point in the narrative—and at this troubled part of the century.

In addition to disappointing her family, at this juncture Laura Díaz does not follow through on social responsibilities either, in spite of her dissatisfaction with her life and her apparent interest in social justice as shown in this discussion with Orlando:

—¿Qué se puede hacer? Son miles, millones...¿por dónde empiezas? ¿qué se puede hacer con toda esta gente?...

—Escoge al más humilde entre todos. A uno solo, Laura. Escoge a uno y salvarás a todos. (205)

["What can one do? There are thousands, millions of them....Where would you begin? What can you do for all these people?"

"Choose the very poorest. Just one, Laura. Choose one and you'll save them all" (171).]

Despite this advice, Díaz steers her gaze, and her feet, away from the people in the poor neighborhoods of Mexico City. Only late in life does she take action, visiting them, photographing them, and showing their images to the public. Until then, her only gesture of social responsibility has been taking in the nun. Perhaps her inability to forgive her husband at that point for being an imperfect hero may be motivated in part because he has spoiled her own single attempt at a heroic, selfless act at mid-life.[7]

Laura Díaz's maturation and emancipation are joined throughout the novel with the passage of the events of her century. For Benjamin, historical reflection and the desire for redemption are axiomatically linked: "Our image of happiness is indissolubly bound up with the image of redemption. The same applies to our view of the past, which is the concern of history" ("Theses" 256). In fact, human redemption is necessary in order to approach a complete, detailed account of the past: "To be sure, only a redeemed mankind receives the fullness of its past...citable in all its moments" (ibid.). The fullness of Laura Díaz's twentieth-century history can thus only be available when she is redeemed.

The redemption begins when Laura Díaz starts to spend time with her son Santiago; she is as drawn to his passion for painting as she is repelled by her other son Dantón's ambition for power. Díaz begins her process of becoming an artist first by living vicariously through him as he paints while slowly dying of an autoimmune disease. "—No quiero ser privada de ti. —No quería privarse, quería decir, de esa parte de ella misma que era su hijo" (382). ["I don't want to be deprived of you." She didn't want to be deprived, she meant, of that part of herself that was her son (327).] Thus, the narrative's vision for deliverance includes the sacrificial death of the son. Redemption originates from a ransom price paid to recover what was lost. In Christian doctrine, the term refers to the recovery of humanity by making amends for sin; Christ the redeemer's suffering frees humanity from its debts. In *Los años*, Díaz's son's death mimics Christ's sacrifice, redeeming Díaz's transgressions, reinstating her as a mother, and awakening her artistic passions. This line of thinking—of the son's merits interceding on another's behalf—is articulated most clearly when Díaz's grandson Santiago dies in the 1968 Tlatelolco massacre, and Laura Díaz argues that his sacrifice has cleansed the sins of corruption of his father Dantón: "Santiago, el hijo, redimió a Dantón el padre" (578) [Santiago the son redeemed Danton the father (497)]. Indeed, a series of three Santiagos die in the novel, each saintly in a different way in accordance with their times.[8]

Just as Benjamin's philosophy of history and of redemption combines Marxism with theology, Fuentes's version blends Hegelian aesthetics with Catholic doctrine. For Hegel, the subject can recognize his absolute (spiritual) freedom via three routes: art, religion, and philosophy: "Now, owing to its preoccupation with truth as the absolute object of consciousness, art too belongs to the absolute sphere of the spirit, and therefore, in its content, art stands on one and the same ground with religion...and philosophy" ("Philosophy of Spirit" 426). For Hegel, each of the three approaches to absolute spirit has its own way of knowing: art is sensuous and intuitive, religion is pictorial, and philosophy, the "purest form," involves rational thinking. Art, which for Hegel ideally produces the "unity of meaning and shape" (440), is Laura's approach to knowledge in the novel. In her late fifties, she shoots her first photo, significantly, that of a woman artist, a memorable shot of Frida Kahlo in her death bed in 1954. Laura then proceeds to support herself as a photographer after her house is destroyed in the 1957 earthquake. Her private, unreleased photo of the deceased Frida Kahlo forms part of a memory crystallized in the lucidity of the protagonist's latter years:

> parte de la riquísima memoria de Laura, el archivo emocional de una vida que súbitamente, a la edad madura, había florecido como una mata de flor tardana pero perenne. La foto de Frida era el testimonio de las fotos que no tomó durante los años de su vida con otros, era un talismán. Al lado de Diego y Frida, sin percatarse, había acumulado, como en un sueño, la sensibilidad artística que tardó la mitad de los años con Laura Díaz en aflorar. (516)

> [part of her rich, rich memory, the emotional archive of a life that had suddenly, in maturity, flourished like a plant that flowers late but perennially. The photograph of Frida was testimony to all the photographs Laura hadn't taken in the years she'd lived with others; it was a talisman. Alongside Diego and Frida, without noticing it, as if in a dream, she had gained the artistic sensibility that flourished much later on, when many of the years with Laura Díaz had gone by (442).]

From the perspective of maturity, she turns her gaze away from herself and her great loves (brother Santiago, son Santiago, lovers Jorge Maura and Harry Jaffe) and looks upon her larger surroundings. She begins with a series of shots of Mexico City, of the migratory flow from the rural areas: "Ése fue el primer gran reportaje gráfico de Laura Díaz; resumió toda su experiencia vital...todo ello lo reunió Laura en una sola imagen tomada en una de las ciudades sin nombre que iban surgiendo como hilachas y remiendos del gran sayal bordado de la ciudad de México" (510). [That was Laura Díaz's first great photo-essay. It summed up the experience of a lifetime...she poured it all into a single image taken in one of the nameless cities springing up like loose threads on the great embroidered sackcloth that was Mexico City (437).] In the novel, Díaz's photography is not only valuable aesthetically but also plays a social function by documenting the troubles of her time and place.

In this late blooming, aging has motivated Díaz to reflect and to respond to the crises of her times; maturity has transformed her into an artist: "Quería despertar con voluntad de ver cada mañana y archivar lo que veía en el lugar más exacto de sus sentimientos, allí donde el corazón y la cabeza se alían. Antes, había visto sin ver. No sabía que hacer con sus imágenes" (512). [She wanted to wake up with a desire to see anew each morning and to file what she was seeing in the most precise place of her feelings, where heart and head joined forces. Before, she'd seen without seeing. She didn't know what to do with her everyday images (438).] As her good friends begin to die off, Laura reflects upon her past and decides to act consciously upon her future: "Laura Díaz empezó a preguntarse, '¿qué haré el año entrante?' y antes, de joven, todo era imprevisible, natural, necesario y, a pesar de todo, placentero. La muerte de Frida, sobre todo, la hizo recordar su propio pasado como una fotografía borrada" (512). [Laura Díaz began to ask herself, "What will I do next year?" Before, when she was young, everything was unforeseen, natural, necessary, and, despite everything, pleasant. But Frida's death especially made her remember her own past as if it were a blurry photo (438).] Aware now of her own mortality, Laura now braves the streets to photograph misfortune:

Salió a fotografiar las ciudades perdidas de la gran miseria urbana y se encontró a sí misma en el acto mismo de fotografiar lo más ajeno a su propia vida, porque no negó el miedo que le produjo penetrar sola, con una Leica, a un mundo que existía en la miseria pero se manifestaba en el crimen, primero un muerto a cuchilladas en una calle de polvo inquieto; miedo a las ambulancias con el ruido ululante y ensordecedor de sus sirenas a la orilla misma del territorio del crimen; las mujeres matadas a patadas por sus maridos ebrios; los bebés arrojados, recién nacidos, a los basureros; los viejos abandonados y encontrados muertos sobre los petates que les servirían de mortajas, clamando por un hoyo en la tierra una semana después de morir, tan secos ya que ni hedor despedían; eso fotografió Laura Díaz y le agradeció a Juan Francisco haberla salvado, a pesar de todo, de un destino así, el destino de la violencia y la miseria circundantes. (514)

[She went out to photograph the lost villages in the great city's misery, and there she found herself, in the very act of photographing something totally alien to her own life. She found herself because she did not deny her fear, all alone with her Leica, of penetrating a world that lived in poverty but revealed itself in crime, first a man stabbed to death on a street of unquiet dust; fear of the ambulances with the howling, deafening noise of their sirens at the very edge of the territory of crime; women stomped to death by drunken husbands; new-born babies tossed on garbage dumps; old people abandoned and found dead on mats that later were used as their shrouds, stuck in a hole in the ground a week later, their bodies so dry that they didn't even smell. Laura Díaz photographed all that and thanked Juan Francisco, despite everything, for having saved her from such a fate, the fate of the violence and misery around her (440).]

These images of the misery she finds in the city are often brutal, like the shots taken by a crime photographer.

Díaz's preferred medium of photography and her crime scene-style shots are indicative of her twentieth-century times. In his essay, "The Work of Art in the Age of Mechanical Reproduction," Benjamin explores the modern transformation of art through the development of photography and film. Benjamin notes that at around 1900, French photographer Eugêne Alget's shots of deserted Parisian streets mark a turning point in art as documentation, as "photographs become standard evidence for historical occurrences, and acquire a hidden political significance" (226). The year 1900 also marks the moment when reproducibility reaches a level at which photography can claim its place as one of the fine arts. The eye, swifter than the hand, takes over artistic production and causes a dramatic public impact. For Benjamin, the aura of a work of art is lost in the age of mechanical reproduction, as an artistic object's uniqueness and permanence, its cult value, is subsumed by the transience and reproducibility of film. However, he does not mourn the loss of the aura of tradition; instead, he describes this destruction as a renewal, and celebrates the cathartic power of film: "For the first time in world history, mechanical reproduction emancipates the work of art from its parasitical dependence on ritual" (224). For Benjamin, redemption once again goes hand in hand with destruction, in this case through the divine weapon of the camera.

As Díaz evolves into a photographer who documents the crisis of urban poverty, it must be said that the novel at times seems to overstate the redemptive power of art, seeing only its constructive aspects and overlooking its destructive capabilities such as its employment in Nazi propaganda posters and films. The anonymous victims of crime are now saved by a photograph, "salvados del olvido por la fotografía de Laura, agradecida de que Jorge Maura la hubiese salvado de la violencia de las ideologías...del sangriento siglo veinte" (514) [saved from oblivion by Laura's photographs. She thanked Jorge Maura for having saved her from the violence of ideologies...of the bloody twentieth century (440)]. The shots save victimized citizens by restoring their remembrance to the history of the "bloody" twentieth century. Furthermore, Laura Díaz's camera cleanses abandoned street children, "sorprendiendo la belleza inexpugnable de la niñez abandonada como si la cámara de Laura limpiase a los niños...niños limpios de mocos, lagañas, pelo emplastado, brazos raquíticos, cráneos rapados por la sarna, manos teñidas por el mapa del pinto, los pies desnudos con su pastel de lodo como calzado único" (514) [surprising their inexpungible beauty of childhood, as if her camera cleansed them…children cleansed of snot, rheum, greasy hair, rachitic arms, heads hairless from mange, hands discolored by *pinta*, the tropical skin disease, bare feet with crusts of mud as their only shoes (440)]. In the novel, Díaz's images reveal the children's beauty beneath their malnourished, slight bodies. Although the implication that art can consistently reverse the damaging effects of history is questionable—Díaz's photographs do not feed the children—the narrative still offers credible examples of how art can have redemptive power.

Now greying and dressed inconspicuously, Laura becomes even more daring, penetrating hospitals and police stations, shooting drug addicts and prostitutes, and frankly documenting the brutalities of an underworld hidden from view. She is also, for the first time in her life, financially independent, selling her shots to newspapers and magazines, producing books, presenting her first exhibition, and signing on with a major agency to sell her photos to private collectors (515). Her work has become a critical triumph, capturing the desolation of poverty and violence but also the joys of birth, religious devotion, and neighborhood celebrations:

La cámara de Laura, al retratar el instante, lograba retratar el porvenir del instante, ésta era la fuerza de su arte, una instantaneidad con descendencia, un ojo plástico que devolvía su ternura y respeto a la cursilería y su vulnerabilidad amorosa a la más cruda violencia, no lo dijeron sólo sus críticos, lo sintieron sus admiradores, Laura Díaz, a los sesenta años, es una gran artista mexicana de la fotografía, la mejor después de Álvarez Bravo, la sacerdotisa de lo invisible (la llamaron), la poeta que escribe con luz, la mujer que supo fotografiar lo que Posada supo grabar. (515–516)

[Laura's camera, depicting the instant, managed to depict the future of the instant; that was the strength of her art, an instantaneity with descendants, a plastic eye that restored tenderness and respect to vulgarity, and amorous vulnerability to the harshest violence. It wasn't only the critics who said it; her admirers felt it, Laura Díaz, almost sixty years of age, is a great Mexican photographer, the best after Álvarez Bravo, high priestess of the invisible, she was called, the poet writing with light, the woman who learned to photograph what Posada could engrave (441).]

This passage provides a glimpse of Fuentes's more optimistic representation of temporality in this particular novel: Laura's photographs

capture an instant in time, simultaneously linking this instant both to
its origins and to its possible future in a way that somehow responds
to the crudest violence with tenderness and respect. While she does
not go so far as to revive the dead and heal the sick, the protagonist
does carry out a civic responsibility by drawing upon her vocation to
document the underside of life in her city and bring it to light, a side
of life that, at the time of the 1968 Olympics, the federal government
did not want the world to see.

Upon reaching around the age of seventy years old, Díaz has finally
found the woman artist's "room of one's own" that Virginia Woolf
describes: "Se encontró, por primera vez en su vida, con una habit-
ación propia, de ella, el famoso 'room of one's own' que Virginia
Woolf había pedido para que las mujeres fuesen dueñas de su zona
sagrada, su reducto mínimo de independencia: la isla de su soberanía"
(527). [She had, for the first time in her life, the famous "room of
one's own" that Virginia Woolf had said women deserved so they
could have their sacred zone, their minimal redoubt of independence:
a sovereign island of their own (453).] With this space to reflect and
create, an epiphany of sorts occurs: "Laura Díaz había aprendido a
amar sin pedir explicaciones porque había aprendido a ver a los
demás, con su cámara y sus ojos, como ellos mismos, quizás, jamás se
verían" (548). [Laura Díaz had learned to love without asking for
explanations because she had learned to see others, with her camera
and with her eyes, as they themselves might never see themselves
(470).] In the narrative, seeing through the lens of a camera has provided the artist with the distance to develop a mature gaze from which
to look compassionately upon her loved ones as well as upon her
sociopolitical surroundings.

> ¿Qué era una fotografía, después de todo, sino un instante convertido
> en eternidad? El flujo del tiempo era imparable y conservarlo en su
> totalidad sería la fórmula de la locura misma, el tiempo que ocurre
> bajo el sol y las estrellas seguiría transcurriendo, con o sin nosotros, en
> un mundo deshabitado, lunar. El tiempo humano era un sacrificio de
> la totalidad para privilegiar el instante y darle, al instante, el prestigio
> de la eternidad. Todo lo decía el cuadro de su hijo Santiago el Menor
> en la sala del apartamento: no caímos, ascendimos. (550)

> [What was a photograph, after all, but an instant transformed into
> eternity? The flow of time was unstoppable, so trying to save it in its
> totality would be a kind of madness—time that went on, under the sun
> and stars, with or without us, in an uninhabited, lunar world. Human
> time meant sacrificing the totality to give privilege to the instant and
> the prestige of eternity to the instant. The painting by Santiago the

Younger in the apartment dining room said it all: we aren't falling, we're rising (472).]

At this point, she is able to see her son Santiago's painting of Adam and Eve as a fresh vision of redemption, a liberation not only from original sin but from the very idea of original sin. In his painting, after partaking of the forbidden fruit, the lovers in paradise have not fallen; instead, they are ascending:

> Gracias al sexo, la rebelión y el amor, Adán y Eva eran los protagonistas del Ascenso de la Humanidad, no de la Caída. El mal del mundo era creer que el primer hombre y la primera mujer cayeron y nos condenaron a una heredad viciosa. Para Santiago el Menor, en cambio, la culpa de Adán y Eva no era hereditaria, no era culpa siquiera, el drama del Paraíso Terrestre era un triunfo de la libertad humana contra la tiranía de Dios. No era drama. Era historia. (518–519)

> [Thanks to sex, rebellion and love, Adam and Eve were the protagonists of the Ascent of Humanity, not its Fall. The evil of the world was believing that the first man and the first woman fell and condemned us to a heritage of vice. For Santiago the Younger, on the other hand, Adam and Eve's guilt was not hereditary, wasn't even guilt, and the drama of the Earthly Paradise was a triumph of human freedom over God's tyranny. It wasn't drama. It was history (444).]

To emphasize his point of human transcendency, on the back of the painting Santiago has written, "El arte no es moderno. El arte es eterno. Egon Schiele" (519).[9] [Art isn't modern. Art is eternal. Egon Schiele (444).] Fuentes's epistemology in the novel makes clear that this eternal quality of art is the principal source of redemptive power.

Underlining this idea of redemptive art, Díaz's old friend Orlando describes Rembrandt's last self-portrait, which depicts him with watery eyes and droopy eyelids, and yet also imparts an affirmation of eternal youth: "La imagen de una juventud eterna, Laura, porque es la imagen del poder artístico que creó la obra entera, la de la juventud, la madurez y la ancianidad. Ésa es la verdadera imagen que nos regala el último retrato de Rembrandt: soy eternamente joven porque soy eternamente creativo" (564). [The image of eternal youth, Laura, because it's the image of the artistic power that created all his work, that of his youth, his maturity, and his old age. That's the true image Rembrandt's last self-portrait give us: I'm eternally young because I'm eternally creative (484).] Rembrandt's creative powers keep him young through the lasting power of his work; again, herein lies the redemption of artistic creation according to Fuentes.

How does this concept link to the Catholic vision of redemption through Christ's sacrifice? In a curious religious discussion with Díaz, Maura offers a double bind situation in which the human subject is doomed: "Dios aconseja lo que no permite: ¡Imitar a Cristo!" (404). [God advising us to do what He will not allow. To imitate Christ! (348)] For Maura, if one tries to emulate Christ, one insults God with one's arrogance. However, in accordance with the novel's vision of redemption, Laura responds with a pragmatic but uplifting note: "No es que no lo permita. Lo vuelve difícil" (404). [It isn't that he doesn't allow it. It's that He makes it difficult (346).] It is hard to imitate a model of grace when, as the century comes to a close, the city continues to change for the worse: "En el aire olía, en las miradas miraba, en la piel sentía, Laura Díaz, tiempos de crimen, inseguridad y hambre, aires de asfixia, invisibilidad de las montañas, fugacidad de las estrellas, opacidad del sol, grisú mortal de una ciudad convertida en mina sin fondo pero sin tesoros, barrancas sin luz pero con muerte" (568). [Laura could smell it in the air, see it in the faces, feel it on her skin—it was a time of crime, of insecurity and hunger, asphyxiating air, invisible mountains, only the fleeting presence of stars, an opaque sun, a mortal fog over a city transformed into a bottomless, treasureless mine, lifeless canyons replete with death (488).]

Yet while the narrative acknowledges adversity, it does not cede to pessimism, instead transmitting a sense of better expectations for Mexico even as her grandson is shot down during the protest of October 1968 in Tlatelolco Plaza:

al lado de su nieto ella también había entendido que toda su vida los mexicanos habían soñado un país distinto, un país mejor...[sus abuelos] soñaron con un país de trabajo y honradez, como el primer Santiago soñó con un país de justicia y el segundo Santiago con un país de serenidad creativa y el tercer Santiago...continuaba el sueño. (554)

[With her grandson she too had come to understand that all her life Mexicans had dreamed of a different country, a better country, [her grandfathers] both dreamed of a country of work and honor, as the first Santiago had dreamed of a country of justice and the second Santiago of a country of creative serenity and the third Santiago...continued the dream (475–476).]

The youngest Santiagos take positive steps toward a possible future: social activism or art, though insufficient to cure society's many ills, at the least offer redeeming paths.

The deaths of the saintly Santiagos over the course of the century bring us back to the image of the angel as redeemer through art or as destroyer through history. Significantly, following her photo of the deceased artist Frida Kahlo, Díaz's second photographic project is that of the Ángel when it has fallen in the 1957 earthquake. Fuentes's narrative conflates the statue of the Ángel de Independencia with its model, "la figura rota del Ángel que fue amante del filósofo" (511) [the broken body of the Angel who was the philosopher's lover (437)]. Antonieta Rivas Mercado was the lover of José Vasconcelos, a significant Mexican intellectual from the time of the revolution, patron of the great muralists and author of *Ulises Criollo* [*Creole Ulysses*]. The reminder of the broken Ángel's human model resonates piteously, as the historical figure Rivas Mercado later attempted to imitate divine annihilation as her own angel of death, committing suicide on the altar of the Notre Dame cathedral: "la estatua hecha pedazos al pie de la esbelta columna, las alas sin cuerpo y el rostro partido y ciego de la modelo para la estatua, la señorita Antonieta Rivas Mercado" (511) [the statue smashed to pieces at the foot of its slender column, the bodiless wings, the split, blinded face of the model, Antonieta Rivas Mercado (437)].

Vasconcelos, as Mexico's philosopher who passed from "noble educator" and sponsor of muralist Diego Rivera to "resentful exile" and adulator of Spanish dictator Francisco Franco, represents, together with his lover the fallen angel's model, the vicissitudes of Mexico from the revolution to the earthquake:

> Vasconcelos era una imagen móvil y dramática del México revoluciona- rio y su amante caída, Antonieta Rivas Mercado, el Ángel de la Independencia, era la imagen fija, simbólica, sobrenatural, de la Patria en cuyo nombre habían luchado los héroes que la veneraron pero también la chingaron. Ambos—el filósofo y su ángel—estaban hoy en ruinas en una ciudad que ellos ya no reconocían y que Laura salió a fotografiar. (511)

> [Vasconcelos was the mutable and dramatic image of revolutionary Mexico, and his fallen lover, Antonieta Rivas Mercado, Angel of Independence, was the fixed, symbolic supernatural image of the nation in whose name the heroes who venerated her had fought, the same ones who'd fucked her. Today, both the philosopher and his angel were in ruins, in a city that neither would recognize and that Laura went out to photograph (438).]

Again, as in the death of Santiago, the narrative makes it appear as if a sacrifice is necessary in order to redeem Mexico; in this case, the sacrifice is that of Antonieta Rivas Mercado, personified in the fallen Ángel statue.

When Laura Díaz's beloved grandson Santiago is shot during the 1968 student protest in the Plaza de Tlatelolco, the narrative again evokes the fall of the Ángel: "entonces la conmoción en la plaza fue como el terremoto que derrumbó al Ángel" (555). [Then the commotion in the plaza was like the earthquake that toppled the Angel of Independence (476).] Santiago, the vessel of redemption in the novel, is sacrificed to save the twentieth century, to liberate Mexico, or perhaps merely to rescue Laura Díaz. The three Santiagos' means of death also represent their times, but the survival of the fourth may represent a new mode of redemption, one that, like the elder Santiago's painting of Adam and Eve, rises not from sin and destruction but from historical free will. The first Santiago, Laura's older brother, shot at the cusp of the Mexican Revolution; the second Santiago, her second-born son, an artist who dies of an autoimmune disease; the third Santiago, her grandson, shot as a student activist. In the novel, these sacrifices permit that the fourth Santiago, the filmmaker and Laura Díaz's great-grandson, survive his assault in Detroit, sheltered by the memory of his photographer great-grandmother. At the close of Laura Díaz's century, her legacy is to produce art that redeems without sacrificing another Santiago, so that the last one can live to tell the story, completing the transition into the twenty-first century.

Conclusion

Mexican Embassy
Je ne passe jamais devant un fétiche de bois, un Bouddha doré, une idole mexicaine
sans me dire; c'est peut-être le vrai dieu. (I never pass by a wooden fetish, a gilded
Buddha, a Mexican idol without reflecting: perhaps it is the true God.)

—Charles Baudelaire

I dreamed I was a member of an exploring party in Mexico. After crossing a high,
primeval jungle, we came upon a system of aboveground caves in the mountains
where an order had survived from the time of the first missionaries till now, its monks
continuing the work of conversion among the natives. In an immense central grotto
with a Gothically pointed roof, Mass was celebrated according to the most ancient
rites. We joined the ceremony and witnessed its climax: toward a wooden bust of
God the Father fixed high on a wall of the cave, a priest raised a Mexican fetish. At
this the divine head turned thrice in denial from right to left.

—Walter Benjamin, "One Way Street," *Reflections*, 67

Benjamin's European view of a primitive periphery shapes his dreamlike
reflections in the epigraph to this chapter. For Benjamin, Mexico is an
unfathomable region of mysterious religious syncretism, ancient caves,
and primeval jungles. As he represents it, a Christian God shakes his
head thrice (like the biblical Peter) to deny a Mexica god. With this
vision of the conflict between religious traditions in the New World,
Benjamin seems to implicitly repeat Baudelaire's question: Which is
the true or authentic God? The epigraph opens a door for us to reflect
upon the paradoxes of Mexican modernity and to return to the questions raised in Aridjis's work in particular, regarding origins at the
moment of Conquest and Inquisition. How would Benjamin's Angel of
History correspond with this mystical Mexican paradigm?

Benjamin's *Angelus Novus* once again appears to be blowing back from the ruins, unable to repair them or to restore the ancient gods as he is thrust into the future. This religious doubt indicated in Benjamin's reflections is not atypical in modern and postmodern thought. Although the roots of the idea of modernity can be traced back to the distinction between ancient and present times during the Christian Middle Ages, the concept of aesthetic modernity developed more fully with nineteenth-century romantic writers such as Stendhal and Baudelaire. As evidenced in the epigraph to this chapter, it was with these writers that religious doubt became a key element in modernity, such that today "the idea of modernity has come to be associated almost automatically with secularism" (Calinescu 13). In light of this modern secularism, with its contradictory roots in medieval spiritualism, another question arises: Does Benjamin's troubled European Angel (in the judeo-messianic tradition) align with the Christian God in his negation of the Mexica deity? If the theoretical European Angel cannot fully address Mexican history, perhaps the peripheral (Mexican) Angel of Independence must stand in its place.

How can this shift of theoretical angels open a space for redemption while acknowledging the Mexica gods within the conquerors' Catholic tradition? An encouraging option would be Argentine-Mexican liberation philosopher Enrique Dussel's alternative "world" or "planetary" view, one that he opposes to the Hegelian, "Eurocentric" view of modernity and history that we have touched upon throughout this book: "For Hegel, the Spirit of Europe (the German spirit) is the absolute truth that determines or realizes itself without owing anything to anyone. This thesis, which I call the Eurocentric paradigm, has imposed itself not only in Europe and the United States, but in the entire intellectual realm of the world periphery" ("Beyond Eurocentrism" 3–4).[1] In other words, in the Eurocentric paradigm, European civilization and cultivated reason have led it to transcend other regions. For Dussel, this reductive notion calls instead for a more nuanced reading: "Philosophy, especially ethics, needs to break with this reductive horizon in order to open itself to the 'world,' the 'planetary' sphere" (4). Such a paradigm change is an ethical imperative in what the theorist calls "transmodernity," an alternative to postmodern interpretations of history and literature; transmodernity would include and affirm the heterogeneous cultural elements that were excluded or "ritually sacrificed" in the colonial model ("World System" 76).

In this sense, the ethical choice is to recognize European modernity as central but as only a part, not the whole, of world modernity. For although modernity begins in Europe (more specifically, in Spain at the time of imperial expansion), it extends simultaneously to Spain's colonial periphery in the Americas and the Caribbean. Thus, despite the ancient importance of China and Mesopotamia, modernity first springs from Spain through the conquest of the New World. We can infer that the process of Inquisition, conquest, and colonization as seen in the historical novels discussed here represents modernity as an effect of these events rather than an afterthought. Dussel's alternate paradigm, then, offers us a vision of modernity and postmodernity as part of a system of including both center and periphery rather than excluding the non-European; again, Europe's centrality stems not from its superiority but rather from its role in the course of conquest and colonization.

Benjamin's Angel of History helplessly flies backward into the future of modernity and postmodernity, the ruins of great ancient— but now peripheral—civilizations left behind. I have stressed in this study the importance of addressing modernity in the periphery (in Mexico in particular as the first colony of major importance in New Spain) as stemming from these events of origin. Dussel's philosophical position from the periphery ambitiously intends "to recoup what is redeemable in modernity, and to halt the practices of domination and exclusion in the world-system" ("World System" 19). This utopian stance aims to liberate the periphery from exclusion, from displacement from the labor force via technology, and from the ecological devastation of the planet. "If 1492 is the moment of the 'birth' of modernity as a concept, the moment of origin of a very particular myth of sacrificial violence, it also marks the origin of a process of concealment or misrecognition of the non-European" ("World Systems" 66). The absolute theological knowing of the conqueror is a limiting perspective linked to the Hegelian, European approach to history. As we have seen in the examination of Aridjis's and del Paso's novels in chapter 3, violence against the colonized is not justifiable as a redemptive sacrifice.

While the fiction addressed in this study cannot claim to change the world, it can certainly have an effect on intellectual history and on how the still-powerful lettered classes respond to these issues of ecological destruction, economic and sociopolitical exclusion, and the effects of globalization and late capitalism. Narrative can work toward constructing new paradigms of national identity and modernity for Mexico. In this vein, the novels analyzed here call upon the reader to remember and recognize damage from the past but to accept the possibility of redemption despite legacies of injustice. The novels rearrange perspectives from the vantage point of our time, demythologizing established heroes, recovering female historical figures, and reassessing the European legacy, thereby recasting notions of national identity in accordance with this peripherical/planetary stance.

In the introduction to *Confronting History and Modernity in Mexican Narrative* I tied the possibility of redemption to the allegorical function of the novels as they linked quandaries of past and present. I use the term allegory simply to indicate an extended metaphor in which a narrative has both a literal level of meaning (in this sense, historical events and figures) as well as a correlated level of agents, occurrences, and ideas (here, those of the present day). The seven novels in this study are examples of how current historical narratives tend to fall into two subgenres: historico-political allegories in the vein of John Dryden's *Absalom and Achitophel* (1681), in which the biblical plot and characters allegorize a political crisis in England in Dryden's time; and satirical allegories in the tradition of Jonathan Swift's *Gulliver's Travels* (1726), in which the protagonist's adventures create a satirical commentary on humanity's foibles and weaknesses. Clusters of characters in the novels studied here also show trends; Hidalgo in *Los pasos* and Madero in *Madero, el otro* represent imperfect, humanized heroes to replace the idealized figures celebrated in Mexico's pantheon; the inquisitors and conquerors in *Memorias del Nuevo Mundo* and *1492*, Maximilian in *Noticias del Imperio*, and Iturbide in *La corte* represent rulers who tried to Europeanize Mexico and overstayed their welcome, but whose vital role in the unfolding of Mexican history is undeniable.

The role of previously marginalized figures such as women also comes to the fore in this study. John Beverly argues that, while the theoretical discussion of postmodernism in Latin America has paid insufficient attention to the women's movement, feminism "may be, in the long run, the most radical, and radicalizing, expression of Latin American postmodernism"(8). In recognition of this feminist expression, we have seen in this book a common pattern of woman characters pulled from the margins to the center and recovered historically; they comprise the women who rule in the domestic (family-nation) realm in *La corte de los ilusos*, Carlota's voice of madness and mourning that dominates the narrative in *Noticias del Imperio*, and Teresa's imperfect heroism as a force for social justice in *La insólita historia*. In centering these women characters who express stronger voices, enjoy an open sense of pleasure in their bodies, and wield a power that embraces community, these novels suggest an alternate paradigm of empowerment from the periphery, in accordance with Dussel's philosophy of trans-modernism. Carmela, the magistrate's wife (La Corregidora) in *Los pasos*, is a leader who boldly warns fellow insurgents that the battles must begin. The seamstress Madame Henriette brings domesticity to the historical forefront in *La corte*, while in the same novel Nicolasa rebels against aristocratic mores with her unproductive eroticism. Carlota in *Noticias* rules capably in Maximilian's stead and, even when she has gone mad, controls the narrative well beyond the time of the empire. Finally, Teresa in *La insólita historia* is proactive both politically and personally; her spiritual practices are unorthodox, she rejects polarities of the pure/impure female body, and she advocates on behalf of the less privileged in her community.

As these narratives adapt to a modern tolerance for ambiguity in such characters as Teresa de Cabora, they provide a vehicle for renewing and reshaping national myths. We have seen in chapter 1 that in the Hegelian interpretation of a hero's destined role, Madero had no choice but to fulfill his responsibility as a historical catalyst for a new era in Mexican history, even when that meant many failures and deaths alongside the limited successes of the decades to come. Chapter 2 examined how works such as Domecq's *La insólita historia* and Beltrán's *La corte de los ilusos* move women from the margins to the center of historical debates, by reconstituting minor domestic genres as part of a broader political discourse and by bringing power to the peripheral space inhabited by female historical figures. In chapter 3, we observed how Aridjis's *1492* and *Memorias del Nuevo Mundo* play a role in keeping alive the awareness of the machinations of biopolitics; Aridjis's work bears witness indirectly to the fragility of the human body not only in the time of the Inquisition and conquest, but also in the modern state. Finally, chapter 4 analyzed Fuentes's *Los años con Laura Díaz*, concluding that while the narrative acknowledges adversity, it does not cede to pessimism, instead transmitting a sense of the possibility of breaking repetitive cycles of destruction. The protagonist Laura and the youngest Santiago take one positive step toward a possible future: art, though insufficient to cure society's many ills, at the least offers one redeeming path.

The deaths of the saintly Santiagos over the course of the twentieth century in Fuentes's novel bring us back to the image of the angel as either redeemer through art or as destroyer through historical processes. How does the work of Menton, Aínsa, and Jitrik on the new historical novel in Latin America respond to this vision of an angel of history? Aridjis's novels *1492* and *Memorias del Mundo Nuevo* tie in with Menton's observation that the 500th anniversary of the 1492 conquest energized and inspired new works of historical fiction, while Solares's incorporation in *Madero, el otro* of eastern religious mysticism found in the *Bhagavad Gita* and in the *Tibetan Book of the Dead* offers an illustration of Aínsa's assertion that social sciences and humanities cross boundaries in today's historical fiction, a result of the blurring of disciplinary borders. And finally, works such as Beltrán's *La corte de los ilusos* offer allegories of present-day political crises, in accordance with Jitrik's theory that frenzied periods such as independence, revolution, or today's neoliberal transition motivate writers to reflect upon the past in order to grapple with the chaotic present.

While some theorists have asserted that modernity and postmodernity have not yet arrived in Latin America, the state of affairs is not so simple; there are central and peripheral zones within each country, and tradition and modern industry coexist; for instance, infrastructure and services in the capital cities are slower to arrive to the rural areas. Dussel's approach to modernity and postmodernity in the Americas is particularly apt for this book when we take into account his understanding of this heterogeneity and his formation as a liberation philosopher. For liberation theologists, the poor are the chosen people of God, and we are called to struggle for their human rights in order to improve conditions for them here on earth rather than asking them to sacrifice and suffer now in hopes for a better life in heaven; in this practice, working on behalf of the poor is the preferred path to redemption. As informed by this alternative Catholic tradition, many recent historical novels, such as Fuentes's *Los años con Laura Díaz*, provide a more nuanced vision of redemption than that espoused by the Vatican (which has been known to reprimand liberation theologists such as the Nicaraguan poet-priest Ernesto Cardenal). The two theoretical angels that frame this book offer recognition that despite the residual effects of a Catholic legacy of guilt and of paradoxically rationalizing the brutalities of the inquisition and the conquest for the sake of "conversion," this legacy can also include a Catholic tradition of forgiveness and a liberation theological model for liberating the disenfranchised.

In contrast with the despair of Benjamin's Angel of History, then, Fuentes's Angel of Independence offers the possibility of creation in the midst of destruction. Although salvation in the novel includes an element of divine sacrifice through the death of the three Santiagos, redemption is primarily possible through two secular means: artistic production and participation in civil society on behalf of others. Still, we must acknowledge that intellectuals in Latin America question the naiveté of a paradigm of emancipation today, as expectations for social justice have been frustrated by the failures of socialism in the last decades of the twentieth century. For example, Chilean social theorist Martín Hopenhayn comments: "The promise of revolution… proposed that intense social mobilization and political struggle would offer future redemption from social injustice, poverty, exclusion, external dependency, and capitalist alienation" (*No Apocalypse* xiii). These mobilizations, however, failed to be as fruitful as promised, and many were still excluded from the benefits of social integration. Hopenhayn asserts that the attempt to construct Latin American modernity by applying a single utopian theoretical model (from right or left) has collapsed in the twentieth- and early twenty first centuries: "Democratic construction agendas also demonstrated that the messianic or redemptive sediments promised in the utopias of radical change did not conform to the slow and painstaking process of building the rule of law" ("Essential Histories" 27). Beyond the failures of revolution in the twentieth century, Hopenhayn finds twenty-first-century alternatives to also be inadequate, arguing that the exaltation of diversity and personal development are false remedies for alienation.

Hopenhayn offers instead an alternate model that is compatible with Dussel's notion of trans-modernity, a model that we can also reasonably draw from our reading of the seven historical narratives in this book, seen for instance in the recognition of heterogeneity in *La insólita historia de la Santa de Cabora* and potential for redemption in *Los años con Laura Díaz*. Hopenhayn's noncoercive, "open and heterodox" utopia would entail ethnic and cultural *mestizaje*, access to postmodern communication resources, solidarity in the face of poverty and exclusion, and participatory democracy (*No Apocalypse* 151). Similarly, Dussel's trans-modernity would put technology at the service of both creativity and tradition, and would be "multicultural, versatile, hybrid, postcolonial, pluralist, tolerant, and democratic" ("World System" 236). This theoretical model is apt for the new paradigm suggested in the novels studied in this book: two angels of history, one European and one Mexican, together extend a new possibility. This new theoretical angel of history and modernity does not turn its face away from historical destruction but also looks ahead to future redemption, in a trans-modern hemisphere of the Americas and a trans-modern planet.

Notes

Introduction: Confronting History and Modernity in Mexican Narrative

1. Translations are my own.
2. Literary critic Maarten Van Delden comments, "If, as Octavio Paz claims, the history of Latin America is the history of different attempts to achieve modernity, then perhaps the history of Latin American intellectual life is the history of different attempts to define modernity" (38).
3. While there were innovative precursors of the current historical novel in the mid-twentieth century, such as Arturo Uslar Pietri's (Venezuela) *Las lanzas coloradas* (1931), Alejo Carpentier's (Cuba) *El reino de este mundo* (1949) and *El siglo de las luces* (1952), Elena Garro's (Mexico) *Los recuerdos del porvenir* (1963), Reinaldo Arenas's (Cuba) *El mundo alucinante* (1969), and Miguel Angel Asturias's (Guatemala) *Maladrón* (1969), and later, the monumental and inventive historical novels such as Fuentes's *Terra nostra* (1975) and Augusto Roa Bastos's (Paraguay) *Yo, el Supremo* (1974), the genre has burgeoned since the 1980s. To illustrate the continued dynamism of the movement, worth mentioning are the following works by Mexican writers published from 1980 to 2008: Carlos Fuentes, *Gringo viejo* (1985), *La campaña* (1990), and *Los años con Laura Díaz* (1999); Fernando del Paso, *Noticias del Imperio* (1987); Jorge Ibargüengoitia, *Los pasos de López* (1982); Homero Aridjis, *1492: Vida y tiempos de Juan Cabezón de Castilla* (1985) and *Memorias del nuevo mundo* (1988); Ignacio Solares, *Madero el otro* (1989), *La noche de Ángeles* (1991), *El gran elector* (1993), *Nen, la inútil* (1995), *Columbus,* (1996), and *La espía del aire* (2001); Eugenio Aguirre, *Gonzalo Guerrero* (1980); Silvia Molina, *Ascención Tun* (1981), *La familia vino del norte* (1987); Arturo Azuela, *Don de la palabra* (1984); Ángeles Mastretta, *Arráncame la vida* (1985) and *Mal de amores* (1996); Herminio Martínez, *Diario Maldito de Nuño Guzmán* (1990), *Las puertas del mundo: una autobiografía hipócrita del Almirante* (1992), *Invasores del paraíso* (1998), and *Lluvia para la tumba de un loco* (2003); Armando Ayala Anguiano, *Como conquisté a los aztecas* (1990); Brianda Domecq, *La vida insólita de Santa Teresa de Cabora* (1990); Julián Meza, *La huella del conejo* (1991); Héctor Aguilar Camín, *La guerra del galio* (1991); Carmen Boullosa,

Son vacas, somos puercos (1991), *Llanto: Novelas imposibles* (1992), *Duerme* (1994), and *Cielos de la tierra* (2000); Paco Ignacio Taibo II, *La lejanía del tesoro* (1992); Elena Ponatowska, *Tinísima* (1992); Francisco Rebolledo, *Rasero* (1993); Jean Meyer, *Los tambores de Calderón* (1995); Marco Antonio Campos, *En recuerdo de Nezahualcóyotl* (1995); Agustín Ramos, *Tú eres Pedro* (1996); Cristina Rivera Garza, *Nadie me verá llorar* (1999); José Antonio Aguilar Rivera, *Cartas Mexicanas de Alexis de Tocqueville* (1999); Daniel Sada, *Porque parece mentira la verdad nunca se sabe* (1999); Jorge Volpi, *En busca de Klingsor* (1999), *El fin de la locura* (2003); Ana Clavel, *Los deseos y su sombra* (2000); Agustín Ramos, *La visita* (2000); Claudia Canales, *El poeta, el marqués y el asesino* (2001); María Rosa Palazón, *Imagen del hechizo que más quiero* (2001); Enrique Serna, *El seductor de la Patria* (2001); Mónica Lavín, *Café cortado* (2001); Martín Casillas, *Las batallas del General* (2002); Fernando Zamora, *Por debajo del agua* (2002); Beatriz Rivas, *La hora sin diosas* (2003); Enrique Serna, *Ángeles del abismo* (2004); Eloy Urroz, *Un siglo trás de mí* (2004); Pablo Soler Frost, *1767* (2004); Francisco Martín Moreno, *México mutilado* (2004). Elena Poniatowska, *El tren pasa primero* (2005); Rodolfo Naro, *El orden infinito* (2007); Álvaro Uribe, *Expediente del atentado* (2007); Eugenio Aguirre, *Isabel Moctezuma* (2008); Hernán Lara Zavala, *Península península* (2008); and from the new "Click" generation, Victor Grovas Hajj's *El viaje del Conde Olivos* (2008).

The aforementioned novels incorporate historical events and/or documents in a fictional narrative; they also utilize postmodern innovations such as pastiche and parody to varying degrees, and generally correspond with the three primary characteristics that I mention in the introduction: the demonumentalization of historical figures, the reassessment of the European legacy, and the repositioning of women as central historical agents. However, it is not my goal here to separate the more daring or challenging texts from the less so; for these distinctions, see Seymour Menton's comparative lists of "New Historical Novels" and "Not So New Historical Novels." Also, while my lists given earlier are representative of recent production of quality, they are not exhaustive, and I encourage the reader to explore further on his or her own.

4. See Angel Rama, *La ciudad letrada* (Hanover: Ediciones del Norte, 1984).
5. *Xicotencatl* (anonymous authorship) was first published in Philadelphia.
6. For the purposes of this study, I define literary postmodernity not as a movement apart from an exhausted modernity but rather as a phase of aesthetic modernity, which originated in the nineteenth century as European artists and writers such as Stendhal and Baudelaire turned away from tradition and normative beauty and instead celebrated the transitoriness of the present. Postmodern artistic production does this to a greater degree, in response to the increasingly rapid changes of late capitalism's global economies. However, as Calinescu argues in *The Five Faces of Modernity* (Duke UP, 1987), despite typically postmodernist questioning of previous knowledge, literary postmodernism does not reject what went before. Instead, amidst its ever-changing present, postmodernist literature seeks to revisit and dialogue with the past, as seen in the novels examined here.
7. See Hayden White, *Metahistory* (Johns Hopkins UP, 1973), and Michel de Certeau, *The Writing of History* (Columbia UP, 1975).

8. See Linda Hutcheon's commentary on the nostalgic and yet parodic and self-reflexive elements of "historiographic metafiction" in *A Poetics of Postmodernism* (New York: Routledge, 1988). For Hutcheon, historiographic metafiction "refutes the view that only history has a truth claim, both by questioning the ground of that claim in historiography and by asserting that both history and fiction are discourses, human constructs, signifying systems, and both derive their major claim to truth from that identity" (93).

   For studies of the resurgence of historical novels in recent decades in Latin America, see Seymour Menton's prominent and highly debated study *Latin America's New Historical Novel* (Austin: UTP, 1993), which enumerates characteristics such as parody and metahistory to distinguish his lists of "new historical novels" from "not-so-new historical novels." See also Noé Jitrik's useful general study of the historical novel as a genre, both in the nineteenth century and in recent decades, *Historia e imaginación literaria* (Buenos Aires: Editorial Biblios, 1995), María Cristina Pons's detailed overview of recent theoretical approaches in the introduction to her study of three historical novels in *Memorias del olvido: La novela histórica de fines del siglo XX* (Madrid/Mexico: Siglo Veintiuno Editores, 1996), and Fernando Aínsa's examination of history and story as well as of the interdisciplinarity that he says gave rise to today's historical novels in *Reescribir el pasado: Historia y ficción en América Latina* (Mérida, Venezuela: Centro de Estudios Latinoamericanos Rómulo Gallegos, 2003).

9. I acknowledge that boundaries may blur here between historical fiction, chronicle, and testimony. Indeed, Victoria E. Campos argues that "chronicle" may be a more appropriate term for describing historical novels in Mexico following the 1968 massacre of student protestors in Tlatelolco, and that the genre closely approaches testimony in its privileging of first-person credibility:

   > Late-twentieth-century historical novels in Mexico have been called by many terms, such as "chronicles," "literature-testimony," "testimonial novels," and "*crononovelas.*" These expressions are not incompatible. Both in the contemporary and Spanish American colonial contexts, the chronicle as well as the testimonial recount the past from the point of view of the narrator's direct experience or contact with eyewitnesses, thus lending the narratives a privileged perspective vis-à-vis the credibility or "truthfulness" of the account given. Moreover, these narrators—again, both contemporary and colonial—engage in dialogue with other perspectives of authority both to imitate the "master text's" discursive form and to "correct the record, giving a truer *relación.*" (48–49)

   For further analysis of the testimonial novel, see George Gugelberger, ed., *The Real Thing: Testimonial Discourse and Latin America* (Durham: Duke UP, 1996).

10. See Harold Bloom, *The Anxiety of Influence* (Oxford: Oxford U P, 1997).

11. The best-known members of the "Crack" group are Jorge Volpi, whose works include the winner of the Biblioteca Breve Seix Barral prize, *En busca de Klingsor* (1999), a mystery/historical novel regarding physicists in Germany during the Nazi period; and Ignacio Padilla, whose *Amphitryon* (2000), also regarding Nazi Europe, won the Premio Primavera. See also Chilean writer Alberto Fuguet's "McOndo" collection of short stories by

young male writers from South America with similar concerns for overcoming the legacy of García Márquez's "Macondo," replacing it with works focusing on the individual subject in an urban environment saturated with international popular culture, Big Mac burgers, and Mac computers (*McOndo*, Barcelona: Grijalbo Mondadori, 1996). Publicity from publishing houses in Spain has recently benefited another "generation" of young male writers, this time from Colombia. Works of dirty realism or urban realism such as Jorge Franco's *Rosario Tijeras* (2000, winner of Spain's Dashiel Hammett prize) and Mario Mendoza's *Satanás* (2002, winner of the Seix Barral Premio Biblioteca Breve) depict sordid violence in the streets of Medellín and Bogotá.

While these well-marketed novelists have female peers such as Rosa Beltrán who are equally skilled and innovative producers of fiction—Puerto Rican writer Mayra Santos Febres comes to mind as a fairly well-known example—the public attention they have received is not as overwhelming, and they are less likely to be included in anthologies or marketed as part of a "generation," perhaps in part because of lingering labels of "literatura light" associated with best-selling popular (women) novelists Isabel Allende and Laura Esquivel.

1   Humanizing the Hero: Ignacio Solares's *Madero, el otro* and Jorge Ibargüengoitia's *Los pasos de López*

1. *Madero, el otro* is the first of Solares's series of three novels of the revolution that include *La noche de Ángeles* (1991), regarding Madero's friend and colleague, the revolutionary general Felipe Ángeles, and *Columbus* (1998), which deals with Pancho Villa's raid on Columbus, New Mexico.
2. All translations are mine except the English version of *Madero el otro*.
3. These books include Enrique Krauze's *Biografía del poder* series (Fondo de Cultura Económica, 1987), *Historia gráfica de México* (INAH, or Instituto Nacional de Antropología e Historia, 1988), and *Así fue la revolución mexicana* (INAH, 1985).
4. Hidalgo the historical figure never studied in Europe. However, Ibargüengoitia may be mixing his protagonist's life with his own here, as critic Vicente Leñero says the writer often does in his works. Ibargüengoitia traveled to the United States on a Rockefeller scholarship, and said in an interview that the fellowship money was good for buying some nice shirts.
5. Ancient heroes such as Odysseus and Gilgamesh show us that to have weaknesses is nothing new. Epic heroes were semi-gods who had defects just as the gods did. Gilgamesh learned that despite his glorious deeds death won out in the end over all heroes. Despite their superhuman qualities and feats they are imperfect like any human being. However, they are different from ordinary humans in that their failings, like their virtues, are larger than life. Heroes are projections of the great and the terrible in humanity.

2   Highlighting Women in History:
Rosa Beltrán's *La corte de los ilusos* and Brianda Domecq's *La insólita historia de la Santa de Cabora*

1. The work of Rosa Beltrán (Mexico, 1960) deserves greater critical attention than the handful of reviews presently devoted to *La corte de los ilusos*. A peer of the young "crack generation" of writers in Mexico, Beltrán completed a doctorate in comparative literature at UCLA and is a full-time member of the faculty at the UNAM in Mexico City. In addition to the prize-winning novel addressed here, her publications include two other novels, *El paraíso que fuimos* (2002) and *Alta infidelidad* (2006), two collections of short stories, *Amores que matan* (1996) and *Cambios cosméticos* (2006), and the literary study *América sin americanismos* (1996).

2. All translations are mine except for the Domecq novel, which is available in English translation (see works cited).

3. See Elisabeth Guerrero, "Urban Legends: Tina Modotti and Angelina Beloff as *flâneuses* in Elena Poniatowska's Mexico City," *Unfolding the City: Women Write the City in Latin America*, Lambright and Guerrero, eds. (University of Minnesota Press, 2007, 189–207).

4. French literary theorist Roland Barthes divides texts into the categories of readerly and writerly; he describes the former as static and predictable while the latter is open and complex, inviting the reader to participate in the act of interpretation and in the construction of meaning. Barthes declares, "the goal of literary work (of literature as work) is to make the reader no longer a consumer, but a producer of the text" (*S/Z* 4).

5. The *Tratado de las obligaciones del hombre* cited earlier can be found in the historical archives; it was written by Iturbide's contemporary, the Guatemalan Juan de Escoiquiz (1747–1820).

6. Indeed Napoleon I and Iturbide share a number of characteristics. The two of them were career soldiers, and for both ambition took priority over political ideals. Like Iturbide, Napoleon also began his rule as a supporter of the revolution, yet soon betrayed the republican agenda by crowning himself emperor, establishing a new family dynasty, and breaking the principle of the separation of powers. He also shared Iturbide's awareness of the importance of appearances, astutely projecting a glorious image that could perpetuate the cult of the hero. As Napoleon himself remarked: "The truth is not half so important as what people think to be true" (qtd. in Ellis 171). The flashy hero's image was key to his power.

7. In the novel, after the coronation, Iturbide's court continues to place show over substance. He cultivates the appearance of nobility by creating the knights of the Order of Guadalupe. For a fee, selected male friends and supporters can obtain a noble title. Truth may seem even stranger than fiction; as in the historical record, Bustamante writes that a spectacle of funerary honors for deceased members of the Order of Guadalupe was a ridiculous sham.

Ironically, none of these newly knighted men had actually died before their "funerary honors" took place.

8. In 1994, the two volume series *Tomochic: la revolución adelantada* appeared in Chihuahua. The historiographic essays included therein provide an alternative to previously available depictions of the Tomochic people as fanatics and disturbers of the public peace. In this volume, the people of Tomochic have strong political motives for their uprising, daring to face the Díaz government and winning the first two battles despite overwhelming odds. Their use of religious rhetoric in the name of the Saint of Cabora emerges not as a blind obsession but rather as a symbol and driving force of resistance. In this historical revision, the *tomochitecos* and Teresa are predecessors of the Mexican Revolution, which officially began in 1910. Historian Rubén Osorio proclaims, "en Estados Unidos, Teresa Urrea, después de los acontecimientos de Tomóchic, va a convertirse en una auténtica revolucionaria mucho antes de que los hermanos Flores Magón y Francisco J. Madero sueñen con derrotar a Porfirio Díaz" (100) [In the United States, following the events of Tomochic, Teresa Urrea will become an authentic revolutionary long before the Flores Magón brothers and Francisco I. Madero dream of defeating Porfirio Díaz.] See also Paul Vanderwood's 1998 study, *The Power of God against the Guns of Government: Religious Upheaval in Mexico at the Turn of the Nineteenth Century.*

9. This technique of juxtaposing conflicting reports illuminates multiple perspectives, a common technique in what theorists of postmodernism such as Linda Hutcheon have described as the new historical novel. Linda Hutcheon's term "historiographic metafiction" refers to fictional narrative that "refutes the natural or common-sense methods of distinguishing between historical fact and fiction. It refuses the view that only history has a truth claim, both by questioning the ground of that claim in historiography and by asserting that both history and fiction are discourses, human constructs, signifying systems, and both derive their major claim to truth from that identity" (93). To give an example of how historiographic metafiction draws attention to the artifice of creating nonfictional as well as fictional accounts, *The Astonishing Story* calls attention to the irony of newspaper articles that claim objectivity yet paint irreconcilably different pictures.

10. Teresa the historical figure challenged not only the Church but also the State. Daring to be a thorn in Porfirio Díaz's side, she signed an editorial published in Lauro Aguirre's newspaper *El independiente* on August 21, 1896 entitled "Mis ideas sobre las revoluciones." In it she disputes accounts that attribute the resistance movement to her role as a mystic leader rather than to political motives: "esos movimientos revolucionarios obedecen a un profundo descontento público contra el despotismo del gobierno" (qtd. in Illades 82). [Those revolutionary movements respond to a deep public dissatisfaction with the government's despotism.] Domecq affirms that after Díaz exiled Urrea in 1892, she became an aware and active participant in Lauro Aguirre's resistance movement. Historian Enrique Krauze confirms that Díaz's rule in Mexico was based upon a paternalistic model: "Quizá la clave del enigma está en una palabra: paternidad. Porfirio se

veía en la figura de un padre inmenso, padre de una grey de niños ambiciosos, dependientes e irresponsables"[Perhaps the key to the enigma is in a word: paternity. Porfirio Díaz saw himself as an immense father figure, the father of a flock of ambitious, dependent, and irresponsible children] (*Porfirio Díaz* 80). Díaz governed Mexico for more than three decades, from 1876 to 1911. He justified this extensive rule by affirming that the Mexican people were not yet ready for democratic elections. First they needed a strong figure to lead them to order, peace, and progress. The historical figure Teresa de Cabora rejects such a "father of the nation," endorsing Lauro Aguirre's constitutional reform plan (1896) as an alternative.

3   Mourning the European Legacy: Homero Aridjis's *1492: Vida y tiempos de Juan Cabezón de Castilla* and *Memorias del Nuevo Mundo*, and Fernando del Paso's *Noticias del Imperio*

1. Ample documentation for the *leyenda negra* appeared in such works as Friar Bartolomé de las Casas's *Brevísima relación de la Destrucción de las Indias* (1552), in which he documented and decried the conquistadors' mistreatment of the natives, and, later, Juan Antonio Llorente's *L'Histoire critique de l'Inquisition espagnole* (1817), in which he examined and critiqued inquisitorial practices.

   In light of the *leyenda negra*, it is ironic that the Inquisition played a role in the creation of Spain's poor reputation in Europe, as it was in part a response to other Europeans' view of Spain as tainted by its long history of Muslim and Jewish presence. The Holy Office was actually seeking to model itself after other European states by attempting to erase all traces of its Semitic past and insisting on religious uniformity.

2. As a poet, Aridjis handles language with an attentive ear for idiomatic expressions and lexicon of the period, such as "asaz" instead of "muy." His ear for language is also notable in the lyricism of descriptive passages. For instance, during the flood of Seville in *1492*, "Los caminos líquidos le salían al encuentro como ríos, los senderos se ahogaban bajo lagunas súbitas y los árboles eran saeteados por miles de semillas blancas, huidizas y frías" (24) [The liquid paths rushed out like rivers, the paths drowned under lakes that appeared without warning, and the trees were pierced with thousands of fleeting, cold, white seeds]. Nevertheless, although meriting this brief footnote, the use of language in the novels is beyond the scope of this essay.

3. Aridjis would perhaps point out that today's government wields biopolitical power in a disregard not only for human life but also for the habitat; for example, in 1986 his group succeeded in convincing the ruling party to set aside sanctuaries for the monarch butterflies, but the officials did not fulfill their promise and permitted massive deforestation, thereby also destroying significant portions of the butterfly habitat.

4. As the nationalizing project began to take form, the Crown also took active measures to compel conversions: as of 1415 in Castile and Aragón, Jews were marked. They were confined to ghettos, prohibited from certain professions, required to wear their hair and beards long and to display a red disc on their clothing. As a result, between 1391 and 1415 half of the Jewish population converted to Catholicism. When the Catholic sovereigns Isabel of Castile and Ferdinand of Aragón came into power, they again reinstated the laws of ghettoization and the red disc in 1480. Although they also ostensibly enforced laws protecting the Jews from attacks, as Pérez recognizes, the institution "probably prolonged and strengthened" anti-semitism (24).

5. In contrast with the marauding Christian peasants, nobles usually attempted to shelter and protect their Jewish neighbors. When the Inquisition was established, these same nobles attempted to protect converts and were highly critical of the institution. "Decidedly, nowhere do the aristocrats appear to have looked kindly upon the Inquisition" (Pérez 33).

6. Agamben differentiates *zoê*, or living, in the simple and natural sense, with *bios*, a particular (perhaps political) classification of human living.

7. Following an arrest, the Inquisition's procedures maintained an air of mystery; the accused could be incarcerated indefinitely while the legal procedures were carried out or until there was enough money for an *auto de fe*; the wait lasted for weeks or months, sometimes in the Americas for years due to the slow transmission of legal documents over the ocean. The prisoner was permitted no visits, no contact with the outside world. In New Spain, prisoners subsisted principally on hot chocolate thickened with corn flour, often the only food they could keep down in their anxious state.

   Initially, the inquisitors would not tell the individual what crime of heresy against the state he or she was accused of committing. Later, he or she would hear testimony against her but would not know who had given this testimony. As was common during this period in Europe, "confessions" were extracted through torture, primarily at the rack. Detainees' property was confiscated and the family was dishonored, their descendants barred from honorable professions. Acquittals were possible but rare; the accused was presumed guilty, and the Holy Office must appear to be infallible.

   In order to maintain order, the accused was not informed of a death sentence until the day of the execution. The *auto de fe* was a public ceremony designed to awe the spectator with pomp as well as fear. The accused must publicly confess and repent. Some had to wear a tunic of shame, the *sambenito*, as illustrated in Aridjis's novel. Others did penance or were lashed. The executions took place immediately after the *auto de fe*, in a nearby location. Those who repented were granted the mercy of being garroted before their bodies were burned at the stake. Those who stood by their Jewish, Protestant, or Illuminist beliefs were burned alive.

8. Today in Mexico the Spanish premodern legacy remains: the Mexican legal system follows Roman law, in which the accused is in effect presumed guilty until proven innocent.

9. Arrests and *autos de fe* diminished considerably after that date, although the Holy Office took on renewed zeal after Martin Luther initiated the protestant reformation, posting his theses in Germany in 1517. With this series of threats to religious uniformity, the Inquisition was able to remain in existence in Spain until 1834 (although briefly disbanded by Napoleon in 1808 and by the liberal constitution of 1820).

10. Unlike in other European states, particularly Germany, suspected witches were rarely burned at the stake in Spain and the New World; they were considered victims of superstition rather than agents of the devil, and public humiliation and lashes were usually their punishment.

11. Unamuno, "La libertad y la fuerza," *Artículos olvidados*, ed. C. Cobb (London: Támesis, 1976), 199–201.

12. Agamben's *homo sacer* plays an even more clear role in the United States at the turn of the twenty-first century, with the state's biometric record keeping and the use of torture in Guantánamo as part of the war on terror.

13. Here I define modernity simply in the sociohistorical sense of a period of technological progress and global exchange.

14. The novel begins in 1861 with an epigraph explaining that in this fateful year President Benito Juárez suspended the foreign debt; this gave Napoleon III a pretext for invading Mexico. This period is known historically as the Intervention or the Second Empire. The novel concludes with a chapter in 1867, when Maximilian is executed, and a chapter in 1927, with Charlotte who has lived on and looks back upon the events she has witnessed. Voices from many levels of Mexican and French society alternate with the voice of the mad Charlotte, enclosed in a European castle in 1927, as she reflects upon her visions of the ill-fated empire.

15. Transculturation is a term coined by Cuban anthropologist Fernando Ortiz in the 1940s and adapted to literary theory by the Uruguayan critic Angel Rama in the 1970s. In contrast with acculturation, in which the dominant culture erases all vestiges of the colonized culture, through transculturation a community incorporates what it finds useful in the colonizing culture, but also retains select elements from its own customs and then creatively adapts and merges the two traditions. As Rama points out, writers such as the Peruvian José María Arguedas and the Mexican Juan Rulfo, can also be agents of transculturation as their writings meld intricate indigenous mythical thought with complex elements of modernist aesthetics adapted from such writers as James Joyce and William Faulkner. Critics Robin Fiddian and Maarten van Delden have further observed that the work of del Paso and Fuentes resides in a point of intersection between Rama's two poles of transcultural writing (Arguedas, Asturias, Rulfo) and cosmopolitan writing (Borges, Cortázar).

16. Freud compares this healthy process of "cathecting" to the unhealthy dynamics of introjection in melancholia, which displays self-revulsion in addition to the usual symptoms of mourning (withdrawal from the outside world, cessation of activities, feelings of dejection, incapacity to love anew). Freud explains this drastic fall in self-esteem as the response to the loss of an object toward

whom there are feelings of ambivalence; rather than losing the loving, libidinal investment in this person who has disappointed, the individual has shifted the reproaches toward the loved one on to his or her own ego. Unconscious anger toward the loved one is disguised as guilt concerning one's own moral failings. Through this identification of the ego with the abandoned object, "the shadow of the object fell upon the ego....In this way the loss of the object became transformed into a loss in the ego, and the conflict between the ego and the loved person transformed into a cleavage between the criticizing faculty of the ego and the ego as altered by the identification" (159). Nevertheless, in *The Ego and the Id* (1924), Freud revised his view of introjection, concluding that rather than being pathological it may be a common characteristic of successful mourning, as a means of giving up the lost object and freeing the libido to form new relationships yet allowing comforting memories or fantasies of the lost object to endure within.

17. For Abraham and Torok, introjection begins with the baby who fills the empty mouth with words as a substitute for the mother's breast.

18. Similarly, the sharing of food in the wake is a healthy protection from incorporation, as the communal experience of sharing food indicates sustaining the survivors and burying the dead rather than symbolically ingesting what has been lost.

4   Redemption of the Present: Carlos Fuentes's *Los años con Laura Díaz*

1.   A Klee painting named "Angelus Novus" shows an angel looking as though he is about to move away from something he is fixedly contemplating. His eyes are staring, his mouth is open, his wings are spread. This is how one pictures the angel of history. His face is turned toward the past. Where we perceive a chain of events, he sees one single catastrophe which keeps piling wreckage upon wreckage and hurls it in front of his feet. The angel would like to stay, awaken the dead, and make whole what has been smashed. But a storm is blowing from Paradise; it has got caught in his wings with such violence that the angel can no longer close them. This storm irresistibly propels him into the future to which his back is turned, while the pile of debris before him grows skyward. The storm is what we call progress. ("Theses on the Philosophy of History," *Illuminations* 259–260)

2. See Christopher Domínguez Michael, "México's Former Future," *Foreign Policy* (March–April 2004): 84, and Ilan Stavans, "The Novelist as Heroine," *TLS: Times Literary Supplement* (May 18, 2001): 9–10.

3. While, in keeping with Georg Lukacs's paradigm for the historical novel, an "everyman" (or here, everywoman) is the hero of the narrative, a number of prominent figures from Mexico's intellectual history also make an appearance

as minor characters: for instance, lawyer and prose writer, Xavier Icaza,   artists Diego Rivera and Frida Kahlo, Mexican poets José Gorostiza and Xavier Villaurutia, Spanish poet Luis Cernuda, filmmaker Luis Buñuel and bullfighter Manolete, and the German phenomenologist Husserl in Europe. Also making a brief cameo appearance is Fuentes's most memorable character, Artemio Cruz, from *La muerte de Artemio Cruz* (1962).

4. In a 1935 letter, during the Nazi occupation, Benjamin similarly described his age as a field of ruins, poised for the last judgment:

"Actually, I hardly feel constrained to make head or tail of this condition of the world. On this planet a great number of civilizations have perished in blood and horror. Naturally, one must wish for the planet that one day it will experience a civilization that has abandoned blood and horror; in fact, I am…inclined to assume that our planet is waiting for this. But it is terribly doubtful whether *we* can bring such a present to its hundred or four hundred millionth birthday party. And if we don't, the planet will finally punish us, its unthoughtful well-wishers, by presenting us with the Last Judgment." (qtd. in Arendt, Introduction to *Illuminations* 38)

5. Indeed, Hegel was so enthused about the possibilities for philosophy in his time that he wrote in the *Phenomenology of Spirit* (1807),

Besides, it is not difficult to see that ours is a birth-time and a period of transition to a new era. Spirit [*Geist*] has broken with the world it has hitherto inhabited and imagined, and is of a mind to submerge it in the past, and in the labour of its own transformation. Spirit is indeed never at rest but always engaged in moving forward. But just as the first breath drawn by a child after its long, quiet nourishment breaks the gradualness of merely quantitative growth—there is a qualitative leap, and the child is born—so likewise the Spirit in its formation matures slowly and quietly into its new shape, dissolving bit by bit the structure of its previous world, whose tottering state is only hinted at by isolated symptoms. (50)

Nevertheless, as Hegel himself noted in his "Philosophy of Absolute Spirit," philosophy does not reach a state of changeless perfection, as it is necessarily a product of its time, even when it views its own time from above: "Philosophy is identical with the spirit of the age in which it appears. . . . Neither does an individual transcend his time; he is a son of it" ("History of Philosophy" 525).

6. Orlando may be a tip of the hat to Virginia Woolf's sexually ambiguous character in the eponymous historical novel.

7. Like Díaz, the other major characters similarly face moral dilemmas: e.g., Harry Jaffe confronts the guilt of having given up his friends' names in the McCarthy trials, while Raquel, a German Jew and a devout Catholic convert, refuses to be saved from the death camps if others cannot also be saved.

8. Notably, two of the twelve biblical apostles were named Santiago (Saint James, from Yago or Jacob, God protects); the elder was the first martyr among the twelve.

9. Fuentes's son, Carlos Fuentes Lemus, like the fictional Laura Díaz's son Santiago, was also a painter who was inspired by Egon Schiele and also died young of a chronic illness (in this case, complications from hemophilia in 1999).

Conclusion

1. At around the time of his exile from Argentina in the early 1970s, Dussel responded to philosopher Emmanuel Levinas's challenge: if Levinas's work was to reflect upon the suffering of the Jews, Dussel's responsibility would be to reflect upon the suffering of the indigenous and slaves in Latin America. His study *Filosofía de la Liberación* followed (México: Edicol, 1977).

Works Cited

Abraham, Nicholas and Maria Torok. "Mourning or Melancholia: Introjection versus Incorporation." *The Shell and the Kernel: Renewals of Psychoanalysis.* Ed. Nicholas Rand. Chicago: U Chicago P, 1994.

Agamben, Giorgio. *Homo Sacer: Sovereign Power and Bare Life.* Trans. Daniel Heller-Roazen. Stanford: Stanford University Press, 1998.

Aguirre, Eugenio. "La novela histórica en México." *Revista de literatura mexicana contemporánea.* 2.6 (1997): 97–101.

Aínsa, Fernando. *Reescribir el pasado: Historia y ficción en América Latina.* Mérida, Venezuela: Centro de Estudios Latinoamericanos Rómulo Gallegos, 2003.

Alamán, Lucas. *Historia de México: desde los primeros movimientos que prepararon su Independencia en el año de 1808 hasta la época presente.* Vol. 2. 5 vols. México DF: Fondo de Cultura Económica, 1985.

Alberro, Solange. *Inquisición y sociedad en México 1571–1700.* México: Fondo de Cultura Económica. 1988.

Anonymous. *The Tibetan Book of the Dead.* Trans. and ed. Francesca Fremantle and Chögyam Trungpa. Berkeley: Shambhala, 1975.

Anzaldúa, Gloria. *Borderlands/La Frontera: The New Mestiza.* San Francisco: Spinsters/Aunt Lute P, 1987.

Arendt, Hannah. *The Origins of Totalitarianism.* New York: Harcourt Brace and Jovanovich, 1973.

Aridjis, Homero. *1492: Vida y tiempos de Juan Cabezón de Castilla.* Mexico: Editorial Diana, 1991.

———. *Memorias del Nuevo Mundo.* Mexico: Editorial Diana, 1991.

———. *1492: The Life and Times of Juan Cabezón.* Trans. Betty Ferber. New York: Summit Books, 1991.

Armenta, Ignacio. "Literatura e Historia: la eterna dicotomía: Entrevista con Rosa Beltrán, autora de La corte de los ilusos." *La Jornada,* June 18, 1995: 4–5.

Avelar, Idelber. *The Untimely Present: Postdictatorial Latin American Fiction and the Task of Mourning.* Durham: Duke UP, 1999.

Bakhtin, Mikhail. *The Dialogic Imagination.* Trans. M. Holquist. Austin: U of Texas P, 1981.

Barrientos, Juan José. "El grito de Ajetreo: Anotaciones a la novela de Ibargüengoitia sobre Hidalgo." *Revista de la Universidad de México* 39.28 (August 1983): 15–23.

Barthes, Roland. *S/Z*. Trans. Richard Miller. New York: Hill and Wang, 1974.

Bartra, Roger. *La jaula de la melancolía*. México: Grijalbo, 1987.

Beardsell, Peter. *A Theatre for Cannibals: Rodolfo Usigli and the Mexican Stage*. London: Associated UP, 1992.

Beltrán, Rosa. *La corte de los ilusos*. Mexico: Planeta, 1995.

———. Interview. "Literatura e historia: la eterna dicotomía: Entrevista con Rosa Beltrán, autora de *La corte de los ilusos*." *La Jornada*, July 1995: 4–5.

———. Interview. "Con el virus de la literatura." With Pilar Jiménez Trejo. *Reforma: El Ángel*, July 2, 1995: 4–6.

Benjamin, Walter. "Critique of Violence." *Reflections*. Ed. Peter Demetz. New York: Schocken Books, 1978.

———. "Theologico-Political Fragment." *Reflections*. Ed. Peter Demetz. Trans. Edmund Jephcott. New York: Shocken Books, 1986.

———. "Theses on the Philosophy of History." *Illuminations*. Ed. Hannah Arendt. Trans. Harry Zohn. New York: Harcourt, Brace & World, 1968: 253–265.

———. "The Work of Art in the Age of Mechanical Reproduction." *Illuminations*. Ed. Hannah Arendt. Trans. Harry Zohn. New York: Harcourt, Brace & World, 1968: 217–253.

Beverly, John, José Oviedo, and Michael Aronna, editors. *The Postmodernism Debate in Latin America*. Durham: Duke UP, 1995.

Bloom, Harold. *The Anxiety of Influence: A Theory of Poetry*. Oxford: Oxford UP, 1997.

Bustamante, Carlos María de. *Cuadro histórico de la revolución mexicana de 1810*. Vol. 4. México DF: Fondo de Cultura Económica, 1985.

Butler, Judith. *Gender Trouble*. New York: Routledge, 1990.

Calinescu, Matei. *Five Faces of Modernity: Modernism, Avant-Garde, Decadence, Kitsch, Postmodernism*. Durham: Duke UP, 1987.

Campos, Victoria E. "Toward a New History: Twentieth-Century Debates in Mexico on Narrating the National Past." *A Twice-Told Tale*. Ed. Santiago Juan-Navarro and Theodore Robert Young. Newark: U of Delaware P, 2001.

Castañeda Iturbide, Jaime. *El humorismo desmitificador de Jorge Ibargüengoitia*. México DF: Nuestra Cultura, Gobierno del Estado de Guanajuato. 1988.

Castillo Ledón, Luis. *Hidalgo: La vida del héroe*. 2 vols. México DF: Instituto Nacional de Estudios Históricos de la Revolución Mexicana, 1985.

del Paso, Fernando. *Noticias del Imperio*. Barcelona: Plaza y Janés, 1987.

Domecq, Brianda. *The Astonishing Story of the Saint of Cabora*. Trans. Kay S. García. Tempe, AZ: Bilingual Press, 1998.

———. *La insólita historia de la Santa de Cabora*. México: Planeta, 1990.

———. *Mujer que publica...mujer pública*. México: Editorial Diana, 1994.

———. "Teresa Urrea: La Santa de Cabora." *Tomóchic: La revolución adelantada: Resistencia y lucha de un pueblo de Chihuahua contra el sistema porfirista (1891–1892)*. Vol. 2. Ed. Jesús Vargas Valdez. Ciudad Juárez, Chihuahua: Universidad Autónoma de Ciudad Juárez, 1994: 11–65.

Dussel, Enrique. "Beyond Eurocentrism: The World System and the Limits of Modernity." *The Cultures of Globalization*. Ed. Fredric Jameson and Masao Miyoshi. Durham: Duke UP, 1998: 1–31.

———. "World System and Trans-Modernity." *Nepantla: Views from South* 3.2 (2002): 221–244.

Ellis, Geoffrey. *Napoleon.* London: Longman, 1997.

Fiddian, Robin. *The Novels of Fernando del Paso.* Gainesville: UP of Florida, 2000.

Foucault, Michel. *History of Sexuality.* Vol. 1. New York: Pantheon, 1978.

Franco, Jean. *Plotting Women: Gender and Representation in Mexico.* New York: Columbia UP, 1989.

Freud, Sigmund. "Mourning and Melancholia." *Collected Papers.* Vol. IV. Trans. Joan Riviere. New York: Basic Books, 1959: 152–170.

Frías, Heriberto. *Tomochic.* Ed. James W. Brown. 3rd ed. México: Porrúa, 1976.

Frye, Northrop. *Anatomy of Criticism.* Princeton: Princeton UP, 1957.

Fuentes, Carlos. Acceptance Speech, Premio Cervantes, 1987: http://www.terra.es/cultura/premiocervantes/ceremonia/ceremonia87.htm. August 11, 2006.

———. *Los años con Laura Díaz.* Mexico: Alfaguara, 1999.

———. *The Years with Laura Diaz.* Trans. Alfred MacAdam. New York: Farrar, Straus and Giroux, 2000.

Fukuyama, Francis. *The End of History and the Last Man.* Toronto: Free Press, 1992.

García Canclini, Néstor. *Culturas híbridas: Estrategias para entrar y salir de la modernidad.* México: Grijalbo, 1989.

González de León, Verónica Sylvia. *La narrativa de Jorge Ibargüengoitia.* Diss. UT Austin. 1982.

Gugelberger, George, ed. *The Real Thing: Testimonial Discourse and Latin America.* Durham: Duke UP, 1996.

Hegel, Georg Wilhelm Friedrich. "Phenomenology of Spirit." *The Hegel Reader.* Ed. Stephen Holgate. Oxford: Blackwell Publishers, 1998.

———. "Philosophy of History." *The Hegel Reader.* Ed. Stephen Holgate. Oxford, UK: Blackwell, 1998.

Hopenhayn, Martín. "Essential Histories, Contingent Outcomes: Latin Americanists in Search of a Discourse." *Radical History Review* 89 (2004): 25–35.

———. *No Apocalypse, No Integration: Modernism and Postmodernism in Latin America.* Trans. Cynthia Tomkins and Elizabeth Horan. Durham: Duke UP, 2001.

Hutcheon, Linda. *A Poetics of Postmodernism: History, Theory, Fiction.* London/New York: Routledge, 1988.

Ibargüengoitia, Jorge. *Estas ruinas que ves.* Mexico DF: Joaquin Mortiz, 1975.

———. *Los pasos de López.* Mexico DF: Ediciones Océano, 1982.

Illades, Lilián. "Teresa Urrea y Lauro Aguirre." in Vargas Valdez: 69–90.

Jitrik, Noé. *Historia e imaginación literaria: Las posibilidades de un género.* Buenos Aires: Editorial Biblos, 1995.

Joseph, Gilbert and Timothy Henderson, Eds. *The Mexico Reader.* Durham: Duke UP, 2002.

Jrade, Cathy. *Modernismo, Modernity, and the Development of Spanish American Literature.* Austin: U of Texas P, 1998.

Kohut, Karl, Ed. *La invención del pasado: La novela histórica en el marco de la posmodernidad.* Frankfurt/Madrid: Vervuert, 1997.

Krauze, Enrique. *Francisco I. Madero: Místico de la libertad.* Mexico City: Fondo de Cultura Económica, 1987.

———. *Siglo de caudillos.* Barcelona: Tusquets, 1994.

———. *Porfirio Díaz: Místico de la autoridad.* México: Fondo de Cultura Económica, 1987.

Levins Morales, Aurora. *Medicine Stories: History, Culture and the Politics of Integrity.* Cambridge, MA: South End P, 1998.

Llorente, Juan Antonio. *L'Histoire critique de l'Inquisition espagnole.* Paris: Treuttel et Wurtz, 1817.

López González, Aralia. "La memoria del olvido: ética y estética del indicio y del zurcido." *Sin imágenes falsas, sin falsos espejos: Narradoras mexicanas del siglo XX.* Ed. Aralia López González. México: Colegio de México, 1990: 499–507.

Ludmer, Josefina. "Las tretas del débil." *La sartén por el mango.* Ed. Patricia Elena González and Eliana Ortega. Río Piedras: Huracán, 1985.

Lukács, Georg. *The Historical Novel.* Trans. Stanley Mitchell. U Nebraska P, 2002.

Martínez, William. "¿Eres o te pareces? La cuestión de la historia en Madero, el otro de Ignacio Solares." *Revista de literatura mexicana contemporánea* 4.10 (July 1999): 79–84.

Mateos, Juan A. *Sacerdote y caudillo.* Mexico DF: Porrúa, 1986.

Menton, Seymour. *Latin America's New Historical Novel.* (Austin: UTP, 1993).

Mergier, Anne. "Como hizo trizas Fernando del Paso un texto de Octavio Paz en la reunión de escritores en París." *Proceso* 750 (March 19, 1991): 46–47.

Mirandé, Alfred and Evangelina Enríquez. *La Chicana: The Mexican-American Woman.* Chicago: U of Chicago P, 1979.

Moi, Toril. *Sexual/Textual Politics.* New York: Routledge, 1985.

Paz, Octavio. *Tiempo nublado.* Barcelona: Editorial Seix Barral, 1986.

Pérez, Joseph. *The Spanish Inquisition: A History.* Trans. Janet Lloyd. New Haven: Yale University Press, 2005.

Pérez de Mendiola, Marina. *Gender and Identity Formation in Contemporary Mexican Literature.* New York: Garland, 1998.

Pohlenz, Ricardo, "De cuando Iturbide fue Emperador." *El Semanario*, June 11, 1995: 6.

Pons, María Cristina. *Memorias del olvido: La novela histórica de fines del siglo XX.* Madrid/Mexico: Siglo Veintiuno Editores, 1996.

Preston, Julia and Damuel Dillon. *Opening Mexico: The Making of a Democracy.* New York: Farrar, Strauss and Giroux, 2004.

Rama, Ángel. *The Lettered City.* Trans. John Charles Chasteen. Chapel Hill, NC: Duke UP, 1996.

———. *Transculturación narrativa de América Latina.* México: Siglo XXI, 1982.

Reyes, Alfonso. "Notas sobre la inteligencia americana." *Obras completas.* Vol. I. Mexico: Fondo de Cultura Económica, 1955: 87.

Rodríguez, Richard and Gloria. "Teresa Urrea: Her Life, as It Affected the Mexican-U.S. Frontier." *Voices: Readings from El Grito 1967–1973*. Ed. Octavio Romero. Berkeley: Quinto Sol, 1973.

Saisselin, Remy. *The Enlightenment against the Baroque: Economics and Aesthetics in the Eighteenth Century*. Berkeley: U of California P, 1992.

Sayer, Chloe. *Costumes of Mexico*. Austin: U of Texas P, 1985.

Solares, Ignacio. *Madero, el otro*. México: Joaquín Mortiz, 1989.

———. *Madero's Judgment*. Trans. Alfonso González and Juana Wong. Toronto: York Press, 1990.

Sommer, Doris. *Foundational Fictions: The National Romances of Latin America*. Berkeley: UCP, 1991.

Sontag, Susan. "Notes on Camp." *Susan Sontag Reader*. New York: Vintage, 1964: 105–119.

Spitta, Silvia. *Between Two Waters: Narratives of Transculturation in Latin America*. Houston: Rice University, 1995.

Stavans, Ilan. *The Scroll and the Cross: 1000 Years of Jewish-Hispanic Literature*. New York: Routledge, 2002.

Unamuno. "La libertad y la fuerza." *Artículos olvidados*. Ed. C. Cobb. London: Támesis, 1976: 199–201.

Van Delden, Maarten. *Carlos Fuentes, Mexico and Modernity*. Vanderbilt UP, 1998.

Vanderwood, Paul. *The Power of God Against the Guns of Government: Religious Upheaval in Mexico at the Turn of the Nineteenth Century*. Stanford, CA: Stanford UP, 1998.

Volpi, Jorge. "Como inventar y destruir un imperio en diecinueve lecciones." *Revista de literatura mexicana contemporánea* 1.2 (January–April 1996): 73–76.

Wilentz, Gay. *Binding Cultures*. Bloomington: Indiana University Press, 1993.

Zea, Leopoldo. *Dependencia y liberación en la cultura latinoamericana*. Mexico: Editorial Joaquín Mortiz, 1974.

Index